Making places in the prehistoric world

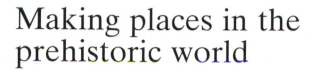

Making places in the prehistoric world: themes in settlement archaeology

Joanna Brück and Melissa Goodman

University of Cambridge

First published in the UK and the USA in 1999
by UCL Press
11 New Fetter Lane
London EC4P 4EE

The name of University College London (UCL) is a registered trade mark used by
UCL Press with the consent of the owner.
UCL Press is an imprint of the Taylor & Francis Group

© Joanna Brück, Melissa Goodman and contributors, 1999

Typeset by Best-set Typesetter Ltd., Hong Kong
Printed and bound in Great Britain by T.J. International

British Library Cataloguing in Publication Data
A catalogue record for this book is available from the British Library.

Library of Congress Cataloging in Publication Data
A catalogue record for this book has been requested

ISBNs: 1-85728-694-4 HB
      1-85728-753-3 PB

Contents

Notes on contributors

Douglass W. Bailey is Lecturer in European Prehistory at the University of Wales at Cardiff. He is an expert in Balkan prehistory, has excavated in Bulgaria and Romania and has published a series of important papers on Neolithic Balkan settlement, society and material culture. One of these, 'Expanding the dimensions of early agricultural tells: the Podgoritsa Archaeological Project (Bulgaria)', has recently been published by the *Journal of Field Archaeology*. Dr Bailey is also a keen proponent of international collaboration between east and west European archaeologists and an edited volume in this direction was published in 1995 (*Prehistoric Bulgaria*). Additional interests include the sociopolitics of archaeology and the use of alternative media for presenting archaeological information.

Joanna Brück is a Research Fellow at Clare Hall, University of Cambridge. She has recently completed a PhD on the use of space in British Bronze Age settlements. Her current research projects focus on the relationship between domestic and ritual practise in the British Bronze Age and on land tenure and residential mobility in the Early Bronze Age of southern England. She lectures on the Bronze Age for the Board of Continuing Education, University of Cambridge, and has also worked as Keeper of Human History at Plymouth City Museum and Art Gallery.

John Carman is an Affiliated Lecturer in the Department of Archaeology, University of Cambridge and a Research Fellow at Clare Hall, Cambridge. His specializations include archaeological heritage management and the archaeologies of war. His books include *Valuing ancient things: archaeology and law* and *Material harm: archaeological studies of war and violence*.

Kathryn Jane Fewster took her first degree in archaeology at the University of Sheffield. She has Masters degrees in both social anthropology (University of Cambridge) and development studies (University of Manchester) and she completed her PhD on ethnoarchaeology at the University of Sheffield. She taught for one year in the Department of Social Anthropology at the University of Durham and is currently involved in ethnoarchaeological research in northwest Spain.

Melissa Goodman is currently completing her doctoral research at the Department of Archaeology, University of Cambridge. Her work concentrates on the role of agriculture and landscape modification in prehispanic societies of the Peruvian Andes. Other research interests include soil micromorphology for the Taraco Archaeological Project at Chiripa, Bolivia.

Christopher Hayden gained his PhD on the archaeology of western Mediterranean islands at the University of Cambridge. He has since spent a year as a Rome Scholar at the British School at Rome. His current research interests are in religion and society in Temple period Malta and in the *domus de janas*, Neolithic tombs in Sardinia.

Joseph J. Kovacik is Project Director for Parsons Brinckerhoff's archaeology section in Albuquerque, New Mexico. His research interests include the social and religious development of the Chaco Anasazi, and the history and philosophy of the science and technology of archaeology. He is currently investigating the creation of archaeological facts and knowledge and writing a theory of 'dirty' archaeology.

Richard A. Krause is a Distinguished Teaching Fellow of the College of Arts and Sciences and a Professor of Anthropology at the University of Alabama. He received his BA and MA from the University of Nebraska and his PhD from Yale University. He has conducted archaeological and ethnographic field research in Alaska, South Africa, Mexico and the Great Plains of North America.

Joshua Pollard is a lecturer in archaeology at the University of Wales College Newport. Since completing his PhD at Cardiff University, he has held a James Knott Fellowship at the University of Newcastle, taught at Queen's University, Belfast, and worked for the Cambridge Archaeological Unit. His research interests are in the British Neolithic, with a specific focus on the interpretation of occupation and social ecology, depositional practices and material culture.

Mary F. Price is a doctoral candidate in anthropology at Binghamton University, SUNY. Her research interests centre on how archaeologists identify and define residential groups in prehistoric small-scale societies. She is particularly concerned with how archaeologists can use the material record to investigate the ways residential groups articulate with larger social groups to create communities and how social norms about social and biological reproduction may dynamically shape the organization of the labour process. At present, she is completing her analysis of residential organization and activity structure at the prehistoric village of Cerro de las Trincheras located in Sonora, Mexico.

Trevor Simmonds gained a Merit pass in the HND in archaeological practice at Bournemouth. He subsequently obtained both his undergraduate degree and a distinction in the landscape studies MA, at Leicester University. He has a developed interest in theoretical approaches to landscape archaeology, British prehistory and the study of multi-period landscapes in northern Britain. He is currently working as a field archaeologist in the northwest of England.

Robert Young graduated from the University of Wales at Cardiff and gained his PhD at Durham University. He is currently a Senior Lecturer in the School of Archaeological Studies at the University of Leicester. His main research interests are theoretical archaeology, British prehistory from the Mesolithic to Bronze Age and landscape archaeology, particularly in the uplands of northern Britain. He is the author of *Lithics and subsistence in north-eastern England* and co-author with Deirdre O'Sullivan of a Batsford English Heritage book on their long-term research project on Lindisfarne, Northumberland.

List of figures

List of tables

Preface

Many of the themes in this volume were first formulated in March 1995 at the conference *Conceptualising Settlement in Prehistoric Archaeology* held at the McDonald Institute for Archaeological Research, Cambridge. The conference was supported by a grant from the McDonald Institute for which we are grateful. It became clear in those lively and sometimes heated discussions that although the assumptions underlying settlement archaeology are problematic, they remain largely unquestioned. We proposed to address this concern through further discussion and the generation of this volume. Both Ian Hodder and J. D. Hill were inspirational at the initial stages of this project and we have appreciated their encouragement. We should like to thank Robin Boast, Chris Scarre and Marie-Louise Sørensen who served as discussants at the conference. We also gratefully acknowledge the input of those who presented papers but, for various reasons, were unable to contribute to this volume: Brian Boyd, Simon Kaner, James McGlade, Stuart Needham, Robin Skeates, Tony Spence and Hanna Zawadzka. The insightful comments and discussion of these and other conference participants helped with the thinking that shaped the direction of this volume.

Three years later we are pleased that several of the conference participants have contributed to this collection. We owe special thanks to Douglass Bailey, John Carman, Chris Hayden, Joshua Pollard, Trevor Simmonds, and Robert Young for their enduring interest in the project and for their patience. We have also been lucky to be able to include the work of Katherine Fewster, Jo Kovacik, Richard Krause and Mary Price. Their papers have added to the scope and range of the volume.

We should like to thank UCL Press for supporting the volume and remaining flexible with the deadline. Roger Jones, Stephen Gerrard, Aisling Ryan and Claire Hart have borne with us over the years explicating the world of publishing. Finally, we should like to thank our partners, Julian Haines and Richard Elgar, for hearing about 'the book' all this time and assuring us that it would, indeed, some day be finished.

Contributors' Acknowledgements

Chapter 1: We should like to thank Jo Safaer Derevenski and an anonymous referee for their insightful comments on earlier drafts of this paper. We have tried to incorporate their suggestions into our discussion but, as always, the responsibility lies with us for any remaining inadequacies.

Chapter 2: This chapter is the outgrowth of two conference papers: 'Community begins at home: rethinking the place of the household in archaeological interpretive models' presented at the Fourth Gender and Archaeology Conference at Michigan State University, 18–19 October 1996 and 'Domestic is as domestic does: the implications of viewing the household as a *domestic* unit' presented at the 61st Annual Society for American Archaeology Meetings, New Orleans, Louisiana. Various people have provided comments on the ideas expressed in these papers. I am grateful to them all but wish to extend special thanks to Susan Pollock, Melissa Goodman and Joanna Brück whose patience, support, and insightful commentary have greatly improved the format and content of this essay. Any errors in data or judgement are, of course, mine.

Chapter 3: This chapter is the outgrowth of two conference papers: 'Community begins at home: rethinking the place of the household in archaeological interpretive models' presented at the Fourth Gender and Archaeology Conference at Michigan State University, 18–19 October 1996, and 'Domestic is as domestic does: the implications of viewing the household as a *domestic* unit' presented at the 61st Annual Society for American Archaeology Meetings, New Orleans, Louisiana. Various people have provided comments on the ideas expressed in these papers. I am grateful to them all but wish to extend special thanks to Susan Pollock, Melissa Goodman and Joanna Brück whose patience, support, and insightful commentary have greatly improved the format and content of this essay. Any errors in data or judgement are, of course, mine.

Chapter 4: The following people have commented on drafts of this paper and I am grateful to them for their constructive criticism and encouragement: Marie-Louise Sørensen, Melissa Goodman, Todd Whitelaw, Julian Thomas, John Barrett, Stuart Needham, Joshua Pollard, Helen Lewis, Mark Knight and Glynis

Jones. Particular thanks are due to Joanna Sofaer-Derevenski for reading several versions and for helping me to clarify my arguments. Several other readers have also offered valuable comments since this chapter was submitted; although I have not been able to take up their advice prior to publication, I certainly intend to do so in my future work on the Early Bronze Age. Finally, Nigel Macpherson-Grant, John Evans, Nicholas Thomas and David Tomalin kindly provided me with unpublished information on some of the sites discussed.

Chapter 5: I should like to thank Richard Bradley, Mark Edmonds and Alasdair Whittle for commenting on an earlier draft of this paper, without implicating them in anything I have said. Joanna Brück and Melissa Goodman deserve special praise for their patience and efficient editorial skills.

Chapter 6: I am grateful to the editors for providing critical comment on various versions of this text and for inviting me to participate in the symposium on settlement in Cambridge. Additional perceptive and useful comment came from Alasdair Whittle. Howard Mason drew figures 6.1 and 6.3; Mike Hamilton produced figure 6.2.

Chapter 7: Thanks to the organisers of the settlement conference for providing the stimulus for this paper and to all those who attended for the useful points they made, in particular to Joanna Brück for many enlightening discussions on the subject of settlements. Much of this paper is based on research for my doctoral thesis that has been greatly clarified by my supervisor, Professor C. Renfrew. I should like to thank many friends in Sardinia and Malta for their help, especially Anna Grazia Russu and Reuben Grima. Many thanks also to the Hayden research foundation for generous financial and other support and to my harshest and most inspiring critic, Caroline Humfress. The infelicities that remain are entirely my own fault.

Chapter 9: I am grateful to Christine Hastorf, William Sillar, Joanna Brück and Richard Elgar for kindly reading and discussing with me earlier drafts of this paper.

Chapter 11: My thanks go to Tim and Sue Fewster for being there when I needed them.

Chapter 12: We should like to thank the following for their comments on earlier drafts of this paper: Tony Brown, Exeter University, and David Mattingly, Jane Webster, Marijke Van der Veen, Deirdre O'Sullivan and Neil Christie, all of Leicester University.

CHAPTER ONE

Introduction: themes for a critical archaeology of prehistoric settlement

Joanna Brück & Melissa Goodman

Introduction

The study of prehistoric settlement enjoys a central position in contemporary archaeology. The prominent role of settlement research within most regional and national traditions is confirmed by the proliferation of field projects and publications focusing primarily on ancient settlements during the 1990s. However, although the variety and abundance of these sites within the archaeological record suggests a need for careful attention to interpretative frameworks, settlements have not benefited from an evaluation of theoretical concerns particular to their study. Thus, there exists a considerable gap between the formulations of settlement presented in site reports and recent developments in archaeological theory. A clear example is the persistence of environmentally determinist interpretations of the relationship between settlement and landscape in many regional traditions. The absence of a critical review of the terminology and representation of settlement also leaves these important areas largely unexamined. The papers in this volume provide a response to these concerns by prioritizing the theoretical challenges that settlements present.

In this introductory chapter, we begin by examining the categories and conventions employed within settlement studies. The apparent neutrality of terms such as 'domestic practice', 'house' and 'household' is questioned and their social and ideological implications are examined. We then move on to discuss the relationship between settlement and landscape and explore how a reorientation away from functionalist models of human behaviour can expand our appreciation of settlements in prehistoric societies. One important line of enquiry is drawn from developments in landscape studies over the 1990s that suggest that landscape is a cultural construct, shaped by myth and tradition, and invested with social meaning (e.g. Bradley 1991b; Bender 1993b; Barrett 1994; Tilley 1994). In this approach, human perception plays an important role in understanding spatial relations at the landscape level. This research suggests that it is through the social construction of

1

place that human–landscape relationships are created and maintained. These considerations have obvious implications for the study of ancient settlements. However, as settlement has not yet formed an explicit focus of concern within this body of research, the application of these insights requires considerable attention to the particular attributes of settlement. Research on settlement is concerned with a wide range of human activities including those essential to daily existence. This emphasis on daily life contrasts with recent approaches to ceremonial monuments in ancient landscapes that emphasize power relations and ideology to the exclusion of other aspects of life (e.g. Barrett 1994; Tilley 1994). Thus, although innovations in landscape studies have much to offer explorations of prehistoric settlement, we argue that there continues to be an important place in archaeological research for a distinctive settlement archaeology.

In the following sections, we identify important themes for a critically informed archaeology of settlement. These include such questions as: how do archaeologists define and identify settlement spatially and conceptually? How have ethnocentric assumptions concerning human behaviour affected settlement archaeology? How can discussions of landscape perception inform research on the location and character of settlements in the past? How do settlements mediate the relationship between humans and landscape and what is their role in land tenure? We cannot claim to exhaustively cover all aspects of settlement research but hope to demonstrate the potential to expand and revitalize the field in the light of recent developments in archaeological theory.

The meaning of settlement

Most archaeologists share a working understanding of what settlement is. Yet on closer examination, the term settlement is more ambiguous and complex than at first sight. At one level, archaeologists employ the term 'settlement' to characterize particular types of site, while at another it is used to describe the process by which a particular group of people inhabits or colonizes a region. In both cases, ethnocentric notions of human behaviour are often uncritically projected into the past. Settlement terminology does not simply reflect the nature of the archaeological data but also the expectations of modern researchers regarding what these data represent. In the following sections, we discuss how the term 'settlement' has been used to describe a particular class of site and we explore how archaeologists have employed concepts such as 'household' and 'domestic practice' to characterize the settlement site.

The settlement site: houses and domestic practice

Settlements form a fundamental element of site typologies. In many archaeological traditions, 'settlement sites' are conceptualized as distinct, bounded categories of space and practice that are distinguishable from the landscape around them and from other types of site within that landscape (see Carman, Chapter 2, this volume). Settlements are usually described as having predominantly domestic or residential functions that may be contrasted with other site types such as cemeteries and monuments. The recognition of settlement sites is therefore dependent on our ability to identify domestic practice in the archaeological record. The primary activities carried out in our own homes include cooking and eating, reproduction and the nurturing of children and it is widely assumed that these are the defining features of settlement sites in all cultural contexts. Such activities serve an essential role in the creation and maintenance of gender ideology, age roles, and kinship relations in modern Western society. The house is the locus of these activities and provides an intuitively recognizable context for such supposedly universal practices. It is not surprising that these associations have led researchers since early this century to focus on houses as a major source of information about the past. For example, Woolley states that 'an ancient building . . . is important, not merely as illustrating the history of architecture but as the setting for the lives of men and women, and as one of their chief forms of self-expression' (1954 [1930]: 76). For Woolley, the comparison of house plans was essential to this study and allowed him to confidently identify separate functional spaces in familiar terms such as kitchens, parlours, lavatories and the like (ibid.: 77).

However, the early optimism of Woolley and his contemporaries has not always been borne out. When it comes to identifying domestic practice and houses in the past, a number of problems are frequently encountered. In some instances, this may be the result of methodological difficulties. For example, Iron Age 'roundhouses' in Britain could have been used as dwellings, byres or for storage, but it is often difficult to distinguish these functions archaeologically. Another concern for archaeologists arises from ethnographic accounts documenting the sequential use of buildings for several different activities within a single generation (e.g. Weismantel 1989). Although each activity may leave archaeological traces, the distinct layers of each short phase of use may collapse into a single archaeological layer over time. In some cases, fine resolution techniques such as soil micromorphology may suggest a sequence of activities (e.g. Matthews & Postgate 1994) but interpretative frameworks must be able to cope with these possibilities. A further complication is the apparent absence of houses from the archaeological record of several cultural traditions, a question that cannot always be explained away as the result of inadequate recovery techniques (see Brück, Chapter 4, this volume). In other instances, abundant structural evidence may be recovered but, as at Catalhoyuk (Melaart 1967; Hodder 1987, 1996), it may be difficult to distinguish between houses and other types of building, for example shrines (see Hayden, Chapter 7, this volume).

At a more fundamental level, many of the problems encountered in contemporary settlement archaeology stem from the interpretative frameworks we employ. The assumption that a discrete set of 'domestic practices' located in 'houses' is a universal characteristic of settlements leads to the expectation that both houses and domestic activities should be easily identifiable archaeologically. However, the structure and elaboration of the house in modern Western society is closely related to a specific ideological construct, the 'home', and depends on ideals of possession and permanence that may be absent in other cultural contexts (see Hayden,

Chapter 7, and Brück, Chapter 4, this volume). A less culturally laden term for residential architecture may be 'dwelling' and, as anthropologists have amply demonstrated, dwellings appear in a variety of forms in different societies (e.g. Oliver 1987; Bourdier & Alsayad 1989; MacEachern et al. 1989). The cultural values and social relations realized through dwellings are equally variable. Employing the appellation 'house' to familiar-looking structures can result in the uncritical imposition of attributes common to Western social life. Boyd's study of Natufian 'houses' provides a good example (1995). Although these stone-footed structures seem to indicate permanent, year-round settlement, the bone assemblages recovered from these buildings in fact provide good evidence for short-term, seasonal use.

The impact of ethnocentric expectations can be further illustrated through inspection of the features used to functionally define structures as houses. The role of the hearth may be the best example as it has played an important role in Western domestic culture for many centuries and occupied a prominent, even central, location within household space in many regional traditions of architecture. In European ideology, the hearth is synonymous with the domestic circle or home. It is symbolically linked to a life-giving force related to motherhood and nourishment that may have its ideological roots in the Greek goddess Hera. However, the primacy of the hearth, or modern kitchen, in Western houses and social life cannot be considered universal defining features of the domestic sphere. There are many cultural contexts where cooking hearths are routinely located outside of dwellings (e.g. Fewster, Chapter 11, this volume) or are found in other locations such as ceremonial architecture.

These observations help to illustrate the difficulty in attempting to construct a universally applicable list of characteristics for domestic practice. In many modern societies, domestic practice is seen as a private, passive, female sphere which can be contrasted with the active, public and male world of politics, ritual and the market economy. Perhaps the clearest examples are in Muslim communities where a strict segregation of the sexes is observed and many women live secluded in purdah. However, among other peoples, activities such as cooking and the socialization of children do not have their own separate spatial sphere and settlements may be focal points for a wide range of ritual, economic and political practices (for discussion see Brück, Chapter 4, Hayden, Chapter 7, and Price, Chapter 3, this volume). In other words, the activities that constitute settlement may differ considerably according to historical context. This suggests that structuralist dichotomies such as public: private or sacred: profane may not always be reproduced through the existence of a separate domestic sphere that can be identified in structural remains (cf. Tiffany 1978; MacCormack & Strathern 1980; La Fontaine 1981; Price, Chapter 3, this volume). If the presence of a distinct domestic domain cannot be taken as a universal, then the association of prehistoric women with passive, domestic social roles must be called into question (Moore 1988: 21–4; Waterson 1990: 169–71).

This challenges us to rethink certain aspects of archaeological research on the internal organization of settlement space. Such studies were originally popularized under the New Archaeology and early investigations into intra-site analysis have become classics in settlement research. A notable example is Clarke's study (1972) of Iron Age buildings at Glastonbury. By analysing the spatial segregation of artefacts and features, Clarke developed a model of domestic organization that related the performance of gender-specific activities to mappable site locations. However, these assignments relied on normative ideas concerning the sexual division of labour. For example, evidence for activities such as the preparation of food was unquestioningly taken to indicate a women's activity area. An emphasis on the identification of universal qualities of intra-site patterning continues to characterize research in this genre (e.g. Kent 1984, 1990).

Similar problems are evident in more recent studies by authors working within a broadly postprocessual framework. These researchers argue that settlement space is invested with cultural meanings that influence how it is ordered, used and valued (e.g. Hodder 1990; Richards 1990; Parker Pearson & Richards 1994a, b). This perspective challenges strictly functional interpretations of activity areas. However, ethnocentric assumptions concerning the nature of domestic practice still show through. A common thread linking many of these writings is the use of structuralism to infer meaning from the archaeological data. For example, Hodder (1990) constructs a conceptual framework for the interpretation of space in European Neolithic houses based on contrasting qualities such as wild: tame, outside: inside and death: life. He draws on these contrasts to suggest that women were conceptually linked with the home in the Neolithic. Using a similar structuralist approach, Parker Pearson (1996) argues that women in Late Bronze Age Britain would have spent much of their time in the inner or back regions of settlement space. He characterizes this as a dirty, private, passive world, the locus of domestic consumption and reproduction. Thus, although the aim of these studies is to access historically contingent, contextualized meaning, the use of supposedly universal structural dualisms often results in the uncritical imposition on to the past of modern Western structures of meaning.

Households

Another important set of preconceptions that affects our understanding of prehistoric settlement arises out of the use of the term 'household'. Ancient households are generally thought to consist of families that function as independent units of production, reproduction and consumption (e.g. Wilk & Rathje 1982). However, anthropological studies have shown that the household does not conform to a distinct set of personnel or activities but is highly variable cross-culturally (e.g. Netting et al. 1984). Supposedly diagnostic household features such as co-residence, kinship relations, the organization of production and sharing of resources are not necessarily coterminous but should be viewed as 'semi-independent variables' (Bender 1967: 493; Rudie 1970; Sanjek 1982; Netting et al. 1984; see Price, Chapter 3, this volume, for discussion). A clear contrast to the archaeological conception of the household can be seen in the residence patterns and socioeconomic practices of many non-Western societies. For example, among the Akan of Ghana, a woman and her children form part of a household comprising matrilateral relatives (Woodford-Berger 1981); her husband often lives elsewhere as a member of a separate household yet his wife provides him with food. Here, a domestic function (the sharing of food) and biological reproduction transgress household boundaries and the nuclear family and household group do not simply map one on to the other. Price (Chapter 3, this volume) draws on similar anthropological studies in her critique of the characterization of households in Americanist archaeological literature. She shows that the frequent equation of settlements with households and households with kin groups has the effect of reducing household and domestic functions to reproduction and naturalizes the relationship between women and the domestic context. In this way, she argues that women's active social roles are denigrated and a universalized image of the patriarchal family is projected into the past (for parallel critiques in anthropology, see Tiffany 1978; Yanagisako 1979; La Fontaine 1981; Strathern 1984; Moore 1988: 21–4).

In anthropology, further debates surround the atemporalized vision of domestic relations often conveyed in discussions of household form. A timeless vision of household relations distorts the impact of real historical conditions on the societies and individuals involved (Fabian 1984). This finds parallels in certain archaeological traditions where there has been a tendency to look at generic household types over long chronological phases without regard to the length of occupation and the impact this might have had on household form and settlement development (see Goodman, Chapter 9, this volume; exceptions include Ellison 1978: 30; Tourtellot 1988). Not only does household membership change over the developmental cycle (Goody 1958, 1972) as members are born, mature and die but economic and social conditions can also impact household membership in the short term. Particularly neglected is exploration of the differences between pioneer and secondary households in newly colonized landscapes (but see Krause, Chapter 8, this volume). However, unlike the artefacts used as cultural markers for chronological change, household groups have been demonstrated to respond quickly to changing social, environmental and economic conditions (Wilk & Netting 1984; Stone et al. 1990; Netting 1993).

These observations suggest that many of the conventions employed in settlement archaeology have the effect of obscuring the potential variability of the prehistoric record. The frequent tendency to apply modern norms to the patterns presented in prehistoric data creates an ethnocentric notion of both settlement activities and membership. As with the term 'house', some categories carry ideals specific to the modern world that makes their application to prehistoric contexts problematic. This indicates that the terminology employed to describe settlements should be evaluated in context. However, we do not advocate a complete abandonment of current categories and conventions. It is impossible to undertake archaeological analysis without grouping the data and so categories must be assigned. However, it would be naïve to assume that the process of categorization can be undertaken in an entirely objective manner (Hodder 1986: 16; Barrett 1991). One potential solution is to use categories as heuristic devices rather than interpretative aids; terms such as 'settlement' must be defined and redefined as they are employed in different cultural and historical contexts. Most importantly, we need to maintain a critical awareness of the effects that categories and conventions can have on our understanding of the past.

Qualities of space: settlement, landscape and environmental perception

Thus far, we have concentrated on the conceptual associations of settlement in archaeology. We will now turn to a different set of issues concerning the complications encountered when trying to physically place settlements within their landscape context. We begin by addressing settlement location and temporal changes in settlement patterns. The nature of human–environment relations is central to this discussion and developments in landscape archaeology over the 1990s provide insights into this issue. We also consider how a focus on settlement can help to broaden the aims of landscape archaeology as currently practised.

In archaeology, the relationship between people and landscape has often been expressed in terms deeply influenced by Cartesian positivism and the political economy of capitalism (Tilley 1994). A mainstay of archaeological practice, the site distribution map, serves to illustrate this point. In these representations, sites are depicted as static points on a Cartesian plane and the landscapes in which they are set are reduced to mapped and measured space. Not only do such two-dimensional representations ignore the impact of perspective on the human experience of space but, more importantly, they strip landscape of cultural meaning (Bender 1993a; Thomas 1993; Barrett 1994: 13–24). In Chapter 2, this volume, Carman relates modern Western ways of conceptualizing human–environment relationships to colonial history; he traces the idea of land as an objectified, measurable and alienable entity that can be colonized, bought and sold to the early modern period. The idea that site-distribution maps are an objective methodology for representing landscape is therefore naïve; they are in fact a tool for the control and appropriation of land and can only be fully understood in relation to the development of the class and gender divisions characteristic of the modern Western world (Harley 1988; Prince 1988; Olwig 1993; Kirby 1996).

Since Willey's seminal study of settlement in the Virú valley in Peru (1953), changes over time in settlement patterns have been widely presented as a chronological series of site-distribution maps. This has the effect of reducing change to a sequence of synchronic snapshots that do not account for the span of time, often centuries, elapsing between them. Such representations simplify the impact of passing time for human individuals in prehistory and ignore the fact that people in the past would have experienced these changes as unfolding events within their lifetimes (see Goodman, Chapter 9, and Kovacik, Chapter 10, this volume). Furthermore, site-distribution maps tend to include only sites dated to the same chronological phase. However, the anthropogenic features that punctuate a landscape are not only those of contemporaneous date but also include any older features that form part of the worldview of the inhabitants. This is most clearly the case with the reuse of sites (see Bailey, Chapter 6, this volume).

Once the settlement pattern for a particular period has been established, researchers have generally sought to explain the location of sites within the landscape. Since the early years of this century, settlement location has been interpreted primarily in terms of the distribution of economic resources such as cultivable soils or flint sources (early examples include Gradmann 1906; Fox 1932). With the development of the New Archaeology, increasingly sophisticated predictive models derived from ecology and geography, for example site-catchment analysis and von Thünen's rings, were explored as a means of evaluating the resource base and land-use patterns of particular settlements. Such models were often uncritically employed as explanatory frameworks of universal applicability, yet they were clearly derived from contemporary economics and management policies. Although no longer so popular, ecological determinist modes of thinking are still widespread in certain regional traditions, as Krause (Chapter 8, this volume) points out for studies of prehistoric settlement patterns in the Great Plains of North America. At a much more implicit level, the relationship between humans and landscape is still often conceptualized in terms redolent of capitalist economics; for example, embedded notions of environmental or economic 'exploitation' continue to occur widely in the archaeological literature. These imply a one-way relationship between humans and the landscape in which nature is objectified, detached from history, controlled and manipulated as a means of maximizing economic returns.

Landscape and cultural meaning

Over the 1980s and 1990s, determinist frameworks for the interpretation of human–environment relationships have been questioned in British archaeology. These researchers recognize that non-capitalist societies have a variety of different ways of articulating the relationship between people and the natural world (e.g. Barrett 1994: 137–41; Tilley 1994). At one end of the spectrum, hunter–gatherers often see themselves as involved in a mutualistic relationship with their environment (e.g. Munn 1970; Brightman 1993). What they receive from it must be regenerated through periodic ritual practice. In contrast, capitalist land ownership is more one-sided, with the aim being to extract as much from the land as possible. Drawing on discussions in behavioural and humanistic geography (e.g. Tuan 1977; Gregory & Urry 1985; Penning-Rosewell & Lowenthal 1986; Cosgrove & Daniels 1988), several British archaeologists have explored how landscape does not simply form a neutral container for human action but acts as a store of cultural meaning (e.g. Evans 1985; Bradley 1991b; Bender 1993a; Tilley 1994). Relationships with landscape are often expressed and maintained through myths that invest particular places with significance; in this way, the natural world becomes both a source of metaphor for social relations and a physical manifestation of cosmological beliefs. In many societies, the culture–nature dichotomy that shapes contemporary human–environment relationships may be less pronounced than in modern Western society (Descola & Pálsson 1996). Where this is the case, landscape may not be distanced and objectified as it is in the modern world (cf. Olwig 1993; Thomas 1993), and economic strategies such as exploitation, intensification or the maximization of subsistence production may have no place in the repertoire of human action (Pálsson 1996).

These observations suggest that approaches that reduce human behaviour to a desire to maximize economic gain and minimize risk and effort must be questioned. Although this may be the rationale behind economic practice in capitalist societies, countless anthropological, historical and even archaeological examples demonstrate that people do not always conform to these behavioural models. For example, the Aztec inhabitants of the Basin of Mexico defied cost-effective norms by living in small dispersed villages despite their economic dependence on inter-village co-operation for intensive, irrigation agriculture (Sanders et al. 1979). This indicates that non-functional variables may be assigned particular value in shaping the nature and location of settlement (see Krause, Chapter 8, this volume). It also suggests that concepts such as 'efficiency' and 'cost-effectiveness' vary from society to society and over time (Hodder 1982: 202). Similarly, what is considered 'marginal' land by one group may not be considered so by another: the forest-dwelling Mbuti pygmies of Zaire perceive the forest as a benign, life-giving force whereas to their Bantu agriculturist neighbours, it is a threatening and dangerous place (Turnbull 1961; cf. Young & Simmonds, Chapter 12, this volume). Problems such as soil deterioration may be solved in different ways; what is perceived as the best solution depends on culturally specific values, aims and rationales and does not always equate with economic maximization (see Young & Simmonds, Chapter 12, this volume). People do not work with a 'real' environment, outside of history, but with their *understanding* of it as constituted through a specific cultural tradition. Thus, there is no fundamental functionalist logic that can be applied to all people at all times. This variability has frequently been recognized in anthropological definitions of economic maximization which have included discussion of perceived gains experienced as 'satisfaction' (e.g. Herskovits 1960: 17; Plattner 1989: 8; see Ortiz 1983 for a discussion of associated issues).

These examples suggest that *experiential* space, not Cartesian space, forms an essential constituent of human social relations. Such issues have long been discussed by geographers of various schools (e.g. Relph 1976; Tuan 1977; Shields 1991; Deutsche 1996; Valentine 1996) but similar concerns have only recently begun to be voiced in the archaeological literature (e.g. Thomas 1993, 1996; Tilley 1994). Human perceptions of landscape have therefore come to be seen as increasingly important in understanding spatial relations at the landscape level. It is the qualitative rather than the quantitative aspects of landscape that inform human action. In Chapter 12, this volume, Young and Simmonds show how long-standing cultural attachment to place can outweigh economic concerns. Despite deteriorating climatic conditions towards the end of the Bronze Age, the settlements of upland Northumbria in northern England were not abandoned. Rather, their occupants responded creatively to changing circumstances, developing a diversified economic base and using kinship networks to overcome environmental limits.

The practical and the symbolic in settlement research

Although the implications of recent discussions of landscape for settlement archaeology are clear, settlement has not yet formed a distinct focus of research within this body of work. Most authors have focused on landscapes possessing prehistoric ceremonial monuments but with little contemporary settlement data (e.g. Bradley 1991b; Barrett 1994; Tilley 1994). Research on ritual landscapes naturally prioritizes particular kinds of questions, for example concerning the nature of ancient cosmologies and the power relations embedded within them. For instance, it has been argued that only an elite minority may have had access to ceremonial monuments; by distinguishing between those allowed inside and those excluded, status differences were reproduced (e.g. Thomas 1991: 41–52; Barrett 1994: 13–24). Thus, much of the recent literature on prehistoric landscapes has laid a strong emphasis on the interpretation of ancient power structures to the exclusion of other aspects of human social life. Although these approaches are clearly valuable, the danger of this is that landscape comes to be seen as the product of an abstract belief-system that appears to have little to do with the materialities of day-to-day life. Such activities as subsistence production or the organization of labour have received little attention within many of these discussions.

An emphasis on environmental perception as a significant variable in shaping human action may help us to avoid the outright rejection of environmental factors that has characterized much archaeological writing on landscape in the 1990s. Not only does this reproduce in the past the radical culture–nature dichotomy that is a particular feature of post-Enlightenment thought (see Jordanova 1980; Lloyd 1984; Bordo 1987), but it also presupposes the universality of the modern fragmentation of practice that disarticulates the ecological from the social. Critiques of positivist approaches within geography (e.g. Gregory 1978; Relph 1981) have facilitated a *re-enculturation* of the environment in geographical writing (e.g. Tuan 1977; Blaikie & Brookfield 1987; Soja 1989; Shields 1991). We argue that in archaeology a focus on settlement will be particularly valuable in helping to redress this balance by explicitly reintroducing the materialities of daily life as a focus of attention. Similar approaches are beginning to be explored elsewhere within the archaeological literature, particularly by environmental archaeologists. Bell (1992), for example, discusses how the perception of and response to 'hazards' such as soil erosion must be understood as socially defined.

One way to avoid the continued dislocation of 'functional' activities from discussions of landscape as a cultural construct is to recognize that human action is always both *practical and symbolic*. Contemporary notions of 'practicality' are culturally constructed; they are part of an historically specific logic that itself forms an ideology. These different logics become articulated as sets of cosmological beliefs and values. By acting practically on the world in day-to-day life, people play out such beliefs. In other words, cosmologies are not abstract belief systems but enable people to understand the world and to get on in it by providing a logic for action and an explanation of the universe. Ideas about what constitutes an appropriate economic strategy are part and parcel of these systems of value and meaning. Thus, modern Western notions of 'efficiency' or 'utility' can be seen as the product of a particular set of historical circumstances. In this sense any practical action is also symbolic because it reproduces the sets of values and social relations that are embedded in cosmological schemes. Settlements, as the locus for a wide range of both daily maintenance and ritual activities, are an obvious source of data for any study of this interrelationship.

Questions of place: boundaries and territoriality

Conceptualization of the interrelationship between settlement and landscape is also called into question when it comes to identifying the location and nature of settlement boundaries. As discussed above with reference to site distribution maps, archaeologists have frequently presented prehistoric settlements as distinct and spatially circumscribed points within the landscape. However, it is often impossible to clearly identify the limits or edges of ancient settlements in spatial terms. In some instances, empirical difficulties may be encountered when it comes to delineating sites on the ground (Wilke & Thompson 1977: 19–20; Cherry et al. 1991: 19–21, 28; Schofield 1991; see Carman, Chapter 2, this volume). For example, artefactual evidence may be distributed irregularly across extensive areas of the landscape, defying resolution into the bounded, artefact-dense localities that we associate with settlement. In other cases, modern Western notions of where a site's boundaries ought to lie are contradicted by the archaeological evidence. For example, Bailey (Chapter 6, this volume) shows how a considerable amount of activity took place outside tell sites in southeastern Europe, transcending the physical limits of the mounds themselves. However, archaeological investigation and discussion in this region has tended to focus exclusively on the tell mounds. The merits of 'off-site' or 'non-site' archaeology as one potential means of overcoming these difficulties have been widely debated (Thomas 1975; Foley 1981; Dunnell & Dancy 1983), particularly in the context of archaeological survey work.

Dunnell (1992) has outlined considerations relevant to this issue. He questions whether sites are 'real' archaeological entities or merely analytical categories, the reality of which becomes erroneously projected into the past (see also Carman, Chapter 2, this volume). There has been a tendency to characterize ancient landscapes as comprising a series of definable nodes of human interest distributed across a uniform background. This allows for greater analytical ease but may also reflect our own place-centred perception of space. The significance of the space between such points is rarely considered beyond its economic value as site-catchment area or economic hinterland (see also Tilley 1994). As discussed above, this clearly relates to capitalist economics and the spatiality of Cartesian thought. The variable nature of the culture–nature divide is also relevant here, especially where it is not articulated as powerfully as it is in modern Western society. In such a context, settlements may not be conceptualized as bounded entities, bastions of culture to be protected from the wilderness outside, but may form part of an extensive and fluid social landscape in which topographical features, animals and humans each play a role in the creation of cultural meaning.

The notion that settlements can be abstracted from their wider landscape context is also problematic when considering issues of residential mobility. The many different places that people encounter over the course of their life-histories all contribute to the construction of selfhood. Humans are never just 'here and now', for some part of their identity is always rooted in past events and in other places. In this way, the spatial rhythms of human life as people move from place to place over the course of a day, a year or a lifetime create very particular ways of experiencing the world (Barrett 1994: 145). The periodicities that were embedded within different lifestyles can be approached archaeologically through studies of residential mobility, subsistence practices, ritual cycles and the like (e.g. Bradley 1991a; Mizoguchi 1993; Barrett 1994; Gosden 1994). For example, Pollard (Chapter 5, this volume) describes how addressing the different temporalities built into the residentially mobile lifestyles of Neolithic Britain can provide new insights into how social identities and inter-group relationships were constituted during this period. Factors such as gendered or age-related divisions of labour meant that not everyone within the community would have followed the same patterns of movement over the annual cycle. He argues that these differences would have resulted in varied experiences and perceptions of life that would have facilitated the reproduction of different categories of social persona.

Land tenure and territoriality

The conceptual and methodological difficulties encountered in trying to detach settlements from the landscapes in which they are embedded introduces a second set of questions. The term 'settlement' is frequently used to describe the process by which people inhabit or colonize an area of landscape. As such, the *act* of settling brings into question the mechanisms through which tenurial relationships are created and reproduced. At this level, settlement studies again move beyond site-centred approaches to consider the relationship between people, place and landscape. In the absence of a context-based approach, archaeologists have tended to reconstruct ancient territorial practices and patterns of land tenure by employing models that project into the past the fixed boundaries and exclusive formalized ownership characteristic of modern nation states. For example, the territories of ancient settlements have been reconstructed using Thiessen polygons.

However, boundaries in other societies are not always as fixed and immutable as they are in the modern Western world. Ingold (1986: 147–56) describes how hunter–gatherers claim tenure over places and paths rather than over areas of land. Their territories do not consist of bounded two-dimensional surfaces and therefore these groups do not identify precise points of transition between adjacent territories (cf. Casimir 1992). The conflict between Aboriginal and post-colonial authorities in Australia over land rights provides valuable insights into different ways of conceptualizing the 'possession' of space. Aboriginal song lines were not legally recognized as a form of land tenure because they were not based on the physical demarcation of space for the use of natural resources. However, Aboriginal individuals and communities maintain ownership through culturally prescribed forms of guardianship actualized by walking through the land in the tracks of mythical ancestors (Berndt 1976; Munn 1986; Morphy 1991).

In many hunter–gatherer societies, ownership of land does not necessarily imply that neighbouring groups may not have access to this space (Ingold 1986; Bahuchet 1992). Although rights to resources are not usually so flexible among settled agriculturists, most societies lie somewhere on a continuum between such an adaptable arrangement and the exclusive rights permanently recorded in the legal documents of capitalist societies (e.g. Sheddick 1954; Nayacakalou 1971; Hoben 1973). Among many agriculturists, a land owner's dominance tails off with distance from a particular reference point, such as a dwelling, leaving a hazy boundary zone that cannot be sharply distinguished from its neighbour. This can be contrasted with the situation in Western society where the power of a land owner remains constant over the whole surface of a well-defined territory. In many societies, rights of land use may be open to contestation or may shift over time. For example, in parts of the Andes, much land is held in common and access to specific parcels is periodically distributed by community leaders (e.g. Isbell 1978; Godoy 1991). Seasonal variations may also contribute to changes in land rights. For example, when fields are in crop they 'belong' to those who have planted them. However, when the same fields are in fallow they may be used by the whole community for grazing. In Chapter 11, this volume, Fewster adds another dimension to these considerations by showing how social and territorial boundaries may be placed to reflect *feelings of social distance* between neighbouring groups. She describes how the Bamangwato of Serowe, Botswana, and their Basarwa neighbours live in close geographical proximity and are economically dependent on one another. Yet, the agropastoralist Bamangwato think of the Basarwa, who until recently have been hunter–gatherers, as inferior and they often describe them as '*tennyanateng*' which can be translated as 'far, far away'. Therefore, perceived 'closeness' can be as much a matter of social distance as measurable physical distance and may be reflected in a community's expression of territoriality.

The construction of place

Given these complications, it may be more fruitful to approach the nature of ancient territoriality by constructing a detailed understanding of the ways in which people in non-capitalist societies relate to the land. This may be expressed through the maintenance and restructuring of cultural meaning, tradition and genealogy. Several of the authors in this volume explore how tenurial practices arise from the complex relationships between social practices and historically constituted landscapes. They show how the construction of place facilitates the creation and reproduction of relationships between humans and the landscapes they inhabit (cf. Williams 1983; Ingold 1986; Tilley 1994). Settlements, as a primary locus for many of the activities through which the social and material conditions of life are maintained and transformed, play a particularly important role in this process. For instance, Bailey (Chapter 6, this volume) interprets the frequent rebuilding and replastering of houses in Bulgarian tells as a means of periodically reaffirming their inhabitants' rights to dwell there; an attempt to create 'a permanence of place that did not in reality exist' for these seasonally occupied locales. The depositional practices identified by Kovacik (Chapter 10, this volume) appear to have played a similar role, forging a link between people and place through reference to the past use and significance of a locale.

Understanding places, including settlements, as historically constituted entities provides one step forward (cf. Ingold 1993; Barrett 1994; Thomas 1996). As Pollard and Kovacik (Chapter 5 and 10, this volume) argue, 'acts of settlement' are not isolated social events but take place within landscapes that are already redolent with meaning. The act of settling at a locale involves reference to the previous use of that place. Conversely, settlements may themselves be commemorated through the construction of later monuments on the same site. In this way, settlements are intimately bound up with the biographies of particular individuals and groups (see Pollard, Chapter 5, this volume). Such biographies are made up of constellations of relationships and events that are inseparable from the places where these are experienced. These relationships and events are strung in a sequence through time such that human identities are constructed in narrative form. Conversely, places can also be seen as possessing biographies (cf. Ingold 1993; Barrett 1994). The people that have dwelt there and the actions that unfolded there all impart meanings to a place. Thus, we may argue that settlements come into being through their embeddedness within networks of human relations that stretch through both space and time.

Conclusion

In this introductory chapter, we have explored settlement as the set of *territorial and social practices* through which relationships between people and the world around them were created and transformed. As the process of 'settling', settlement can be seen as the creation of place through culturally specific sets of activities relating individuals and groups to landscapes and to each other within those landscapes. In effect, this involves a reorientation of settlement studies away from received notions of spatial or functional characteristics and towards defining and understanding the range of intercultural variability in residential practice. The ambiguity we have noted in the manner in which the term 'settlement' is used and characterized demonstrates that a single definition will not work in all cases. The terms and descriptive categories prehistorians employ have particular effects on interpretation and require consideration. The contributions to this volume therefore explore a dynamic and contextual conceptualization of settlement constituted primarily within the social time of human experience rather than the 'objective' time of archaeological chronologies.

This approach underlines the fact that settlement and landscape cannot be divorced from one another. Similar issues are clearly relevant to both landscape and settlement studies, for example the nature of human–environment relations. The character of individual settlement sites can only be fully understood through reference to their landscape context. At the same time, the physical and conceptual boundaries between site and landscape are often difficult to locate archaeologically and in many societies are more fluid and contextual than in the modern Western world. Nonetheless, it would be a mistake to subsume settlement studies entirely within landscape archaeology. A focus on settlement can contribute uniquely to studies of ancient landscape in several ways. As we have discussed, humans categorize and differentiate space according to culturally constituted perceptions of its qualitative value. Studies of the social construction of place therefore remain central to understanding human–landscape relations in the past. As settlements are the locations where many of the activities central to the social and material reproduction of life are performed, they play a major role in this process. Furthermore, settlement provides an important point of contact between the 'practical' and the 'ideological' components of human existence. By focusing at this level, it may therefore be possible to avoid the current disjunction in landscape studies between those approaches that view landscape as a manifestation of cosmological beliefs and those that locate it firmly within the realm of functional behaviour. Finally, studies at an intra-site level also raise questions that have not generally been a focus of interest in landscape archaeology. These include the construction of gender relations, the categorization of human practice, the organization of space within the intimate, lived experience of day-to-day life, the relationship between domestic and ritual activity and the nature of the household group as well as many others. We therefore argue that there continues to be an important place in archaeological research for a distinctive settlement archaeology.

Clearly, there is considerable potential to expand and revitalize settlement studies in the light of current developments in archaeological theory. The issues discussed in this volume are necessarily disparate and cannot address all aspects of settlement research. Yet, we hope that these themes in settlement archaeology will go some way towards stimulating renewed interest in what remains a central source of archaeological evidence on the prehistoric world.

References

Bahuchet, S. 1992. Spatial mobility and access to resources among the African pygmies. In *Mobility and territoriality: social and spatial boundaries among foragers, fishers, pastoralists and peripatetics*, M. Casimir & A. Rao (eds), 205–57. New York: Berg.

Barrett, J. C. 1991. Bronze Age pottery and the problem of classification. In *Papers on the prehistoric archaeology of Cranborne Chase*, J. Barrett, R. Bradley, M. Hall (eds), 210–30. Oxford: Oxbow Monograph 11.

Barrett, J. C. 1994. *Fragments from antiquity: an archaeology of social life in Britain, 2900–1200 BC*. Oxford: Blackwell.

Bell, M. 1992. Archaeology under alluvium: human agency and environmental process. Some concluding remarks. In *Alluvial archaeology in Britain*, S. Needham & M. Macklin (eds), 271–6. Oxford: Oxbow Monograph 27.

Bender, D. 1967. A refinement of the concept of household: families, co-residence and domestic function. *American Anthropologist* **69**, 493–504.

Bender, B. 1993a. Landscape – meaning and action. See Bender (1993b), 1–17. Oxford: Berg.

Bender, B. (ed.) 1993b. *Landscape: politics and perspectives*. Oxford: Berg.

Berndt, R. 1976. Territoriality and the problem of demarcating socio-cultural space. In *Tribes and boundaries in Australia*, N. Peterson (ed.), 133–61. Canberra: Australian Institute of Aboriginal Studies, Social Anthropology Series 10.

Blaikie, P. & H. Brookfield (eds) 1987. *Land degradation and society*. London: Methuen.

Bordo, S. 1987. *The flight to objectivity: essays on Cartesianism and culture*. Albany: State University of New York Press.

Bourdier, J. P. & N. Alsayad (eds) 1989. *Dwellings, settlements and tradition: cross-cultural perspectives*. Lanham, Maryland: University Press of America.

Boyd, B. 1995. Writing histories of occupation: perceptions of settlement in the Later Epipalaeolithic and Early Neolithic Levant. Paper presented at the conference 'Conceptualising Settlement in Prehistoric Archaeology', Cambridge, England.

Bradley, R. J. 1991a. Ritual, time and history. *World Archaeology* **23**, 209–19.

Bradley, R. J. 1991b. Rock art and the perception of landscape. *Cambridge Archaeological Journal* **1**, 77–101.

Brightman, R. 1993. *Grateful prey: Rock Cree human–animal relationships*. Berkeley: University of California Press.

Casimir, M. 1992. The dimensions of territoriality: an introduction. In *Mobility and territoriality: social and spatial boundaries among foragers, fishers, pastoralists and peripatetics*, M. Casimir & A. Rao (eds), 1–26. New York: Berg.

Cherry, J. F., J. L. Davis, E. Mantzourani 1991. *Landscape archaeology as long-term history: northern Keos in the Cycladic Islands*. Los Angeles: Institute of Archaeology, University of California.

Clarke, D. L. 1972. A provisional model of an Iron Age society and its settlement system. In *Models in archaeology*, D. L. Clark (ed.), 801–69. London: Methuen.

Cosgrove, D. & S. Daniels (eds) 1988. *The iconography of landscape*. Cambridge: Cambridge University Press.

Descola, P. & G. Pálsson (eds) 1996. *Nature and society: anthropological perspectives*. London: Routledge.

Deutsche, R. 1996. *Evictions: art and spatial politics*. Cambridge, MA: Massachusetts Institute of Technology Press.

Dunnell, R. C. 1992. The notion site. In *Space, time and archaeological landscapes*, J. Rossignol & L. Wandsnider (eds), 21–41. New York: Plenum Press.

Dunnell, R. C. & W. S. Dancy 1983. The siteless survey: a regional scale data collection strategy. In *Advances in method and theory*, vol. 6, M. B. Schiffer (ed.), 267–88. New York: Academic Press.

Ellison, A. 1978. The Bronze Age in Sussex. In *Archaeology in Sussex to AD 1500*, P. Drewett (ed.), 30–37. London: Council of British Archaeology Research Report 29.

Evans, C. 1985. Tradition and the cultural landscape: an archaeology of place. *Archaeological Review from Cambridge* **4**, 80–94.

Fabian, C. 1984. *Time and the other: how anthropology makes its object*. New York: Columbia University Press.

Foley, R. 1981. Off-site archaeology: an alternative approach for the short-sited. In *Pattern of the past: studies in honour of David Clarke*, I. Hodder, G. Isaac, N. Hammond (eds), 157–83. Cambridge: Cambridge University Press.

Fox, C. 1932. *The personality of Britain: its influence on inhabitant and invader in prehistoric and early historic times*. Cardiff: National Museum of Wales / The Press Board of the University of Wales.

Godoy, R. 1991. The evolution of common field agriculture in the Andes: a hypothesis. *Comparative Studies in Society and History* **33**(2), 395–414.

Goody, J. (ed.) 1958. *The developmental cycle in domestic groups*. Cambridge: Cambridge University Press.

Goody, J. 1972. The evolution of the family. In *Household and family in past time*, P. Laslett & R. Wall (eds), 103–24. Cambridge: Cambridge University Press.

Gosden, C. 1994. *Social being and time.* Oxford: Blackwell.

Gradmann, R. 1906. Beziehung zwischen Pflanzengeographie und Siedlungsgeschichte. *Geographische Zeitschrift* **12**, 305–25.

Gregory, D. 1978. *Ideology, science and human geography.* London: Hutchinson.

Gregory, D. & J. Urry (eds) 1985. *Social relations and spatial structures.* London: Macmillan.

Harley, J. B. 1988. Maps, knowledge and power. In *The iconography of landscape: essays on the symbolic representation, design and use of past environments*, D. Cosgrove & S. Daniels (eds), 277–312. Cambridge: Cambridge University Press.

Herskovits, M. 1960. *Economic anthropology: a study in comparative economics.* New York: Alfred Knopf.

Hoben, A. 1973. *Land tenure among the Amhara of Ethiopia: the dynamics of cognitive descent.* Chicago: Chicago University Press.

Hodder, I. 1982. Towards a contextual approach to prehistoric exchange. In *Contexts for prehistoric exchange*, J. E. Ericson & T. Earle (eds), 199–211. New York: Academic Press.

Hodder, I. 1986. *Reading the past: current approaches to interpretation in archaeology.* Cambridge: Cambridge University Press.

Hodder, I. 1987. Contextual archaeology: an interpretation of Çatal Hüyük and a discussion of the origins of agriculture. *Bulletin of the Institute of Archaeology* **24**, 43–56.

Hodder, I. 1990. *The domestication of Europe: structure and contingency in Neolithic societies.* Oxford: Blackwell.

Hodder, I. (ed.), 1996. *On the surface: Catalhoyuk 1993–95.* Cambridge: McDonald Institute for Archaeological Research.

Ingold, T. 1986. *The appropriation of nature.* Manchester: Manchester University Press.

Ingold, T. 1993. The temporality of the landscape. *World Archaeology* **25**(2), 152–74.

Isbell, B. J. 1978. *To defend ourselves: ecology and ritual in an Andean village.* Austin, TX: Institute of Latin American Studies, University of Texas at Austin.

Jordanova, L. J. 1980. Natural facts: a historical perspective on science and sexuality. In *Nature, culture and gender*, C. MacCormack & M. Strathern (eds), 42–69. Cambridge: Cambridge University Press.

Kent, S. 1984. *Analyzing activity areas: an ethnoarchaeological study of the use of space.* Albuquerque: University of New Mexico Press.

Kent, S. (ed.) 1990. *Domestic architecture and the use of space: an interdisciplinary cross-cultural study.* Cambridge: Cambridge University Press.

Kirby, K. 1996. Re: mapping subjectivity: cartographic vision and the limits of politics. In *BodySpace: destabilizing geographies of gender and sexuality*, N. Duncan (ed.), 45–55. London: Routledge.

La Fontaine, J. 1981. The domestication of the savage male. *Man* **16**, 333–49.

Lloyd, G. 1984. *The man of reason: 'male' and 'female' in Western philosophy.* London: Methuen.

MacCormack, C. & M. Strathern (eds) 1980. *Nature, culture and gender.* Cambridge: Cambridge University Press.

MacEachern, S., D. Archer, R. Garvin (eds) 1989. *Households and communities.* Calgary: University of Calgary Architectural Association.

Matthews, W. & J. N. Postgate 1994. The imprint of living in an early Mesopotamian city: questions and answers. In *Whither environmental archaeology?*, R. Luff & P. Rowley-Conwy (eds), 171–212. Oxford: Oxbow Monograph 38.

Melaart, J. 1967. *Çatal Hüyük.* London: Thames & Hudson.

Mizoguchi, K. 1993. Time in the reproduction of mortuary practices. *World Archaeology* **25**(2), 223–35.

Moore, H. 1988. *Feminism and anthropology.* Oxford: Polity Press.

Morphy, H. 1991. *Ancestral connections.* Chicago, IL: Chicago University Press.

Munn, N. D. 1970. The transformation of subjects into objects in Walbiri and Pitjantjatjara myth. In *Australian Aboriginal anthropology: modern studies in the social anthropology of the Australian Aborigines*, R. Berndt (ed.), 141–63. Perth: University of Western Australia Press.

Munn, N. D. 1986. *Walbiri iconography.* Chicago: Chicago University Press.

Nayacakalou, R. R. 1971. Fiji: manipulating the system. In *Land tenure in the Pacific*, R. Crocombe (ed.), 206–26. Oxford: Oxford University Press.

Netting, R. 1993. *Smallholders, householders: farm families and the ecology of intensive, sustainable agriculture*. Stanford: Stanford University Press.

Netting, R., R. Wilk, E. Arnould (eds) 1984. *Households: comparative and historical studies of the domestic group*. Berkeley: University of California Press.

Oliver, P. 1987. *Dwellings: the house across the world*. London: Phaidon.

Olwig, K. 1993. Sexual cosmology: nation and landscape at the conceptual interstices of nature and culture; or what does landscape really mean? See Bender (1993b), 307–43.

Ortiz, S. 1983. What is decision analysis all about? The problems of formal representations. In *Economic anthropology: topics and theories*, S. Ortiz (ed.), 249–97. London: University Press of America.

Pálsson, G. 1996. Human–environmental relations: orientalism, paternalism and communalism. In *Nature and society: anthropological perspectives*, P. Descola & G. Pálsson (eds), 63–81. London: Routledge.

Parker Pearson, M. 1996. Food, fertility and front doors in the first millennium BC. In *The Iron Age in Britain and Ireland: recent trends*, T. Champion &. J. Collis (eds), 117–32. Sheffield: J. R. Collis Publications.

Parker Pearson, M. & C. Richards 1994a. Ordering the world: perceptions of architecture, space and time. In *Architecture and order: approaches to social space*, M. Parker Pearson & C. Richards (eds), 1–37. London: Routledge.

Parker Pearson, M. & C. Richards 1994b. Architecture and order: spatial representation and archaeology. In *Architecture and order: approaches to social space*, M. Parker Pearson & C. Richards (eds), 38–72. London: Routledge.

Penning-Rosewell, E. & D. Lowenthal (eds) 1986. *Landscape meanings and values*. London: Allen & Unwin.

Plattner, S. (ed.) 1989. *Economic anthropology*. Stanford, Stanford University Press.

Prince, H. 1988. Art and agrarian change, 1710–1915. In *The iconography of landscape: essays on the symbolic representation, design and use of past environments*, D. Cosgrove & S. Daniels (eds), 98–118. Cambridge: Cambridge University Press.

Relph, E. 1976. *Place and placelessness*. London: Pion.

Relph, E. 1981. *Rational landscapes and humanistic geography*. London: Croom Helm.

Richards, C. 1990. The Late Neolithic house in Orkney. In *The social archaeology of houses*, R. Samson (ed.), 111–24. Edinburgh: Edinburgh University Press.

Rudie, I. 1970. Household organisation. Adaptive process and restrictive form: a viewpoint on economic change. *Folk* **11/12**, 185–200.

Sanders, W. T., J. R. Parsons, R. S. Santley 1979. *The Basin of Mexico: ecological processes in the evolution of a civilization*. New York: Academic Press.

Sanjek, R. 1982. The organisation of households in Adabraka: toward a wider comparative perspective. *Comparative Studies in Society and History* **24**, 57–103.

Schofield, A. J. 1991. *Interpreting artefact scatters: contributions to ploughzone archaeology*. Oxford: Oxbow Books.

Sheddick, V. 1954. *Land tenure in Basutoland*. London: Her Majesty's Stationery Office.

Shields, R. 1991. *Places on the margin: alternative geographies of modernity*. London: Routledge.

Soja, E. 1989. *Postmodern geographies: the reassertion of space in critical social theory*. London: Verso.

Stone, G. D., R. M. Netting, M. P. Stone. 1990. Seasonality, labour scheduling and agricultural intensification in the Nigerian Savanna. *American Anthropology* **92**(1), 7–23.

Strathern, M. 1984. Domesticity and the denigration of women. In *Rethinking women's roles: perspectives from the Pacific*, D. O'Brien & S. Tiffany (eds), 13–31. Berkeley: University of California Press.

Thomas, D. H. 1975. Nonsite sampling in archaeology: up the creek without a site? In *Sampling in archaeology*, J. W. Mueller (ed.), 61–81. Tucson: University of Arizona Press.

Thomas, J. 1991. *Rethinking the Neolithic*. Cambridge: Cambridge University Press.

Thomas, J. 1993. The politics of vision and archaeologies of landscape. See Bender (1993b), 19–48. Oxford: Berg.

Thomas, J. 1996. *Time, culture and identity: an interpretive archaeology*. London: Routledge.

Tiffany, S. 1978. Models and the social anthropology of women. *Man* **13**, 34–51.

Tilley, C. 1994. *A phenomenology of landscape: places, paths and monuments*. Oxford & Providence: Berg.

Tourtellot, G. 1988. Developmental cycles of households and houses at Seibal. In *Household and community in the Mesoamerican past*, R. Wilk & W. Ashmore (eds), 97–120. Albuquerque: University of New Mexico Press.

Turnbull, C. 1961. *The forest people*. London: Jonathan Cape.

Tuan, Y.-F. 1977. *Space and place: the perspective of experience*. London: Arnold.

Valentine, G. 1996. (Re)negotiating the 'heterosexual street': lesbian productions of space. In *BodySpace: destabilizing geographies of gender and sexuality*, N. Duncan (ed.), 146–55. London: Routledge.

Waterson, R. 1990. *The living house: an anthropology of architecture in southeast Asia*. Singapore: Oxford University Press.

Weismantel, M. 1989. *Food, gender and poverty in the Ecuadorian Andes*. Philadelphia: University of Pennsylvania Press.

Wilk, R. & R. Netting 1984. Households: changing forms and functions. In *Households: comparative and historical studies of the domestic group*, R. Netting, R. Wilk, E. Arnould (eds), 1–28. Berkeley: University of California Press.

Wilk, R. & W. Rathje 1982. Household archaeology. *American Behaviorial Scientist* **25**(6), 617–39.

Wilke, S. & G. Thompson 1977. *Archaeological survey of Western Kent County, Maryland*. Annapolis: Maryland Historical Trust.

Willey, G. 1953. *Prehistoric settlement patterns of the Virú Valley, Peru*. Washington, D.C.: Smithsonian Institution, Bureau of American Ethnology Bulletin **15**.

Williams, N. 1983. Yolngu concepts of land ownership. In *Aborigines, land and land-rights*, N. Peterson & M. Langton (eds), 94–109. Canberra: Australian Institute of Aboriginal Studies.

Woodford-Berger, P. 1981. Women in houses: the organisation of residence and work in rural Ghana. *Antropologiska Studier* **30/31**, 3–35.

Woolley, L. 1954. *Digging up the past*, 2nd edn. Harmondsworth: Penguin.

Yanagisako, S. J. 1979. Family and household: the analysis of domestic groups. *Annual Review of Anthropology* **8**, 161–205.

CHAPTER TWO

Settling on sites: constraining concepts

John Carman

This volume concentrates on the concept of 'the settlement' as it applies in prehistoric archaeology. Somewhat perversely for an opening chapter, I want to focus on the other half of this conceptual equation: the idea of the settlement *site*.

My aim in writing the paper is to pursue the wider objective of introducing concerns derived from the field of archaeological heritage management (AHM; otherwise cultural resource management or CRM) into 'mainstream' or 'research' archaeology texts. Since the concept of the 'settlement' is not a specific concern of AHM, but the nature and use of the concept of 'site' is such a concern, the two concepts will be compared and juxtaposed in order to gain some insight into what the combined term 'settlement site' may refer to. The first part of this chapter thus constitutes a ramble through the conceptual history of the 'settlement site' in English language usage, in research archaeology, in UK and US law and in the management practices of archaeology. In the course of this discussion, the concept inevitably becomes involved with ideas about landscape and the colonization of space – some of it other peoples'. Drawing on and developing these themes, the chapter then goes on to outline a possible alternative to 'site-based' settlement archaeology and some of its implications. Among these is the recasting of the 'settlement' concept from that of a fixed location in space to an extended process over time.

Settlements and sites

Binford (1989: 3) has asserted that archaeologists 'do not study . . . ancient settlements . . . We study artifacts.' In contrast with this, my focus is on the basic ideas and concepts archaeologists use and where they come from with particular reference to those found in English law and in archaeological heritage management (Carman 1996b). One approach to this is to look at the origins and changing meanings of terms as they are used over time.

At first glance, and acting on intuitive judgement alone, the words 'site' and 'settlement' would appear to be quite closely related. They both start with the letter 's' and the following vowels are not that different: the 'i' of 'site' may be a simple transformation of the 'e' in 'settle'. They each follow with a 't', and only the fact that in 'settle' that 't' is in fact a 'tl' diphthong suggests that perhaps the words may not be that closely related after all. If they are related, then it seems that in the concept of the 'settlement site' we are faced with a tautology: two terms used together that both mean the same thing. Tautologies are, of course, very powerful things. In saying the same thing twice but in different words or expressions, they contain a self-reinforcement that discourages examination of the concept. So much so that the concept becomes self-evidently meaningful and what it actually refers to and any hidden assumptions that it contains are rarely, if ever, brought to light.

In fact, the terms 'site' and 'settlement' are not that closely related after all (except maybe in their joint derivation from some original source in the Indo-European language). 'Site' comes from Anglo-French *site* or Latin *situs* meaning local position, and perhaps derives ultimately from the past participle stem of the Latin verb *sinere*, which means to leave or allow to remain. In 1461 the word 'site' meant 'the ground or area upon which a building, town, etc. has been built, or which is set apart for some purpose. Also, a plot, or number of plots, of land intended or suitable for building' (Oxford English Dictionary 1984). By 1567 it referred to 'the situation or position of a place, town, building, etc.' (ibid.) and by 1691 it meant 'the place or position occupied by some specified thing, frequently implying original or fixed position'. 'Settlement' (the verb 'settle' plus the suffix 'ment' that turns it into a noun) derives from Old English *setlan* and one of its meanings is defined as 'an assemblage of persons settled in a locality'. In 1697 it meant specifically 'a community of the subjects of a state settled in a new country; a tract of country so settled, a colony, especially one in its earlier stages' (ibid.).

Both these terms thus contain two ideas that they share. The one is to do with the original position and deliberate placement in that position. The other is to do with agglomerations of people and buildings to contain them. Despite their different origins, both terms thus came to mean the same thing, and their use together in the idea of the 'settlement site' accordingly creates a tautology. Moreover, this common meaning emerged very much at the same time. The concept of the site as an original and deliberate location appeared in 1691. The settlement as colony (the deliberate placement of people and their buildings in a new land) appeared only six years later in 1697. The last years of the seventeenth century was the culmination of a period in which such communities were planted in, among other places, the New World and Ireland (Gillespie 1993). Such settlements and colonies and sites are always new communities being actively created, frequently with some religious, political or commercial purpose behind them.

The concept of the settlement site as a distinctive category thus includes the idea of an original foundation, a pioneer settlement, something only just made, and fragile. It also follows that we are looking for something similar to the kind of settlement we would expect to find in the New World: a distinct location, a particular place, and quite firmly bounded. In consequence, any visual picture of a prehistoric settlement site we may carry about in our heads may owe a great deal to adventure stories set in the American wilderness. This should not be surprising since the concept of 'landscape' as the object that acts as a container to sites, settlements and hence settlement sites (Carman 1996a) is itself a product of this period of colonization. The term emerged in the early modern period, that is the same period as that in which 'site' and 'settlement' were first used synonymously. It meant 'a background of scenery in a portrait or figure painting' in 1676, less specifically 'a view of something' by 1711, and came also to mean 'a map' by 1723 (OED 1984).

Maps seek to contain and regulate space by reducing it to figurative conventions; thus, they allow the marking of non-natural, non-physical boundaries on that space. They are a technology of control over land and as such they lend themselves to use as a tool of ownership. It is less immediately clear from the dictionary definitions of 'landscape' that paintings are a technology of control, but the best evidence is available from looking at such a work. Gainsborough's mid-eighteenth century painting of 'Mr and Mrs Andrews' shows from left to right: Mr Andrews with his gun over his arm and his dog at his feet, Mrs Andrews seated beside him, and a view of fields and orchards stretching away and behind to their distant house. An alternative title might be 'Mr Andrews and his prized possessions' as the image is of all the things belonging to Mr Andrews gathered around him, from sporting rifle and dog, wife and income-producing property, to country mansion. For Olwig, 'landscape painting represents a concept of nature that subtly colonizes the earlier concepts of nature, nation, land and . . . culture . . . Landscape was framed and reified as a cultural object, to be bought and sold' (1993: 331) and was to become the primary tool of identity formation in colonial America (ibid.: 334–8). This metaphorical colonization of one abstract concept by another was matched in practice by the colonization of previously common land by private landowners, and the colonization of distant lands by Europeans, all in the same period of history.

Sites in archaeological heritage management

The term 'site' is used extensively in legislation affecting the material of archaeology and in the semi-official literature produced by archaeological heritage management agencies. Despite the primacy of law in archaeological heritage management (Cleere 1989: 10), lawyers do not have a definition of 'site' other than one derived from archaeological texts (O'Keefe & Prott 1984: 162–3). As understood for the purposes of English preservation legislation, a site is usually not a site in itself but is instead the site of something else, except when it can be an ancient monument in its own right (National Heritage Act 1983, s. 33[8] and 34[3]). This is the same view of the concept as is taken in the (UK) *Thesaurus of Archaeological Site Types* that advises us to 'specify the site type wherever possible' (Royal Commission on Historic Monuments for England/English Heritage 1992: 122).

The law also places boundaries around sites. In US legislation, archaeologically identified 'sites' are legally designated as 'landmarks' that are treated as single, distinct locations (US Department of the Interior 1989–90: 28).

In England, both ancient monuments and sites are understood as clearly demarcated spaces that have hard edges that can be identified. A monument comprises a physical feature, deliberately placed where it stands or penetrates the earth, together with the land on which it stands or which is penetrated by the feature. A site is the location and physical form of such a feature and any land allowing it to remain in place (the ground under a built structure, the roof and walls of a digging or cave). Intuitively and by observation, we all know that objects have hard edges; buildings and churches have walls and so on. Nonetheless, it is not clear that a site or a monument can be easily distinguished from its surroundings, and yet the law treats them as if this is the case. The same applies to the site of a crashed, stranded or sunk aircraft, vehicle or vessel.

To add to the confusion, 'References . . . to the site of a monument – (a) are references to the monument itself where it consists of a site; and (b) in any other case include references to the monument itself' (Ancient Monuments and Archaeological Areas Act, s. 61[11]). This tortuous and tautological provision from current English law has a wonderfully beguiling and cabalistic quality. What these words simply mean is that the site of a component of the archaeological record can both contain and be contained within that component and also comprises the component itself. This is three quite different things all at once. What this amounts to is a circularity in the legal understanding of these terms. A monument can include its site, but at the same time the site of a monument can comprise the monument, and a site may indeed constitute an ancient monument in its own right. In other words, the site is the monument and the monument is the site. To talk of one is to encompass the other. This returns us to the tautology that lies at the heart of the notion of the 'settlement site'.

At this point, it is worth complicating the issue still further by pointing out that there are in archaeology two quite distinct understandings of the concept of 'site'. First, sites may be understood as places where relatively more archaeological material is found than in the landscape surrounding them, although such material is scattered all over that landscape. Second, they may represent nodes of more concentrated activity within a larger area over which activities were conducted in the past. Both of these ideas of the nature of the site are reflected to some extent in the understandings of the concept of site enshrined in English and US legislation, although the former is by far the dominant one.

The idea of site as a relatively dense concentration of archaeological material represents the site as a contemporary phenomenon that is the concern of the archaeologist. This is the understanding contained within the English legal definitions of monument (AMAA79, s. 61[7–11]) and ancient monument (NH83, s. 33[8]) as timeless, as related to the form identifiable now (as upstanding, earth-penetrating, or by geographical extent), and as dependent on a specifically ascribed historic, architectural, traditional or archaeological interest to make it worthy of legal attention (AMAA79, s. 61[12]). Similarly, US legislation calls for a survey of sites to determine 'which possess exceptional value as commemorating or illustrating' US history (Historic Sites Act 1935, s. 2[b]) and those which are 'significant in American history' (National Historic Preservation Act 1966, s. 101[a][1][A]).

The second idea – that of a specific locus of past human activity – is what is meant by a 'settlement site'. Accordingly, a 'settlement site' is a specific, clearly defined location with certain things deliberately placed within it: an original, fixed point in place and time. This is precisely the view taken in the official guidance documents produced in England for the purposes of archaeological heritage management. The *Thesaurus of Archaeological Site Types* (RCHME/English Heritage 1992: 118) advises use of the term 'settlement' in preference to 'habitation site' or 'occupation site'. The more specific versions of the term listed include seven specified types of self-evident forms ('enclosed', 'hut circle', 'linear', 'moravian', 'platform', 'scooped' and 'unenclosed' which are all forms of 'settlements'); one rather general term ('open site'); five that refer to non-prehistoric phenomena ('hamlet', 'town', 'vicus', 'vill', 'village'); and one other ('constructed camp'). Related terms include 'cave', 'flint scatter' and 'house'. However, having so listed all the things that make up settlement sites for archaeological purposes, the term is not then defined in either the *Thesaurus* or any other dictionary of archaeological terms.

The idea of using the term 'settlement' for all examples of settlement types, whatever a settlement might be thought to be, is actually a very recent one. The only heritage management text that uses the term as advised in the *Thesaurus* is Darvill's (1987) *Ancient Monuments in the Countryside*. Others show an interesting shift across the chronological and cultural periods of prehistory.

The Ordnance Survey (1973) publication *Field Archaeology in Britain* is a guide to the types of archaeological remains we might encounter in the British landscape. The terminology used as we progress forward in time is quite diverse. Caves constitute examples of 'occupation sites' in the Palaeolithic (ibid.: 33). The Mesolithic site of Starr Carr is simply a 'site' (ibid., 35). In the Neolithic we encounter 'dwellings' for the first time, with the 'settlements' at Skara Brae and Rinyo in Orkney described as 'villages' (ibid.: 51) where much is made of 'Neolithic pioneering activity'. Here we are back again with the idea of the settlement as a colony in a wild, untamed land. By contrast, the Bronze Age has 'houses' (ibid.: 68) and 'unenclosed villages' (ibid.: 69). The Iron Age then sprouts a whole plethora of specifically 'settlement' types: 'defended settlements' (ibid.: 72); 'smaller units of settlement' that are 'the equivalent of villages, hamlets, manors and homesteads' (ibid.: 79); 'palisaded settlements' (ibid.: 82); and 'platform settlements' (ibid.: 84) among others.

The much more recent English Heritage publication *Exploring Our Past* lays down a list of academic priorities in archaeology for the 1990s based around 'processes of change' including 'settlement evidence' (English Heritage 1991: 34). However, the publication does not speak of 'settlements' until there are 'established farming communities' in the Neolithic. At that stage, discussion and description slip into a language of 'settlement types' and 'the settlement-dominated landscape of later prehistory' (ibid.: 36). Earlier periods do not have settlements. Instead, they have 'occupation sites' from the lower Palaeolithic through to the post-Glacial periods (ibid.: 35); 'occupation sites and areas' in the late Palaeolithic and Mesolithic (ibid.: 35–6); and '*in situ* occupation debris' in the Palaeolithic (ibid.: 38). It is the shift from 'hunter–gatherer to farmers' that results in 'established farming communities' (ibid.: 36) and thus settlements.

In introducing these two publications it is not my intention to criticize them for their substantive content but to demonstrate the use of the idea of 'settlement site' and how it is inevitably bound up with concepts of domestication, civilization, the taming of the wild, and the planting of new people in an empty and unused land. In short, in archaeology as in other branches of history, it is a very colonialist discourse that the concept of the 'settlement site' invites us (and perhaps forces us) to join (Young 1990). What we need to break us out of this and to avoid the power of the tautology is another way of looking.

Leaving the site

'Off-site' (Foley 1981) or 'non-site' archaeology (Dunnell and Dancey 1983) consists of an approach:

> that takes into account the full range of archaeological material on or in a landscape, treating the material that is distributed across it as a spatially continuous variable [and subsuming] within it the information contained in a site [which is defined as] a concentration of humanly modified materials. (Foley 1981: 11)

Accordingly:

> it is predicted that a landscape should contain . . . a continuously distributed scatter of artefacts, exhibiting properties of differential spatial densities [and] these density distributions may be expected to conform to the distribution and frequency of prehistoric human activities. (ibid.: 32)

As off-site archaeology develops, the concept of 'site-based' archaeology can be expected to lose importance. At the same time, the concept of site as defined in terms of past activity is currently giving way to the alternative of the 'activity area'. This is defined as 'a place within a site where a relatively limited set of tasks was performed with a limited set of artifacts' (Rigaud & Simek 1991: 200), and such areas are always intra-site phenomena (Kroll & Price 1991: 1–3; Kent 1990: 1). In terms of archaeological practice, then, as the site is replaced by the landscape as the focus of archaeological attention, with the site relegated to no more than a nodal concentration within a widespread artefact distribution, these now less important sites themselves become no more than bundles of 'activity areas' that are the new focus of archaeological attention. Accordingly, while at one ('macro') level the site merges into the landscape, at another ('micro') level it is broken down into activity areas. The result is a simultaneous shift 'up scale' away from the site to the landscape and 'down scale' from the site to the activity area.

This has two consequences for settlement archaeology. First, emphasis is shifted away from a focus on defining the kind of site under study. The site becomes merely a nodal concentration of artefacts that may (but does not necessarily) imply a locus of activity in the past. Second, instead of seeing a static concentration of people in the past, what is envisaged is people who are perhaps doing more things at one particular place than another, and spending more time at one place than another, but who are nevertheless generally understood to be constantly on the move. If archaeology is, as some wish it to be, the history of the long term (Hodder 1987), then this approach that does not focus on statics but on dynamics may be the way forward. It does mean the death of the 'settlement site' concept, but it also contributes to the end of a colonialist discourse in the historical sciences.

To encourage this process and to carry it further requires a change of key terminology and thereby a change in the concepts in use. The settlement that may remain the focus of inquiry needs to become instead of a 'site', a 'place' – not simply a location in measured and mapped space but the meanings and associations that location has for people in the past and the present. Unlike sites, places need no fixed boundaries and can be considered to be not material phenomena but experiential ones (cf. Carman 1998). Accordingly, we are led out of archaeology as the study of the contemporary material record of past activities (Binford's 'artifacts': 1989: 3) and into the study of people in the past, not as 'dead' archaeology but more as 'living' anthropology (Barrett 1995). The focus on movement and on lived experience may encourage a more 'phenomenological' methodology (Tilley 1994), one that focuses on physical movement through culturally-constructed space as a form of 'objectified' ritual (Barrett 1991; Thomas 1991).

Similarly, in denying conceptual space for the boundary that encompasses the site, and reconceptualizing the site as a cultural (rather than a physical) phenomenon, the distinction between the managerial categories of 'site', 'monument' and 'landscape' is also annulled. While under English law a site can be a monument and *vice versa*, this only applies so long as the site is also a monument as defined by that law. Features such as flint scatters are excluded because they do not meet the definition of a monument as a phenomenon that is a physical feature built on or out of the land. However, flint scatters are the kinds of phenomena deliberately sought in off-site or non-site archaeology; their non-monument status is precisely the attribute required by this approach. Since a flint scatter represents not a discrete and bounded entity but a surface of 'continuous variation' (Wheatley 1995: 170), it takes on some of the attributes normally accorded to a landscape that, as discussed above, is more than a mere physical landform since it is always a creation of culture (Olwig 1993).

Moreover, unlike a site or a flint scatter, a landscape is perhaps not properly thought of as a discrete feature containing other discrete features; rather, it is the set of relationships that gives those features their meaning and binds them together. Accordingly, changes in individual features, their addition or removal, does not affect the existence of the landscape. Whatever the fate of its individual components, the landscape always remains present. The focus of landscape archaeology is therefore on a phenomenon that is in constant flux rather than a static object fixed in time. Together with a concern for the movement of people across space, the concern is also with the constant change of that space through time. In changing, new relationships are forged between the features constituting that space, and new meanings represented by that space for the people to whom it has meaning as 'place'.

In thus moving conceptually from site to place, the settlement as a category ceases to be considered a physical entity and becomes instead a cultural phenomenon. In this reordering, the legal distinction between the categories of site, monument and landscape is broken down to allow types of features previously denied legal status to re-emerge with a heightened importance and a new role to play in interpretation. Thus, a simple challenge to the concept of 'settlement site' has the capacity not only to refresh the practices of 'settlement archaeology' itself but to provide new models for the archaeology of landscapes and to encourage change in the management structures and regulatory mechanisms of archaeology as a field. Quite what the new research models and changed legal structures will look like when in place remains to be seen, and are therefore beyond the scope of this chapter. However, what they can be expected to allow is archaeological research approaches to be brought into close alignment with management schemes and *vice versa*.

Conclusion

This chapter is an attempt to reveal the hidden assumptions and ideas contained in the concept of the 'settlement site' as used in archaeology. What emerges is that the term is a tautology that, because of its historical development, engages us willy-nilly in a colonialist understanding of 'the settlement' in the distant past. This colonialist understanding is reflected in the use of the term in the literature of archaeological heritage management and policy-making.

This colonialist discourse is one of plantations and static foundations. An alternative can be found in the archaeology of regional survey, 'off-site' or 'non-site' archaeology. This frees us from a static vision of people in fixed locations and puts them on the move through space and time. By so doing, it leads us out of the discourse of colonialism and into the study of long-term history. It also provides a means whereby the rigid structures of the management of archaeology can be reordered.

References

UK Legislation

Ancient Monuments and Archaeological Areas Act 1979   AMAA79
National Heritage Act 1983   NH83

US Legislation
Historic Sites Act 1935   HSA35
National Historic Preservation Act 1966   NHPA66

Barrett, J. 1991. Towards an archaeology of ritual. In *Sacred and profane: proceedings of a conference on archaeology, ritual and religion, Oxford 1989*, P. Garwood, R. Skeates, J. Toms (eds), 1–9. Oxford: University Committee for Archaeology, Monograph 32.

Barrett, J. 1995. *Some challenges in contemporary archaeology*. Oxbow Lecture 2. Oxford: Oxbow.

Binford, L. 1989. *Debating archaeology*. San Diego: Academic Press.

Carman, J. 1996a. Object values: landscapes and their contents. In *Landscapes – perception, recognition and management: reconciling the impossible? Landscape archaeology and ecology*, vol. 2, M. Jones & D. Rotherham (eds), 51. Sheffield: Landscape Conservation Forum.

Carman, J. 1996b. *Valuing ancient things: archaeology and law*. London: Leicester University Press.

Carman, J. 1997. Bloody meadows: the places of battle. In *The familiar past?*, S. Tarlow & S. West (eds), 233–45. London: Routledge.

Cleere, H. F. (ed.) 1989. *Archaeological heritage management in the modern world*. London: Unwin Hyman.

Darvill, T. 1987. *Ancient monuments in the countryside: an archaeological management review*. London: English Heritage, Archaeological Report No.5.

Dunnell, R. C. & W. S. Dancey 1983. The siteless survey: a regional scale data collection strategy. In *Advances in archaeological method and theory*, vol. 6, M. B. Schiffer (ed.), 267–87. New York: Academic Press.

English Heritage. 1991. *Exploring our past: strategies for the archaeology of England*. London: English Heritage.

Foley, R. 1981. *Off-site archaeology and human adaptation in East Africa*. Oxford: British Archaeological Reports, International Series No. 97.

Gillespie, R. 1993. Explorers, exploiters and entrepreneurs: early modern Ireland 1500–1700. In *An historical geography of Ireland*, B. J. Graham & L. J. Proudfoot (eds), 123–57. London: Academic Press.

Hodder, I. (ed.) 1987. *Archaeology as long-term history*. Cambridge: Cambridge University Press.

Kent. S. 1990. Activity areas and archaeology: an interdisciplinary view of the relationship between use of space and domestic built environment. In *Domestic architecture and the use of space: an interdisciplinary cross-cultural study*, S. Kent (ed.), 1–8. Cambridge: Cambridge University Press.

Kroll, E. M. & T. D. Price 1991. Introduction. In *The interpretation of archaeological spatial patterning*, E. M. Kroll & T. D. Price (eds), 1–3. New York: Plenum Press.

O'Keefe, P. J. & L. V. Prott 1984. *Law and the cultural heritage: vol. 1, discovery and excavation*. Abingdon: Professional Books.

Olwig, K. 1993. Sexual cosmology: nation and landscape at the conceptual interstices of nature and culture; or what does landscape really mean? In *Landscape: politics and perspectives*, B. Bender (ed.), 307–43. Oxford: Berg.

Ordnance Survey. 1973. *Field archaeology in Britain*. Southampton: Ordnance Survey.

Oxford English Dictionary 1984. *Shorter Oxford English dictionary*. Oxford: Clarendon Press.

Rigaud, J.-P. & J. F. Simek 1991. Interpreting spatial patterns at the Grotte XV: a multiple method approach. In *The interpretation of archaeological spatial patterning*, E. M. Kroll & T. D. Price (eds), 199–220. New York: Plenum Press.

Royal Commission on Historic Monuments for England and English Heritage. 1992. *Thesaurus of archaeological site types*. London: Royal Commission on Historic Monuments for England/ English Heritage.

Thomas, J. 1991. Reading the body: beaker funerary practice in Britain. In *Sacred and profane: proceedings of a conference on archaeology, ritual and religion, Oxford 1989*, P. Garwood, R. Skeates, J. Toms (eds), 33–42. Oxford: University Committee for Archaeology, Monograph 32.

Tilley, C. 1994. *A phenomenology of landscape: places, paths and monuments*. Oxford & Providence: Berg.

us Department of the Interior 1989–90. *Federal historic preservation laws*. Washington: US Department of the Interior.

Wheatley, D. 1995. The impact of information technology on the practice of archaeological management. In *Managing archaeology*, M. A. Cooper, A. Firth, J. Carman, D. Wheatley (eds), 163–74. London: Routledge.

Young, R. 1990. *White mythologies: writing history and the West*. London: Routledge.

CHAPTER THREE

All in the family: the impact of gender and family constructs on the study of prehistoric settlement

Mary F. Price

Introduction

Households have become an increasingly vital area of study for archaeologists interested in examining prehistoric settlement. The appeal of households, and domestic groups in general, can be measured by the plethora of new studies directed toward residential space (e.g. Gilman 1987; MacEachern et al. 1989; Kent 1990; Blanton 1993).[1] In the United States, this surge in popularity is due in part to an article published in 1982 entitled *Household Archaeology* (see also Willey 1953; Winter 1976). Authored by Richard Wilk and William Rathje, this study uses ethnographic source materials to outline an approach for estimating archaeological household size based on economic measures. Progressive at the time of its publication, Wilk and Rathje's (1982) study continues to offer valuable insights for prehistorians, particularly as they relate to considerations of domestic group activity structure. This investigative thread has been elaborated on by many subsequent authors but is clearest in studies taking an ecological view of households (e.g. Coupland & Banning 1996).

In this chapter, I examine the influence of a key tenet of Wilk and Rathje's model (1982) on contemporary investigations of domestic settlement. Specifically, I question the assumption made by the authors that separates domestic personnel structure from domestic activity structure. Wilk and Rathje isolate household activity from household personnel because of their concern with how to approach these analytical units in the material record. However, in downplaying the importance of domestic personnel structure for the study of archaeological households, and by extension for other domestic units, Wilk and Rathje unwittingly construct a situation in which such details are not critically evaluated in the explicit formulation of archaeological approaches to domestic groups. While this division may be valuable from a methodological standpoint, it encourages prehistorians to rely on implicitly constructed social formations with which to interpret the personnel structure of archaeological domestic groups. These analogies find their base in a circular logic which predicates the identification and interpretation of habitational remains on the existence and location of particular familial forms, most commonly the nuclear family. Despite disclaimers to the contrary in Wilk and Rathje (1982) and elsewhere (e.g. Ashmore & Wilk 1988; Santley & Hirth 1993b), in practice, these groups remain the basis for archaeological reconstructions of domestic activity structure and settlement (Doyel 1987; Bawden 1990; Aldenderfer 1994; Rogers & Smith 1995). By default, these social analogues generally correspond to groups that mirror contemporary Western and androcentric norms. The problems inherent in this division are magnified by the application of ethnographic cases to prehistoric ones in which a similar uncritical eye has been applied to the nature of domestic group relationships (e.g. Fortes 1958).

In fairness to Wilk and Rathje (1982), it is important to note that their investigation occurred prior to any critical interest in issues of social identity such as gender in American archaeology (cf. Conkey & Spector 1984). This comment also holds for the ethnographic sources utilized by these two authors. As a result, they should not necessarily be expected to have dealt with such issues according to contemporary standards. Instead, Wilk and Rathje's (1982) article is critiqued here to serve as a foil for the analyses of subsequent authors who draw directly from or parallel the ideas presented in it. The structure of this chapter reflects this goal and is divided between a general critique of Wilk and Rathje, on the content and structure of domestic activities, and a discussion of related issues underlying co-residence as a feature of domestic groups.

My goal in this enterprise is to contribute to the development of an explicit body of archaeological theory designed to deal with the family as an historical and context-specific set of social relations. From this vantage point, the vital question to be addressed is not whether there are cases where families or other kin groups resided in archaeological domestic units. Certainly there were such cases prehistorically. Instead, the interpretive problems for archaeologists lie in a reliance on functional typologies to define archaeological domestic groups and in the tendency to naturalize the connection(s) between domestic space or domestic action and social units such as the family.

The family base of the household economy: evidence from Wilk & Rathje's (1982) study of archaeological households

The limitations present in the model forwarded by Wilk and Rathje (1982), while partly attributable to tacitly expressed parallels between family and household, also relate to the tenets of an ecological paradigm. The authors are particularly concerned with examining households along an adaptive continuum. They hold that, generally speaking, 'relative household size is sufficient to defin[e] a range of economic circumstances for which different size groups are the most effective survival vehicles' (ibid.: 632). One main goal of their research is to isolate, by way of inference, what types of subsistence economy produce what kinds of house-holds. They also aim to discern any material patterning that may be visible as a result of the activities of these groups. Thus, their definition of household focuses on actions performed in a domestic context.

Borrowing from the work of Netting et al. (1984)[2], Wilk and Rathje list five categories of activity that apply to domestic groups. These are production, distri-bution, consumption, transmission and reproduction. The authors place special emphasis on the importance of production and distribution in their model. These activities appear to be highlighted because they have been determined to consti-tute the economic functions of archaeological households. Wilk and Rathje (1982: 622) define production as that 'human activity that procures or increases the value of resources'. Distribution is the process of moving resources from producers to consumers; the authors also take distribution to include the consumption of those resources (ibid.: 624). Transmission is used to categorize a specific form of distri-bution that involves the transference of rights, roles and property between genera-tions and hence refers to a genealogical connection.

Wilk and Rathje note a range of flexibility in household functioning. Using ethnographic examples, the authors posit that on an evolutionary scale, a di-chotomy exists between productive–distributive households and the inheritance household (which emphasizes transmission). Both are viewed as the product of population pressure with the two household forms distinguished by the relative scarcity of labour to land. When labour is the scarce resource, Wilk and Rathje theorize that households emphasizing production and distribution will predomi-nate. When it is land/property that is scarce, focus will be placed on maintaining land within the householding group. In the examples cited by Wilk and Rathje (1982: 628–9), this falls to consanguineal and affinal kin with special emphasis placed on the social bonds created through marriage as well as on those endowed on children. However, for archaeological inquiry, the authors shy away slightly from the utility of transmission because of the difficulty in connecting extinct genealogical connections with spatial/social units, except in special cases (e.g. periods that have documentary or figurative sources available). Despite this caution, the authors maintain transmission as a key factor in the examination of prehistoric household organization (ibid.: 631–2).

The importance of children in domestic functioning is raised again under the guise of reproduction. Cast as the least flexible of household activities, reproduc-tion in the form presented by Wilk and Rathje (1982: 630) is limited to the rearing and socialization of children. The centrality of child-rearing to their construction of reproduction attributes a stability to this household function that devalues it within their analytical framework. Hence, reproduction, as an operation fulfilled by households, is not one which generally leads to the foundation of large house-holds but rather is an integral by-product of such configurations (i.e. large house-holds have the resources, whether economic or social, to physically reproduce themselves whereas small households may not) (ibid.: 631). The auxiliary role ascribed to reproduction in this model also isolates reproductive labour from productive labour in domestic contexts. Wilk and Rathje (1982: 630–31) focus on the pooling of female labour as the solution to childcare that, in their view, liberates women to engage in subsistence production, most notably agriculture. In effect, reproduction is not seen to play a temporally sensitive or synchronically dynamic role. Interestingly, it is the only area in which women and their labours are discussed explicitly in Wilk and Rathje's argument.

While Wilk and Rathje place reproduction in the proverbial 'backseat' analytically, for my purposes it retains great significance on two counts. First, the identification of reproduction as a ubiquitous household function confuses the activities of households with those defined for families. Second, Wilk and Rathje's formulation of the inner workings of reproduction conflates biological reproduction with other forms of reproduction. Regarding the first case, cultural anthropologists have long been concerned with the connections between households and families (e.g. Bender 1967). Particularly valorous is Sylvia Yanagisako's article (1979) because it critiques the related issues of the universal functionality of households and families, as well as the male bias present in much of the work directed toward domestic groups. Her principle argument challenges the appropriateness of functional definitions of the family as well as of the household. Yanagisako asserts that these functional definitions are conceptually connected by the assumption that cross-culturally families and households exist primarily to ensure human survival.

In Yanagisako's review of the ethnographic literature, she notes that when the family is defined its basic characteristics consistently highlight the primacy of genealogical relationships and reproductive activity, a depiction that also fits the literature on households. In her survey, Yanagisako notes the tendency among analysts to define family in terms of mothers and their offspring. She challenges this equation that reduces the core family universally to women and their children (Yanagisako 1979: 189). Such a claim presupposes that peoples everywhere recognize the mother–child relationship as the basis for emic definitions of the family. Yanagisako (ibid.: 191) disputes this point, countering that variability exists not only in gender ideologies that connect (or fail to connect) womanhood to motherhood but also in the functional criteria attributed to motherhood.[3] The problems inherent in this logic have been recognized for other genealogical ties (e.g. sibling ties as the family core). However, Yanagisako contends (ibid.: 197) that the conceptual foundation for defining the core family as a mother and her children is based on the unquestioned notion that nurturance, by the mother, is a prerequisite for the biological survival of human offspring to adulthood and that the social recognition of this 'fact' is universal. Extending her critique to the place of kinship in household and family definitions, she notes that kinship has historically also been constrained to fit a biological reproductive model focusing on genealogical connections to the detriment and/or denial of role relationships (ibid.: 198).

The reductionism embedded in functional definitions of family and household extends beyond any 'inherent' connection between mother and offspring to those activities in which households and families are seen to share, namely those related to the bearing and rearing of children. In a comment directed to the work of Jack Goody in particular, Yanagisako (1979: 199) points out that diversity in the organization of reproductive pursuits is quite limited, based on:

> assumptions about the way in which the physiological and psychological concomitants of childbearing, childrearing, and food preparation structure the activities of domestic units. The reluctance to recognize that in different societies widely varying and shifting assemblages of people [apart from family and household] participate in these activities bespeaks of an unstated absorption with the biological requirements of sexual reproduction. [brackets mine].

Hence, the imposition of biological reproduction as a function of families and households constrains the ability of anthropologists to analyze these social groups as historically contingent.

In considering Wilk and Rathje's (1982) essay in light of Yanagisako's (1979) work, several parallels come to mind. The appearance of reproduction in Wilk and Rathje's list of household functions and their emphasis on child-rearing seem to betray their preoccupation with biological reproduction. By structuring the discussion of reproduction in terms of women 'nurturing' their children and/or those from other mother–child dyads, they insert an inherently Western notion of family into their conception of archaeological households that privileges the genealogical bond above other social bonds. In addition, the influence of biological reproduction plays out in Wilk and Rathje's assumption that the pooling of female labour is necessarily responsible for fulfilling this child-raising function. Accentuating female involvement over that of males again plays on an essentialized construction of 'woman as nurturer' based on her biological endowment. This portrayal also extends into the spatial dimension following the assumption that women care for their children in domestic contexts. This construction slides easily into the long-held dichotomy in the West between a public and private sphere (for historical dialogue on the critique of this dichotomy within anthropology see Comaroff 1987; Lamphere 1997). While the public sphere forms the locale where all socially relevant decision-making and activity takes place, the private sphere corresponds to the protected and nurturing familial domain, dominated by women and children. The private sphere is not an arena of social change; rather it is a space marked by stability. Note should be made that 'private' and 'domestic' are freely interchanged in this division. From this vantage point, it is not surprising that Wilk and Rathje consider reproduction to be the least elastic household function and the least researchable archaeologically.

It could be argued that this critique, while valid, is not pertinent to Wilk and Rathje's (1982) model, as reproduction is not considered in their key criteria for determining household organization archaeologically. I would counter that these issues, most visible in their construction of reproduction, also appear in their construction of other household functions. For example, the authors list food-processing as a basic form of production that is almost invariably conducted in a household setting (Wilk & Rathje 1982: 622). However, if it follows that families exist in order to rear children, we must contend that food-processing is also a function of family groups as children must eat in order to survive. When considered in relation to Wilk and Rathje's discussion of transmission, the argument that food-processing is a basic kind of household production relies on the premise (if we continue with their assumption of nurturance and biological connection) that demands the presence of family groups in domestic settings. Their position on this issue is rather ambiguous and places them in the contradictory situation of claiming that inheritance is not always limited to genealogical relatives while simultaneously privileging substantial examples that demonstrate exactly this form of transmission. This would imply that in their mind archaeological household groups encompass genealogical groups. I imagine that this was not Wilk and Rathje's explicit intent; rather it most likely is simply an unexpected by-product of trying to reconstruct social groups using material remains. Regardless, this example demonstrates the confusion generated by trying to disentangle the activities of domestic groups, whose implicit characteristics, like those of households, are so bound up with the family.

Beyond a folk model of domestic space: lessons from reproduction and labour allocation

Yanagisako's comments on the centrality of the genealogical connection between mothers and offspring also points to the second disabling factor in Wilk and Rathje's concept of reproduction. The underlying concern with sexual reproduction that Yanagisako critiques in anthropological treatments of family and household accents the point made by many feminist anthropologists. Their arguments point to a reliance on a 'folk theory of biological reproduction' (Yanagisako & Collier 1987: 31) that not only limits the definitional scope of reproduction as a social construct but conflates one form of reproduction with all forms of reproduction (e.g. Edholm et al. 1977; Moore 1994: Ch. 5).

Some feminist scholars (e.g. Harris 1984; Harris & Young 1981; Moore 1992) argue that when we speak of reproduction, we really discuss three separate but related phenomena: biological reproduction, the reproduction of the labour force, and social reproduction. While recognizing that these aspects are interrelated, some (Harris 1984) call for an analysis of how these connections articulate with one another, a feat only possible if these components are analyzed discretely. Accordingly, the most common source of confusion among traditional analysts lies in equating the reproduction of the labour force with biological reproduction (Harris & Young 1981). Biological reproduction refers to the physiologically based creation of a new human being while reproduction of the labour force deals with the socialization of children. While initially this distinction may appear minor, further consideration deems it rather significant.

The reproduction of the labour force moves beyond biological endowments, for the criteria to reproduce the next generation cannot be subsumed solely under issues of sustenance. This recognition, as Henrietta Moore (1994: 90–93) argues, enlightens us to the connections between social reproduction, which implies the transmission and recreation of a cultural lifeway from one generation to the next, and the other forms of reproduction. In her perspective, the production of people is a socially constructed phenomenon that involves not only the creation of biological individuals but the production of social identities 'in ways that are congruent with socially established patterns of power' (ibid.: 93). Thus, the roles and activities in which a person can labour within their lifetime are contingent on their relative status as well as the rights and responsibilities available (whether through achievement or ascription) to a person based on factors such as age, sex, class, group membership, etc.

A focus on the reproduction of the labour force locates social reproduction at the core of human social relations and places the relations of reproduction on an equal footing with those of production. It locates reproductive forces in a number of locales and social institutions, ranging from the household to the state. This perspective calls investigators to consider the historicity and political nature of reproductive labour. It also requires that we recognize that reproductive labour is production; and that in studying the relations of reproduction, we should consider the same criteria for reproductive labour as for productive labour. Issues of time and scheduling (Picazo 1997), as well as social identity and power, become important factors, as do questions related to labour allocation (Harris & Young 1981: 128).

For Moore (1994), concern for the context and exercise of social identities in the labour process demands reflection on the impact of gender ideologies and other forms of difference (i.e. race, class, ethnicity, etc.) that draw on social identities. Gender concepts, for example, are not mere superstructural epiphenomena unclearly articulated with political and economic processes but are formative of them. To fail to connect these analytical threads, in Moore's view (1994: 92), unravels any understanding or explanatory power anthropologists might gain of institutions such as the household. It denies the extent to which social constructs, including the gendered division of labour, conjugal arrangements, residence rights and inheritance laws, forge gender ideologies. These points are vital for the formulation of any archaeological model that treats domestic groups, as they pinpoint criteria that must be evaluated (e.g. how do these factors impact the spatial configuration and nature of houses and activity areas?) in order to design usable interpretive analogues. Wilk and Rathje's study offers a glimpse of the veracity of this statement.

While Wilk and Rathje's (1982) model of archaeological households does not ignore the subject of labour allocation, it does suffer from the artificial separation they create between productive and reproductive labour. This analytical detachment belies their position on the relevance of social identity (or lack thereof) for archaeological inquiry. Labour allocation is broached only in the realm of their concept of productive household functions under the guise of task-scheduling, which they cite as the most important variable in determining household size and efficiency (Wilk & Rathje 1982: 622–4). Scheduling is organized along a complexity continuum in which the most intricate arrangements (complex simultaneous tasks) involve overlapping tasks requiring the participation of many individuals. As part of their concern with evolutionary change, the authors posit that the formation of large households is a function of the need to efficiently organize labour in the face of an increased diversity of tasks engaged in by a given householding group. This crisis in turn results in the necessary creation of a household head.

Gender, as a kind of social identity, is not a formal variable in Wilk and Rathje's analysis but is a requirement for their construction of household decision-making under the guise of the household head. The distinction made between productive and reproductive labour generally limits the location and participation of women in 'production' and decision-making (except in special cases) because of their naturalized role in reproduction.[4] The authors imply that women are embroiled in a scheduling conflict that would inhibit their ability to engage in the range of decision-making attached to a household head. A result of their under-differentiated portrayal of reproduction, Wilk and Rathje express this in their notion that women cannot participate in subsistence production unless they pool their labour to cover childcare needs. The implication of this line of reasoning is that women are unencumbered only a portion of the time to engage in alternative pursuits (i.e. both kinds of activities cannot go on simultaneously). It also presumes that all women rest in the same structural position *vis-à-vis* children, namely that all women are biologically and socially held responsible for nurturing children. This occurs for two principal reasons. First, their discussion fails to consider the diverse social identities held by women (for example as a result of their age, affiliation or endowment) that might prohibit their participation in childcare during a given period (i.e. consideration of a division of labour within a given gender over time).[5] Second, Wilk and Rathje's inadequate formulation of reproduction denies it analytical import when compared with the attention given to production. The result is that the authors do not develop a formal scheme to treat the scheduling and allocation of reproductive labour.

Another assumption embedded in the household head proposition, as presented in *Household Archaeology* (1982), is that the pooling of resources and labour in households will benefit all members of the household equally. In terms of their ethnographic examples, Wilk and Rathje give the impression that they would reject this proposition for both small and large householding groups; however, on closer consideration it is clear that this is a partial truth. Their use of material to discuss the creation, fissioning, and extended life span of different size households takes qualified consideration of household members, emphasizing variability among male members. Where mentioned in the cases cited, it is male offspring in differing configurations who stand to inherit.[6] As transmission marks a central force in the foundation, location and viability of householding groups for Wilk and Rathje, the authors leave their argument open to question because they do not explicitly address gender as a factor in transmission nor in internal group decision-making. In this manner, the potential for male bias to creep into archaeological consideration of these issues increases greatly. It becomes easy to 'read' off the record that male household members, by their predilection to inherit, are the agents who foster the creation of spatial patterning, domestic or otherwise.

Wilk and Rathje's (1982: 633–7) acquiescence to this point seems clear in their test case which attempts to use contemporary Kekchi Maya household and kin organization as an appropriate analogue for Lowland Maya domestic groups during the prehistoric Early Formative Period. The goal of the test case is to point out that the geographical and temporal variability present in Lowland Maya settlement is the result of differing relations of production. However, the basis for using the Kekchi Maya relates to the location of both groups in similar ecological conditions. Wilk and Rathje take this ecological parallel to imply that the Kekchi Maya and Swasey phase groups (1000–2000 BC) utilized related 'adaptive' mechanisms to mold themselves to their surroundings. Inheritance is not a formative principle in Kekchi domestic organization. Instead, they focus on spatial mobility that results from a perceived commonality in the organization of production, distribution, transmission and reproduction centered on households. Despite this, the agents in this example remain men. According to the authors, Kekchi household mobility is predicated on the personal mobility of Kekchi men 'who move their families from place to place in response to the local shortage or availability of well-fallowed land' (ibid.: 633–4). For the Kekchi Maya this quote alludes to a male head of family who, in this particular case, also corresponds to the head of household. While this characterization may be accurate for the contemporary Kekchi, on what basis do we, as archaeologists, evaluate this organizational structure for archaeological application? In the context of Wilk and Rathje's model (1982), we cannot do so because intra-group relationships have not been explicitly addressed in the equation.

If for no other reason, their use of analogy is problematic because it determines that comparable environmental conditions necessarily produce similar social relations. Their devotion to ecology does not require that they evaluate other circumstances (e.g. colonialism, nationalism) with a potential effect on the spatial patterning and socioeconomic structure of Kekchi Maya domestic organization. This step seems necessary if the goal is to make some sort of connection between an ethnographic and prehistoric case. By not being source critical, the authors are free (whether deliberately or not) to impose a male-centered view of household mobility on to a distant temporal situation. They opt to apply this model without real consideration of the personnel involved. Contextually speaking, people as agents (or perhaps better stated as people other than adult males) are inconsequential in the face of population pressure, adaptive modes and environmental factors.[7] Cultural ecology is not the only factor influencing male bias in Wilk and Rathje's model; rather this impression also originates from their use of ethnographic sources.

The kinds of studies that Wilk and Rathje utilize to formulate their concept of prehistoric household operation rely on materials employing a classical perspective on kinship analysis (e.g. Goody 1972). Their use of this material fosters another analytical gap easily filled by male bias, as this work relies heavily on Euro-American concepts of male/female roles in kinship networks (for critique see Yanagisako and Collier 1987). In these studies, women are distanced from holding the position of household head because androcentric interpretations of kinship underlie notions of postmarital residence. These implicitly treat women as pawns in alliance-building by household and lineage heads as well as presupposing that the interests of male and female kin coincide. Recent kinship studies question this generalization by challenging the idea that transmission and residence can be reduced to economic factors.

Nazzari's study (1996) investigating changing lineage strategies among Portuguese colonists in colonial Brazil suggests that variability in naming and inheritance patterns can be attributed to issues of migration, racial hierarchy and class as much as economic issues. In her example, colonial elite families shifted traditional naming patterns for a time from one that privileged sons in inheritance to one emphasizing daughters. Major influences in this change were the presence of a male dominated immigrant flow and cultural notions regarding blood purity. The demographic shift sparked by the influx of European men inadvertently gave daughters and wives increasing power and importance as a daughter's chance of marrying a European and 'whitening' the lineage was far greater than those of sons. It is intriguing to consider the impact of location on such bonds. The geographical context inhabited by a group looking to reproduce kin relations is significant in understanding some of the conditions in which innovation can occur (for marriage practices see Stoler 1991). The location of Nazzari's study in a colonial context crystallized the other aspects influencing naming practices. These factors would not have had the same impact in Europe at that period. This line of inference could prove fruitful for archaeological investigations as issues of demographic change and settlement have long been of import.

In another discussion, Cunningham (1996) examines the relationship between Mende kinship structures and postmarital residence in Sierra Leone. The author notes that in the village of Kpetema power relations within households were not distinguished only by gender but by compound location. In her survey of 37 households, Cunningham identified the key factor in intra-household power relations to be not lineage affiliation but whether or not a woman remains in her natal village following marriage. Having access to influential kin as well as to her village cohort from the Bundu Society,[8] a married woman residing in her natal community could exact more control over her spouse than could a woman who moved in from another village. The benefits of remaining in one's own village include increased personal autonomy, as measured by access to land, control of proceeds from market sales, and the ability to avoid physical and emotional abuse from a woman's spouse.

These studies point to the necessity of considering the relationship between constructs of social identity (as represented by the intersecting factors of kin, class, race and gender) and the use of space. Arguably, Wilk and Rathje do make some mention of class issues in their discussion, indicating that in some way they value the investigation of social identity for interpreting archaeological domestic units. However, in my reading this interest arises not from concern for the impact of social identity on social relations internal to domestic groups but as a factor in gauging household efficiency. Of greater alarm, however, is that generally speaking subsequent work on archaeological households has not moved far (if at all) from Wilk and Rathje's model in terms of its ecological determinism and gender bias (for an exception see McAnany 1992). As a result, many recent studies (see below) are constrained by the same uniformitarian assumptions regarding household structure based on implicit notions of family and kin relations. To illustrate this point, I next consider a vital area for considering domestic settlement that falls into this predicament – co-residence.

Discussion: family-based assumptions embedded in the notions of co-residence

The topics of co-residence and the domestic cycle are two ways in which a growing number of archaeologists attempt to deal with domestic settlement. Archaeologically, the treatment of co-residence is by far the most central to any understanding scholars may achieve of domestic groups. Co-residence describes individuals, generally assumed to be kin, who reside together on a regular basis in a localized area such as a house or residential compound. Because archaeologists excavate the remains of past dwelling spaces,[9] it is the material remains left by co-residential groups that they encounter (McGuire 1992: 158–61). Hence, co-residence is attractive to archaeologists because it facilitates connecting people and their activities to a place. As a result, co-residence has become an important source of scholarly debate. On one side lie those who argue that co-residence or at least a 'sense of place' (Coupland & Banning 1996: 2) is a requirement in studying archaeological domestic groups (Blanton 1993: 4). These scholars are juxtaposed to those who, like Wilk and Rathje (1982: 621), reject the applicability of co-residence but fail in their attempt to perform domestic analyses without relying on it in practice (Wilcox et al. 1981; Lowell 1991; Stanish 1992).

Both positions are problematic; nonetheless, I find the second more contentious because it rejects discussion of key methodological issues in identifying archaeological domestic groups through the incorporation of a theoretical disclaimer. Authors falling into this second group contradict their theoretical position through their use of methodology which connects domestic groups, and households specifically, to socially circumscribed spaces based on the shared set of activities discussed above, and most especially on maintenance tasks such as childcare. As noted, the theoretical snags embedded in Wilk and Rathje's presentation of domestic activity conflates household with family and makes it difficult to tease one out from the other. By extension, this must also hold for the spatial dimension of domestic settlement since the presence of these 'ubiquitous' activities is the basis for identifying archaeological households.

In response to this debate concerning archaeological households and co-residence, some scholars advocate the use of the residential corporate group in archaeological inquiry (cf. Hayden & Cannon 1982). The residential corporate group concept describes a kin group that lives together and that has inalienable rights to land and/or resources that can be inherited only within the group (e.g. land held by a matriline is passed only to members of the matriline). These archaeologists postulate that households generally are not an effective tool for dealing with residential groups in prehistory because of the problem of establishing co-residence (Doelle & Wallace 1991; Wilcox 1991; Wills & Leonard 1994). Rather than leave archaeologists in a quandary about how to interpret residence, proponents argue that where deemed appropriate, the residential corporate group concept accomplishes what archaeological households cannot. Namely, it establishes a clear link between a kin-based social group with inherent economic priorities and a co-residential location. The corporate group concept also carries an important methodological advantage. Some advocates suggest that, in comparison to the archaeological household, the residential corporate group reduces the inherent variability between individual habitation assemblages (owing to preservation, social differences, looting, etc.) to a level at which temporally patterned variability can be detected (Cowgill et al. 1984; Fish & Donaldson 1991).

While in some cases the residential corporate group may allow archaeologists to side-step the prickly issue of co-residence, as an analogue, it is not free from analytical problems similar to those in using the household. The social correlate for the residential corporate group developed out of ethnographic studies involving corporate lineages. The presumption underlying a corporate lineage is that interests in land, resources or other property are held in common among members of the group and that these resources remain within the group across generations. Hence, the key criterion for using the corporate group as an archaeological analogue rests on the issue of transmission. More specifically, these arguments turn on the assumption that transmission within a group creates a recognizable spatial pattern in architecture and artefacts across generations that archaeologists can detect through excavation.

The spotlight on transmission bespeaks a connection between genealogical affiliation and corporate group ties based on biological reproduction and the nuclear family. In practice these connections are enacted where the residential corporate group concept is used to deal with the patterned distribution of houses into clusters or the recognition of a large residential structure internally divided. The smaller constituent parts, whether in the form of a house or a hearth area, are interpreted as the loci of nuclear family units (Wilcox et al. 1981; Bawden 1990; Coupland & Banning 1996). In some cases, these areas are equated to women and children (Isbell 1997). Thus, the residential corporate group becomes defined archaeologically as the agglutination of nuclear family units, the particular articulations between which are not problematized. At this level, the interpretation of intra-group relations and decision-making, when dealt with, explicitly falls into the pattern described for Wilk and Rathje – the use of a faulty analogue imbued with presentist notions of family and kin relations.

For example, in their seminal study on residential corporate groups, Hayden and Cannon (1982: 148) note that the criteria for generating an estimate of corporate group strength relate to the organization, productive capacity, stylistic variability and nature of leadership within the group. While nuclear families are integral to these discussions, as they form the basis for the corporate group, there is no consideration of how an individual or group of individuals take a leadership role in group decisions and task assignments. Instead, they assume that environmental and/or economic factors will require the creation of these individuals. Their discussion of stylistic variability as a factor of residential coherency and group strength also rests on a kin foundation. They propose that group strength can be measured through craft homogeneity. The degree of consistency in craft style results, they argue, from differences in rules of postmarital residence. Notably the authors press scholars using the approach to demonstrate that the artefacts can be tied to the corporate group and present evidence that the crafts were likely to have been learned prior to marriage (Hayden & Cannon 1982: 148). Through their discussion they also intuitively point out that postmarital residence is not temporally stable but dynamic and variable. This viewpoint would imply that kin relations, internal decision-making and power relations within such groups are also temporally malleable. Unfortunately, Hayden and Cannon do not vest any analytical strength in investigating such notions archaeologically.

The centrality of factors such as postmarital residence and marriage is not limited to the archaeological household and residential corporate group but also find their way into the study of domestic or developmental cycles. This construct has been applied to both household and corporate group by archaeologists (e.g. Rice 1987; Tourtellot 1988). Yet another concept borrowed from cultural anthropology (Goody 1958), the basis for the domestic cycle begins with the establishment of a new household (which can mean either a single family household or multiple family household like a corporate group) founded on marriage. The cycle follows a household from its foundation through subsequent stages that include growth and fissioning. Archaeologically, compound growth, manifested in the construction of additional structures, is measured through two mechanisms: 'domestic growth' and 'accretionary growth' (Howard 1985: 314). The former refers to population increase as the result of biological reproduction and the influx of new affinal members while the latter addresses compound growth through the addition of new members from parts of the site where building space is lacking.

Two basic interpretations are derived from these ideas regarding domestic unit growth. One argues that postmarital residence patterns determine growth trajectories such that most, if not all, households, go through this type of increase. The other argues that growth depends on the ability of a 'household head' to manage and attract new labour to the group (e.g. Doelle et al. 1987: 89). Both are similar in that they rely on a normative concept of the household based on the notion of a nuclear family. Part of this assumption gives proponents the basis to argue for average family size throughout the cycle. Averaging allows archaeologists to engage in statistical analyses to manipulate domestic data. The results serve as a foundation for analysts to infer the size of the household, co-residential group, and/or the residential corporate group labour pool (e.g. Lightfoot 1994).

The downside of this typology is that neither option questions the nature of obligations at the domestic level. The first option relies on postmarital residence patterns as a prime factor in group size while the second directs its attention to the managerial capabilities of a 'household head'. The typology resulting from the former assumes that most, if not all, householding groups are based on kinship and that they have equal ability to enact such transactions. The question of what relations or things constitute this ability is not addressed. The latter case of the household head also assumes a kin form for domestic groups. The difference lies in that not all household heads have the same ability to manipulate resources. Interestingly, the evaluation of the household head's managerial capacity is treated in terms of individual characteristics. Hence, the success and/or failure of the household unit, measured in terms of temporal growth, depends solely on the personal characteristics of the household head. The assumed gender of the household head gives an added dimension to the focus on 'individual' capacity in domestic cycle discussions. While not always gendered in prehistoric cases, the implication by default and/or language is consistently male (e.g. Doelle et al. 1987: 89). However, as in the cases of the household and the residential corporate group, to fail to deal with the issue of kinship leaves the analyst free to refrain from asking these sorts of questions and leaves him or her open to imposing such a structure implicitly.

Some authors also pose the argument that co-residence is less of a variable in the majority of prehistoric cases due to the economic organization of these societies. In this perspective, the global expansion of capitalism is credited as the source which inserts variability into domestic organization. Hirth (1993), in a volume dedicated to West Mexican households, illustrates this perspective well.[10] Hirth makes a distinction between societies engaged in precapitalist modes of production and those impacted by a capitalist mode. He notes that rates of change between these modes are radically different based on the presence or absence of production and transportation technologies that make it possible to mobilize resources on a large scale. Hirth (1993: 23) ties the inability of pre-industrial and prehistoric households to respond to or enact change in these ways directly to issues of kinship and the structure of household activities; specifically to 'strong beliefs about family composition and child-rearing practices [that] are powerful influences which tend to stabilize the structure and composition of the household'. While Hirth does not explicitly mention co-residence, it is clear that his notion of household in most prehistoric circumstances presupposes a stability in household structure based on alleged family-related functions such as childcare. This position leaves the impression that co-residence is a pervading concomitant of householding groups in prehistoric contexts. An approach like Hirth's draws an artificial division between distinct modes of production, at least in relation to reproduction. It offers historicity and dynamism to those domestic groups sitting on one side of the divide while simultaneously claiming stagnation and constancy for the others.

Conclusion

Wilk and Rathje's (1982) article has been used here to point out several issues that continue to hinder contemporary archaeological approaches to the study of domestic groups. In reflecting on these concerns, the position could be forwarded that the normative assumptions made regarding prehistoric domestic groups are a 'necessary evil' in the context of archaeological inquiry. Indeed, some basis for the interpretation of domestic remains is necessary and there are copious historic and ethnographic cases in which a family group corresponds to a householding group. I agree that allowances must be made in the study of archaeological materials because of the nature of the data available; however, what needs to be reconciled for archaeological domestic groups is not just a factor of method. This situation is evident as we do not need to challenge the connection between domestic groups and co-residence to question the Wilk and Rathje-inspired (1982) characterization of prehistoric households.

Several feminist-oriented works dealing with the gendered division of labour in the face of societal reorganization point to domestic variability in a number of temporal and organizational contexts. Studies by Elizabeth Brumfiel (1991) and Christine Hastorf (1993) note the extent to which the organization of domestic labour believed to have been performed by women, specifically food-processing and preparation, was altered by state incorporation and centralization. Similarly, Cathy Lynne Costin (1996) focuses specifically on the reorganization of craft production, particularly cloth manufacture (a domestic activity), in the context of Inca expansion. Brumfiel's article is especially laudable in its consideration of domestic contexts as potential sources of social dynamism. Her argument addresses both the varying constraints imposed by the Aztec state, as well as the creative and proactive responses initiated by domestic actors – in her study these are believed to be women.

Organizational variability in the past does not appear to have been limited to societies coping with a state apparatus or on the verge of state incorporation. In the American Southwest, for example, Alison Rautman (1997) discusses changes in regional exchange relationships that occurred among Puebloan groups during the Pithouse to Pueblo transition. Using pollen remains and ceramics derived from residential contexts in two sites in central New Mexico (one Pithouse period (AD 800–1250) the other Pueblo period (AD 1200–1500)), she infers that the residential and spatial changes represented by the Pithouse to Pueblo transition embody a scalar change in society. This alteration, she argues, both impacts on and is impacted by the actions of individuals in a domestic context. The significance she attributes to domestic space and domestic actors follows from her view that the social relationships between individuals are the local architects of regional exchange.

The fact that none of these studies question the issue of co-residence or the relationship between domestic and family contexts is telling on two levels. The feminist studies mentioned here point to the reach of androcentric thought in archaeological theories of the domestic division of labour and the use of space. To be able to highlight variability in a situation that has been constructed as diversity-resistant speaks volumes. These studies point out that archaeologists do not have to question the issue of genealogical connection in order to assess variability in domestic group organization. Such malleability is inherent as women and men who reside together are regularly modifying their labour, time and relationships to recreate a socially valued lifeway, whether consciously or not (e.g. Bender 1990). Hence, these studies support the notion that gender is a critical factor in domestic group maintenance and the social reproduction of society.

Conversely, these feminist analyses highlight a potential difficulty in addressing the gendered division of labour without also questioning correlative categories of analysis such as household and family. In archaeological cases where documentary sources are available for the period or where the case study sits in protohistory (e.g. Brumfiel 1991; Costin 1996), the explicit connection between family, co-residence and household can be demonstrated to be valid. However, for societies with greater temporal depth, written and figurative sources may be sparse or absent. To follow the assumption which indiscriminately connects women and children to 'domestic' space, in the long run, risks committing the same errors as studies critiqued in this chapter – gender bias and the use of faulty analogy. Wilk and Rathje (1982) and others overlook the contributions made by women in the context of reproductive activities because of cultural assumptions about the nature and scale of these tasks. However, the opposite seems just as problematic. While women in contemporary and historic cases are generally associated with 'domestic' maintenance activities, to impose such a set of relationships on the distant past risks naturalizing this connection as part of the human condition and effectively undermining the feminist enterprise (cf. Conkey 1991).

Great potential exists for ameliorating some of the ills discussed here. Because of space constraints I can only mention them but feel it necessary so as not to seem overly deconstructionist in tone. One of the strengths of many current forays into domestic settlement is that authors rely on multiple lines of evidence with which to evaluate their assertions regarding past lifeways (e.g. Seymour & Schiffer 1987). The power of this methodological stance can be augmented in two ways. First, archaeologists need to seriously consider the personnel content of domestic groups moving beyond the 'faceless blob' syndrome expressed by Ruth Tringham (1991). The problem confronting analysts lies in how current terms, used to study domestic groups, are constructed. To limit determinism, the evaluation of social analogues (e.g. household or residential corporate group) needs to move away from views where social identity (e.g. class, ethnicity, gender) is overly determined by economic and environmental factors.

As argued elsewhere (Brumfiel 1992), issues of social identity and difference need to be addressed on an equal footing with ecological factors as sources of variability in the archaeological record. In the case of archaeological domestic groups, this task requires the development of a body of theory expressly designed to examine our gendered notions of 'family' in relation to households, corporate groups, etc. The absence of such a framework cripples the powerful perspectives present in studies, such as Wilk and Rathje's (1982), that combine action, space and place. They are weakened because key issues of social difference, gender in particular, are not explicitly and critically incorporated into their analyses. To consider such variables would not only strengthen archaeological interpretations but would demand that prehistorians challenge their notions of domestic space.

Instead of thinking of domestic space as private in nature and localized only around the dwelling and its immediate activity areas, scholars would need to examine more distant activity areas as potentially being part of domestic space (e.g. resource procurement/processing areas). While not fully developed, some current investigations seem to toy with this idea (e.g. Rice 1987; Santley & Kneebone 1993; Bayman 1994). Such questioning is crucial for our attempts to articulate domestic groups with larger social groups such as the community; this is particularly so in cases where household management may be the management of the public economy (e.g. Leacock 1978).

Finally, in order to develop an expressly archaeological theory (or theories) of family, archaeologists must exercise diligent criticism of the ethnographic and historic bases for their work prior to usage (cf. Stahl 1993). In addition to source criticism, archaeologists can mediate the extent to which they impose an ethnocentric form of domestic group on to the past by engaging in a practice increasingly common to feminist archaeologists. These scholars (e.g. Claassen 1991), offer multiple interpretations of case-study data as a means of fully considering alternative explanations. When accompanied by the critical analysis of social identities, the employment of multiple interpretations can give prehistorians more latitude in how they think about their data. Contrary to the sentiments of many, rather than opening interpretation up to claims of hyper-relativism or equifinality, recent work has detailed the extent to which multiple interpretations are bound by the parameters of data (Brumfiel 1996). Hence, they are more than attempts to impose contemporary political ideologies on to the past. Although the source material for these alternative interpretations may be relatively contemporary (and hence, open to scrutiny), nonetheless, critical borrowing poses an opportunity for archaeologists to engage current debates elsewhere (Maynes et al. 1996) regarding the historicity and internal variability of various domestic formations. This interaction would also give archaeologists the opportunity to influence the formulation of constructs used by other social analysts to investigate more recent domestic groups. As American archaeology remains heavily indebted to other social disciplines for its concepts, such increased involvement alone may go a long way toward combating the spectre of family in studies of domestic settlement.

Notes

1. I have limited the scope of this paper to American archaeology deliberately, both because of space constraints and my familiarity with regions in the Americas. A recent article by Steadman (1996) provides an extensive overview on a more inclusive geographic scale.
2. The reader may be concerned that the Netting et al. volume post-dates the Wilk and Rathje (1982) article by two years. This discrepancy is a factor of actual publication dates rather than the circulation of ideas in a public forum. In their article, Wilk and Rathje acknowledge the influence of Robert Netting's ideas of households on their own research. The strength of his influence stems from two symposia held in 1981. One was organized by Wilk and Rathje at the 46th Annual Society for American Archaeology Meeting. The session was entitled 'The Archaeology of the Household' and Robert Netting was an invited participant. The papers presented at the SAA household session were published in a 1982 special issue of *American*

Behavioral Scientist. The other symposium, entitled 'Households: Changing Form and Function', was held at the Wenner-Gren Foundation. Both Netting and Wilk were present here and the papers delivered at this meeting resulted in the 1984 book edited by Netting et al. Because the latter resulted in an edited monograph, many factors contributed to this work being published substantially later than the Wilk and Rathje article. Nonetheless, the ideas contained therein form the basis for Wilk and Rathje's perspective in the 1982 article discussed here.

3. Hawaiian women living in the nineteenth century, for example, do not appear to have conceived of femininity in terms of a Western notion of motherhood or wife (Grimshaw 1989). Their divergence in views was partly a factor of Hawaiian social organization that privileged a woman's role as sister, daughter and niece over that of wife. This distinction gave them greater sexual, productive and social mobility (*vis-à-vis* American missionary wives) but brought Hawaiian feminine pursuits into direct conflict with Christian ideology as forwarded during the colonial period by American missionaries (both male and female). On the subject of motherly functions, the social role of nanny offers a counterpoint to the natural connection between mothering and childcare (i.e. Boon 1974).

4. Wilk and Rathje (1982: 631) follow their evolutionary theme by postulating the transformation of women's labour in more 'complex' social formations. They see the ultimate liberation of women's labour in state-level societies where the nuclear family predominates and state institutions such as schools take over socialization. The implication of this third position is that women cease to labour to fulfil household responsibilities once they are called into a larger labour pool, a view that has come under increasing debate (e.g. Wallerstein and Smith 1992).

5. By extension, it also ignores the variable role(s) of men in childcare and socialization. See, for example, Herdt 1982.

6. Relying on the work of Jack Goody and others, Wilk and Rathje (1982: 627–30) argue that this holds for cases in which property inheritance is invested in one child, seen to encourage the cross-generational maintenance of the household, or divided among many, believed to foster the fissioning of households. In the latter case, Wilk and Rathje presume that it will be male offspring who found splinter households.

7. This raises the questionable implication that internally driven change is not a factor in domestic groups (whether historic or prehistoric) (for a critique see Pauketat 1996). Theoretically and methodologically, this does not ask prehistorians to flesh out the articulations between domestic social organization, domestic activity (and by extension space) and other social institutions.

8. The Bundu society is a religious-based female society to which 95 per cent of women in Sierra Leone belong. Because of the supernatural affiliation of the society, women are said to be guaranteed respect from all societal members (Cunningham 1996: 340). Cunningham also notes that these societies pervade most West African societies as well as many others across the continent.

9. I use this term to refer to both house structures as well as any domestic associated activity areas.

10. Some authors do not provide as well-positioned a statement as Hirth (1993). However, they do assume an overly stable structure for prehistoric households which is tied to issues of socialization and genealogical connection (e.g. Howard 1985; Henderson 1987).

References

Ashmore, W. & R. Wilk 1988. Household and community in the Mesoamerican past. In *Household and community in the Mesoamerican past*, R. R. Wilk & W. Ashmore (eds), 1–11. Albuquerque: University of New Mexico Press.

Aldenderfer, M. S. (ed.) 1994. *Domestic architecture, ethnicity, and complementarity in the south central Andes*. Iowa City: University of Iowa Press.

Bawden, G. 1990. Domestic space and social structure in pre-Columbian northern Peru. In *Domestic architecture and the use of space: an interdisciplinary cross-cultural study*, S. Kent (ed.), 153–71. Cambridge: Cambridge University Press.

Bayman, J. M. 1994. *Craft production and political economy* at the Marana platform mound community. PhD thesis, Department of Anthropology, Arizona State University.

Bender, B. 1990. The dynamics of hierarchical societies. In *The evolution of political systems: sociopolitics in small-scale sedentary societies,* S. Upham (ed.), 247–63. Cambridge: Cambridge University Press.

Bender, D. 1967. A refinement of the concept of household: families, coresidence, and domestic functions. *American Anthropologist* **69**, 493–504.

Blanton, R. 1993. *Houses and households: a comparative study.* New York: Plenum.

Boon, J. A. 1974. Anthropology and nannies. *Man* **9**, 137–40.

Brumfiel, E. 1991. Weaving and cooking: women's production in Aztec Mexico. See Gero & Conkey (1991), 224–54.

Brumfiel, E. 1992. Breaking and entering the ecosystem – gender, class, and faction steal the show. *American Anthropologist* **94**, 551–67.

Brumfiel, E. 1996. The quality of tribute cloth: the place of evidence in archaeological argument. *American Antiquity* **61**, 453–62.

Claassen, C. 1991. Gender, shellfishing, and the shell sound Archaic. See Gero & Conkey (1991), 276–300.

Comaroff, J. L. 1987. Sui genderis: feminism, kinship theory and structural 'domains'. In *Gender and kinship: essays toward a unified analysis,* J. F. Collier & S. Yanagisako (eds), 55–85. Stanford, California: Stanford University Press.

Conkey, M. 1991. Does it make a difference? Feminist thinking and archaeologies of gender. In *The archaeology of gender*, D. Walde & N. D. Willows (eds), 24–35. Calgary, Alberta: Archaeological Association of the University of Calgary.

Conkey, M. & J. Spector 1984. Archaeology and the study of gender. In *Advances in archaeological method and theory*, vol. VII, M. B. Schiffer (ed.), 1–38. Tucson: University of Arizona Press.

Costin, C. L. 1996. Exploring the relationship between gender and craft in complex societies: methodological and theoretical issues of gender attribution. In *Gender and archaeology*, R. Wright (ed.), 111–40. Philadelphia: University of Pennsylvania Press.

Coupland G. & E. B. Banning (eds) 1996. *People who lived in big houses: archaeological perspectives on large domestic structures.* Monographs in World Prehistory 27. Madison, Wisconsin: Prehistory Press.

Cowgill, G. L., J. H. Altschul, R. S. Sload 1984. Spatial analysis of Teotihuacan: a Mesoamerican metropolis. In *Intrasite spatial analysis in archaeology*, H. Hietala (ed.) 154–95. Cambridge: Cambridge University Press.

Cunningham, K. 1996. Let's go to my place: residence, gender and power in a Mende community. In *Gender, kinship, and power: a comparative and interdisciplinary history*, M. J. Maynes, A. Waltner, B. Soland, U. Strasser (eds), 335–49. New York: Routledge.

Doelle, W. H. & H. D. Wallace 1991. The changing role of the Tucson Basin in the Hohokam regional system. In *Exploring the Hohokam: prehistoric desert peoples of the American Southwest*, G. J. Gumerman (ed.), 270–345. Dragoon, Arizona: Amerind Foundation.

Doelle, W. H., F. W. Huntington, H. D. Wallace 1987. Rincon phase community reorganization in the Tucson Basin. In *The Hohokam village: site structure and organization*, D. E. Doyel (ed.), 71–95. Glenwood Springs, Colorado: Southwestern and Rocky Mountain Division of the American Association for the Advancement of Science.

Doyel, D. E. (ed.) 1987. *The Hohokam village: site structure and organization.* Glenwood Springs, Colorado: Southwestern and Rocky Mountain Division of the American Association for the Advancement of Science.

Edholm, F., O. Harris, K. Young 1977. Conceptualising women. *Critique of Anthropology* **3**(9/10), 101–30.

Fish, S. K. and Donaldson 1991. Production and consumption in the archaeological record: a Hohokam example. *Kiva* **56**, 255–75.

Fortes, M. 1958. Introduction. In *The developmental cycle in domestic groups*, J. Goody (ed.), 1–14. Cambridge: Cambridge University Press.

Gero, J. & M. Conkey (eds) 1991. *Engendering archaeology: women and prehistory*. London: Basil Blackwell.

Gilman, P. 1987. Architecture as artefact: pit structures and pueblos in the American Southwest. *American Antiquity* **52**, 538–64.

Goody, J. (ed.) 1958. *The developmental cycle in domestic groups*. Cambridge: Cambridge University Press.

Goody, J. 1972. The evolution of the family. In *Household and family in past time*, P. Laslett & R. Wall (eds), 103–24. Cambridge: Cambridge University Press.

Grimshaw, P. 1989. New England missionary wives, Hawaiian women and 'the cult of true womanhood'. In *Family and gender in the Pacific: domestic contradictions and the colonial impact*, M. Jolly & M. Macintyre (eds), 19–44. Cambridge: Cambridge University Press.

Harris, O. 1984. Households as natural units. In *Of marriage and the market*, K. Young, C. Wolkowitz, R. McCullagh (eds), 49–68. London: CSE Books.

Harris, O. & K. Young 1981. Engendered structures: some problems in the analysis of reproduction. In *The anthropology of pre-capitalist societies*, J. Kahn & J. Llobera (eds), 109–47. Atlantic Highlands, New Jersey: Humanities Press.

Hastorf, C. 1993. Pre-hispanic political change and the role of maize in the central Andes of Peru. *American Anthropologist* **95**, 115–38.

Hayden, B. & A. Cannon 1982. The corporate group as an archaeological unit. *Journal of Anthropological Archaeology* **1**, 132–58.

Henderson, T. K. 1987. *Structure and organization at La Ciudad*. Arizona State University Anthropological Field Studies 18. Tempe, Arizona: Arizona State University Press.

Herdt, G. H. 1982. *Rituals of manhood: male initiation in Papua New Guinea*. Berkeley: University of California Press.

Hirth, K. 1993. The household as an analytical unit: problems in method and theory. See Santley & Hirth (1993a), 21–36.

Howard, J. B. 1985. Courtyard groups and domestic cycling: a hypothetical model of growth. In *Proceedings of the 1983 Hohokam symposium: part I*, A. E. Dittert Jr. & D. E. Dove (eds), 311–26. Phoenix, Arizona: Phoenix Chapter of the Arizona Archaeological Society.

Isbell, W. H. 1997. Household and ayni in the Andean past. *Journal of the Steward Anthropological Society* **23**(1–2), 247–305. Urbana: University of Illinois.

Kent, S. (ed.) 1990. *Domestic architecture and the use of space: an interdisciplinary cross-cultural study*. Cambridge: Cambridge University Press.

Lamphere, L. 1997. The domestic sphere of women and the public world of men: the strengths and limitations of an anthropological dichotomy. In *Gender in cross-cultural perspective*, 2nd edn, C. B. Brettell & C. F. Sargent (eds), 82–92. Upper Saddle River, New Jersey: Prentice Hall.

Leacock, E. 1978. Women's status in egalitarian societies: implications for social evolution. *Current Anthropology* **19**, 247–75.

Lightfoot, R. R. 1994. *The Duckfoot site*, vol. 2. Occasional Papers of the Crow Canyon Archaeological Center 4. Cortez, Colorado: Crow Canyon Archaeological Center.

Lowell, J. C. 1991. *Prehistoric households at Turkey Creek Pueblo, Arizona*. Anthropological Papers of the University of Arizona 54. Tucson, Arizona: University of Arizona Press.

MacEachern, S., D. J. W. Archer, R. D. Garvin (eds) 1989. *Households and communities: proceedings of the 21st annual Chacmool conference*. Calgary, Alberta: University of Calgary Press.

Maynes, M. J., A. Waltner, B. Soland, U. Strasser (eds) 1996. *Gender, kinship and power: a comparative and interdisciplinary history*. New York: Routledge.

McAnany, P. A. 1992. A theoretical perspective on elites and the economic transformation of classic period Maya households. In *Understanding economic process*, S. Ortiz & S. Lees (eds), 85–103.

McGuire, R. H. 1992. *A Marxist archaeology*. New York: Academic Press.

Moore, H. 1992. Households and gender relations: the modeling of the economy. In *Understanding economic process*, S. Ortiz & S. Lees (eds), 131–48.

Moore, H. 1994. *A passion for difference: essays in anthropology and gender*. Bloomington, Indiana: Indiana University Press.

Nazzari, M. 1996. The waxing and waning of matrilineality in Sao Paulo, Brazil: historical variations in an ambilineal system, 1500–1900. In *Gender, kinship, and power: a comparative and interdisciplinary history*, M. J. Maynes, A. Waltner, B. Soland, U. Strasser (eds), 305–18. New York: Routledge.

Netting, R., R. R. Wilk , E. J. Arnould 1984. *Households: comparative and historical studies of the domestic group*. Berkeley: University of California Press.

Ortiz, S. & S. Lees (eds) 1992. *Understanding economic process*. Lanham: University Press of America.

Pauketat, T. 1996. The foundations of inequality with a simulated Shan community. *Journal of Anthropological Archaeology* **15**, 219–36.

Picazo, M. 1997. Hearth and home: the timing of maintenance activities. In *Invisible people and processes: writing gender and childhood into European archaeology*, J. Moore & E. Scott (eds), 59–67. London: Leicester University Press.

Rautman, A. 1997. Changes in regional exchange relationships during the Pithouse-to-Pueblo transition in the American Southwest: implications for gender roles. In *Women and prehistory: North America and Mesoamerica*, C. Claassen & R. A. Joyce (eds), 100–18. Philadelphia: University of Pennsylvania Press.

Rice, G. 1987. La Ciudad: a perspective on Hohokam community systems. In *The Hohokam village: site structure and organization*, D. E. Doyel (ed.), 127–58. Glenwood Springs, Colorado: Southwestern and Rocky Mountain Division of the American Association for the Advancement of Science.

Rogers, J. D. & B. D. Smith (eds) 1995. *Mississippian communities and households*. Tuscaloosa: University of Alabama Press.

Santley, R. S. & K. G. Hirth (eds) 1993a. *Prehispanic domestic units in western Mesoamerica: studies of the household, compound, and residence*. Boca Raton, Florida: CRC Press.

Santley, R. S. & K. G. Hirth 1993b. Household studies in western Mesoamerica. See Santley & Hirth (1993a), 3–17.

Santley, R. S. & R. R. Kneebone 1993. Craft specialization, refuse disposal, and the creation of spatial archaeological records in prehispanic Mexico. See Santley & Hirth (1993a), 37–66.

Seymour, D. & M. B. Schiffer 1987. A preliminary analysis of pithouse assemblages from Snaketown, Arizona. In *Method and theory for activity area research*, S. Kent (ed.), 549–603. New York: Columbia University Press.

Stahl, A. B. 1993. Concepts of time and approaches to analogical reasoning in historical perspective. *American Antiquity* **58**, 235–60.

Stanish, C. 1992. *Ancient Andean political economy*. Austin: University of Texas.

Steadman, S. R. 1996. Recent research in the archaeology of architecture: beyond the foundations. *Journal of Archaeological Research* **4**(1), 51–93.

Stoler, L. A. 1991. Carnal knowledge and imperial power: gender, race and morality in colonial Asia. In *Gender at the crossroads of knowledge*, M. di Leonardo (ed.), 51–102. Berkeley: University of California Press.

Tourtellot, G. 1988. Developmental cycles of households and houses at Seibal. In *Household and community in the Mesoamerican past*, R. R. Wilk & W. Ashmore (eds), 97–120. Albuquerque: University of New Mexico Press.

Tringham, R. 1991. Households with faces: the challenge of gender in prehistoric architectural remains. See Gero & Conkey (1991), 93–131.

Wallerstein, I. & J. Smith 1992. Households as an institution of the world-economy. In *Creating and transforming households: the constraints of the world-economy*, I. Wallerstein & J. Smith (eds), 3–23. Cambridge: Cambridge University Press.

Wilcox, D. R. 1991. Hohokam social complexity. In *Chaco and Hohokam: prehistoric regional systems in the American Southwest*, P. L. Crown & W. J. Judge (eds), 253–76. Santa Fe: School of American Research Press.

Wilcox, D. R., T. R. McGuire, C. Sternberg 1981. *Snaketown revisited: a partial cultural resource survey, analysis of site structure and an ethnohistoric study of the proposed Hohokam-Pima national monument*. Archaeological Series 155. Tucson: Arizona State Museum.

Wilk, R. R. & W. L. Rathje 1982. Household archaeology. *American Behavioral Scientist* **25**, 617–39.

Willey, G. R. 1953. *Prehistoric settlement patterns in the Virú valley, Peru*. Washington, DC: US Government Print Office.

Wills, W. H. & R. L. Leonard 1994. *The ancient southwestern community: models and methods for the study of prehistoric social organization*. Albuquerque: University of New Mexico Press.

Winter, M. C. 1976. The archaeological household cluster in the valley of Oaxaca. In *The early Mesoamerican village*, K. V. Flannery (ed.), 25–31. New York: Academic Press.

Yanagisako, S. 1979. Family and household: the analysis of domestic groups. *Annual Review of Anthropology* **8**, 161–205.

Yanagisako, S. & J. F. Collier 1987. Toward a unified analysis of gender and kinship. In *Gender and kinship: essays* toward *a unified analysis,* J. F. Collier & S. Yanagisako (eds), 14–50. Stanford, California: Stanford University Press.

CHAPTER FOUR

What's in a settlement? Domestic practice and residential mobility in Early Bronze Age southern England

Joanna Brück

Introduction

The Early Bronze Age of southern England[1] is one of the most intensively re-searched areas in British archaeology. Yet, evidence for Early Bronze Age settle-ments is peculiarly lacking. Very few settlements have ever been discovered and their absence from the archaeological record is one of the classic problems of British Bronze Age studies (Childe 1940: 98; Simpson 1971: 131). In this chapter, I argue that the apparent invisibility of settlements in this period is not a feature of the archaeological record but results from our own engagement with the data. It is a product of contemporary expectations, values and perceptions and of the way in which Early Bronze Age sites have been categorized. I consider how a critique of current conceptual frameworks may provide fresh insights into this question and I propose an alternative model that may enhance our understanding of the data.

Early Bronze Age sites

An initial step will be to briefly describe the full range of Early Bronze Age sites. The Early Bronze Age of southern England is particularly famous for a series of spectacular upstanding monuments that have long formed the focus of antiquarian and archaeological interest, notably round barrows, henges,[2] stone circles and stone rows (e.g. Colt Hoare 1812; Ashbee 1960; Wainwright 1989; Barrett 1994). These are generally interpreted as ritual sites on the basis of finds and/or morphol-ogy. For example, the internal ditches and external banks surrounding henges have made it difficult to ascribe a functional role to these sites (e.g. Colt Hoare 1812: 18), while the astronomical alignments preserved in many stone rows and circles have encouraged archaeologists to explore their potential cosmological significance (e.g. Burl 1976; Ruggles & Whittle 1981). In the case of round barrows, the presence of human burials identifies these as funerary monuments.

Other types of Early Bronze Age site have proved much more elusive. Outside of the various kinds of ritual sites, evidence for the presence of Early Bronze Age people in the landscape exists largely in the form of extensive artefact scatters of flint and ceramic material. Surveys demonstrate that in many areas, there is a continuous, if low density distribution of Early Bronze Age artefacts across much of the landscape, interspersed with denser concentrations (e.g. Richards 1990: fig. 159). On excavation, Early Bronze Age artefact scatters provide little structural evidence. Features such as pits and postholes are scarce and, even when present, these rarely form any interpretable pattern.

The important point here is that although it has long been recognized that these different types of sites can tell us about the Early Bronze Age *settlement pattern* (i.e. the general distribution of the population across the landscape), none of them have been unequivocally identified as actual *settlements*.

How have archaeologists explained this lack of settlements?

During the first half of this century, the lack of settlement evidence convinced many archaeologists (e.g. Childe 1940: 98–9; Hodges 1957) that, throughout much of Britain, Early Bronze Age people were nomadic pastoralists living in light tents that would leave no trace in the archaeological record. However, over the 1960s and 1970s, more and more evidence for the cultivation of cereal crops came to light, including plough marks, pollen from buried soils and grain impressions on ceramics. This cast the pastoralist model into doubt (Bradley 1972). Since then, the assumption that settled agriculture was the established means of subsistence has dominated much of the literature (e.g. Case 1977: 76; Burgess 1980; Darvill 1987: 105). Although it is generally recognized that other resources (for example, shellfish at coastal sites) were also used, these are often thought to have been of relatively minor importance. Thus, it is widely assumed that substantial houses and farmsteads like those of the Middle Bronze Age and later periods must once have existed (e.g. Simpson 1971; Darvill 1987: 103). That these have not been found has largely been explained through postdepositional processes. In particular, it has often been argued that Early Bronze Age settlements were located in parts of the landscape that have been subject to severe erosion or later inundation by colluvial/ alluvial sediments (e.g. Bradley 1970b: 264–5; Simpson 1971: 131; Gibson 1992: 42– 3). In other words, the invisibility of Early Bronze Age settlements is understood to be a real feature of the archaeological record.

There are several problems with arguments that posit postdepositional disturbance. For much of southern England, the heaviest erosion has been suffered by the higher parts of the chalk downlands, yet Middle Bronze Age and later settlements are frequently found in these very areas. Colluvial and alluvial processes do not provide us with an easy explanation either. Test pits excavated in the river valleys of Hampshire by John Evans (pers. comm.) have produced Roman layers directly overlaying the Mesolithic. Even where Early Bronze Age sites have been found beneath layers of colluvium, for example at New Barn Combe, Isle of Wight (D. Tomalin, pers. comm.), and Holywell Combe, Kent (N. Macpherson-Grant, pers. comm.), these have not produced houses but rather comprise scatters of artefacts and occasional features very similar to sites in other parts of the landscape.

Bradley (1970b: 264) has proposed a further possible explanation. He suggests that the building techniques used might have left no trace in the archaeological record: for example a method of construction employing sill beams would not have left subsoil features. Given the plentiful evidence for post-built architecture in both the preceding and succeeding periods, this is perhaps unlikely, although the use of this method to construct post circles of apparently ritual significance at henges may have precluded its employment in contemporary domestic architecture. However, I argue below that the evidence from Early Bronze Age sites in general does not support a sharp distinction between ritual and secular practice, making this explanation inherently unlikely.

How settlement has been defined

I should like to turn the tables by suggesting that we have been asking the wrong questions. Rather than wondering what factors have rendered Early Bronze Age settlements archaeologically invisible, I argue that we need to start at a much more fundamental level. We must examine the criteria that are used to identify settlements in the archaeological record (see also Hayden, Chapter 7, this volume). We must also ask whether it is possible to justify the assumption that the kind of sites that we are expecting to find actually existed in the Early Bronze Age.

The definition of settlement that is widely employed within British prehistoric archaeology is problematic, yet largely implicit. This means that any understanding of how settlement has been defined must be reached from a rather oblique angle. An important hint is provided by the data recovered from sites such as henges and round barrows. Many of these sites provoke considerable interpretative dilemmas. Although they are generally characterized as locations of ritual significance, it is difficult to accommodate all of the evidence recovered from them within such a monothetic interpretative framework (see also Gibson 1982: 1–2; Lane 1986). For example, hearth sweepings, quern fragments and cooking vessels are frequently found in the ditches of henge monuments, such as Mount Pleasant, Dorset (Wainwright 1979: 35–47). The presence of sherds or knapping debris under a round barrow or in its surrounding ditch presents a similar problem. These are generally explained in one of two ways. The first interprets such finds as evidence of preceding or succeeding domestic/economic activities, unconnected with the barrow itself (e.g. Smith 1965a: 32–40). For example, it is often argued that flint-knapping waste results from the expedient use of nodules accidentally unearthed during barrow-digging activities (e.g. Barrett et al. 1991: 128). Alternately, such material is interpreted as votive deposits of an expressly ritual nature associated with the mortuary rites (e.g. Hughes 1996: 48; cf. Brown 1991: 105–7).

The interpretation of structural evidence has similarly proved problematic. Circular post-built structures beneath barrows are a particularly good example. On analogy with later prehistoric roundhouses, some authors have argued that these can be interpreted as houses predating the barrows in question (e.g. Piggott 1940; Gibson 1980). Other researchers have proposed that the structures should be interpreted as mortuary buildings, constructed specifically for the funeral rite (e.g. Fox 1941: 114; Ashbee 1960: 65). What is happening here is that ritual and non-ritual practices are being defined as mutually exclusive. One explanation is assumed to preclude the other. This suggests that archaeologists expect to be able to neatly assign sites to such categories of practice as domestic, ritual, economic or political.

These observations suggest that a settlement is generally considered to be *a spatially and functionally distinct type of site* (see Carman, Chapter 2, this volume for a critique of the concept of a 'settlement site' from a different angle). In terms of function, it is the presence of domestic activities that identifies and characterizes a settlement. In other words, domestic activities are considered to be the primary feature of a settlement. The archaeological identification of domestic activities requires the existence of a recurrent package of functionally distinct artefacts. Although it is widely accepted that this package will vary both historically and culturally, the universal existence of a core group of domestic activities, notably food preparation, food consumption, reproduction and childcare, is often assumed. In morphological terms, the presence of a house is generally considered essential to the identification of domestic sites in the archaeological record. The definition of a settlement as a functionally distinct type of site, that is a domestic site, is closely linked to a second common assumption: namely that settlements are spatially discrete entities, distinguishable from categories of locale whose major roles lie in other realms, such as ritual, political or economic practice.

To date, however, archaeologists have been unable to identify a distinct class of sites that matches these expectations. What I propose here is that this definition of settlement does not fit the Early Bronze Age data. This is because it is based, first, on an historically particular categorization of human practice, and second on a set of presuppositions concerning the nature and significance of the house. Within an Early Bronze Age context, the modern concept of 'domestic' is itself called into question, both from the viewpoint of the identification of functionally distinct artefacts and the notion of spatially discrete domestic arenas. I therefore argue that archaeologists are unable to find Early Bronze Age settlements because sites of this type did not exist during this period.

Can we identify a functionally and spatially distinct package of domestic artefacts?

In order to demonstrate this, two questions must be considered: a) can a distinct package of domestic artefacts be identified in the Early Bronze Age data, and b) is this package consistently associated with any one category of site (defined in morphological terms)?

These questions can only be investigated by looking at the full range of Early Bronze Age sites in the study area. A database of over 50 Early Bronze Age sites of different types was compiled by means of a literature review. This provides the data presented in tables 4.1–4.4. I have included as many sites as possible in each table. However, the information presented was not available for all of the sites. For example, information on the percentage of different tool types present within a flint assemblage was available for only six sites (table 4.4) whereas details concerning the presence/absence of different categories of finds were available for 24 sites (table 4.1). For each of the tables, sites are listed according to site type. The appendix at the end of the paper provides a list of references for each of the sites in the tables (the relevant appendix number is placed in brackets after the name of the site in the table).

The identification of Early Bronze Age domestic artefacts has always proved particularly difficult. Material that archaeologists often intuitively label as domestic, for instance pottery, flint scrapers or hearth debris, becomes less easy to classify on closer inspection. For example, vessels used to store and serve food on a day-to-day basis seem to have been identical in form to those employed at feasts and placed in the graves of the dead. Research on Beaker ceramics demonstrates how difficult it is to distinguish a distinct domestic component (Whittle 1981: 312–13; Gibson 1982: 69–76): even Beaker coarsewares are not confined to any one type of site, but are found accompanying burials, at henge monuments and as components of artefact scatters. This suggests that a single artefact type may fulfil roles in what we would consider to be different spheres of practice. Similarly, hearth debris may signify domestic activities, but it might also have been produced in the context of feasting or the preparation of a ritual meal. Again, such material is found at a variety of different types of site (see table 4.1), hinting at a multiplicity of meaning and function. It is therefore extremely difficult to identify individual artefacts that unambiguously indicate domestic activities.

Even those artefacts that may have had a more specialized function, for example 'thumbnail' scrapers, bone awls or quernstones, are found at many different types of locale (table 4.1). This suggests that particular kinds of activities were not confined to specific categories of site but were carried out at a variety of different places across the landscape. Although it is not possible to ascribe a single function or significance to artefacts such as potsherds or flint knives, the fact that these are found at many morphologically different types of site may indicate a similar non-specific distribution for some of the activities (including food preparation and consumption) in which such objects played a role.

If it is difficult to identify individual artefacts that unambiguously indicate domestic activities, this problem is compounded when we try to identify a repeated assemblage, or distinct package of domestic items. What is evident when we consider the finds from Early Bronze Age sites is the degree of variability in the nature, co-occurence and relative proportion of different artefacts. Tables 4.2–4.4 detail the flint assemblages from several well-documented sites. This material is not without its problems. In particular, the excavation and sampling strategies employed at different sites vary substantially, rendering it problematic to compare

Table 4.1 Presence/absence of different materials at different types of Early Bronze Age site.

Site name	Type of site	Hearth	Pottery	Flint	Animal bone	Burnt flint	Hammer	Quern/rubbing stone	Comb	Awl/point
Belle Tout (4)	Artefact scatter	✔	✔	✔			✔			
Bullock Down (5)	Artefact scatter		✔	✔						
Downton (10)	Artefact scatter	✔	✔	✔		✔				
Hengistbury Head (13)	Artefact scatter		✔	✔		✔				
Rackham (20)	Artefact scatter	✔				✔		✔		
Wilsford Down (24)	Artefact scatter		✔	✔	✔	✔				
Arreton Down (1)	Scatter under round barrow		✔	✔	✔	✔				
Ashey Down (2)	Scatter under round barrow		✔	✔	✔					
Avebury G55 (3)	Scatter under round barrow		✔	✔	✔			✔		✔
Cowleaze (8)	Scatter under round barrow		✔	✔						
Lamb Down (15)	Scatter under round barrow		✔	✔	✔					
Overton Hill (18)	Scatter under round barrow		✔	✔	✔					
Snail Down (21)	Scatter under round barrow		✔	✔						
W. Kennet Ave. (23)	Scatter along stone row		✔	✔	✔					
Dean Bottom (9)	Single pit		✔	✔	✔				✔	✔
Stockbridge (22)	Single pit		✔	✔	✔				✔	✔
Coneybury Henge (7)	Henge		✔	✔	✔	✔				
Durrington Walls (11)	Henge	✔	✔	✔	✔	✔				✔
Mt. Pleasant (16)	Henge	✔	✔	✔	✔	✔	✔			✔
Church Hill (6)	Ring ditch	✔	✔	✔	✔	✔				
Playden (19)	Ring ditch	✔	✔	✔		✔				
Holdenhurst (14)	In ditch of earlier monument	✔	✔	✔						
North Marden (17)	In ditch of earlier monument	✔	✔	✔	✔	✔				
Windmill Hill (25)	In ditch of earlier monument	✔	✔	✔						✔

these directly, as does the fact that assemblages from subsurface features will have undergone very different postdepositional processes to those recovered from surfaces. Nonetheless, this should not prevent us from making some useful preliminary observations about the variability of the data.

To begin with, we may note that there is considerable variability among what are morphologically similar sites. For example, the finds from henges suggest that the same suite of activities were not carried out at all such sites. Although the flint assemblage from Coneybury henge, Wiltshire (Richards 1990), and Mount Pleasant, Dorset (Wainwright 1979), included a similar percentage of cores and retouched artefacts (table 4.2), Mount Pleasant produced many more scrapers

Table 4.2 Early Bronze Age flint assemblages: cores, flakes and retouched artefacts as percentage of total flint artefacts (Ret = retouched artefacts).

Site name	Type of site	Finds considered	Cores (%)	Flakes (%)	Ret (%)	Total flint artefacts
Rackham (20)	Artefact scatter	Complete assemblage	1	95	4	12,473
Wilsford Down (24)	Artefact scatter	Complete assemblage	3	95	2	21,343
Arreton Down (1)	Scatter under round barrow	Complete assemblage	1	96	2	13,367
Dean Bottom (9)	Single pit	Complete assemblage	4	93	3	1,472
Coneybury (7)	Henge	Ditch and surface of interior	2	95	3	14,760
Mt. Pleasant (16)	Henge	Ditch, Site IV and Palisade trench	1	96	3	19,761
Windmill Hill (25)	In ditch of earlier monument	Trench B upper secondary ditch silts	2	93	5	814

Table 4.3 Early Bronze Age flint assemblages: scrapers as percentage of total retouched flint artefacts.

Site name	Type of site	Finds considered	%	Total scrapers
Rackham (20)	Artefact scatter	Complete assemblage	89	397
Wilsford Down (24)	Artefact scatter	Complete assemblage	43	182
Arreton Down (1)	Scatter under round barrow	Complete assemblage	43	133
Dean Bottom (9)	Single pit	Complete assemblage	44	23
Firtree Field (12)	Pit group	Complete assemblage	91	Unknown
Coneybury (7)	Henge	Ditch and surface of interior	40	195
Mt. Pleasant (16)	Henge	Ditch, Site IV and Palisade trench	78	445
Windmill Hill (25)	In ditch of earlier monument	Trench B upper secondary ditch silts	47	19

than Coneybury (table 4.3). Hence, sites that appear similar in some respects may look very different in others.

The flint assemblages also suggest the existence of task-specific sites (Bradley 1972: 197, 1978b: 56; Holden & Bradley 1975: 101–3). Bradley (1972) has argued that Late Neolithic and Early Bronze Age sites fall into two major groups, one with a considerably higher percentage of flint scrapers than the other. Table 4.3 demonstrates this well. Scrapers form a large proportion of the retouched flint from three of these sites (c. 80–90 per cent), whereas they form a much smaller proportion of the retouched flint from the remaining five sites (c. 40–50 per cent). Bradley (1978b: 56) suggests that scrapers would have been employed in such tasks

Table 4.4 Early Bronze Age flint assemblages: different tool types as percentage of total retouched flint artefacts.

Site name	Type of site	Finds considered	Scrapers (%)	Knives (%)	Axes/adzes (%)	Arrowheads (%)	Fabricators (%)	Piercers (%)	Serrated flakes (%)	Notched flakes (%)	Bevelled flakes (%)	Retouched blades (%)	Core tools (%)	Hammers (%)	Chopping tools (%)	Miscellaneous (%)	Total retouched flint artefacts
Rackham (20)	Artefact scatter	Complete assemblage	89	8	<1	1	<1	–	–	<1	–	–	–	–	–	<1	448
Wilsford Down (24)	Artefact scatter	Squares R, T, K/L	36	6	–	6	1	1	3	–	–	–	–	–	–	46	184
Arreton Down (1)	Scatter under round barrow	Complete assemblage	43	<1	1	7	<1	5	1	28	–	–	4	–	<1	10	310
Dean Bottom (9)	Single pit	Complete assemblage	44	10	–	2	–	8	–	–	–	–	–	–	–	37	52
Mt. Pleasant (16)	Henge	Complete assemblage	78	<1	2	4	1	1	4	–	–	7	–	1	<1	<1	568
Windmill Hill (25)	In ditch of earlier monument	Trench B upper secondary ditch silts	47	23	2	5	2	2	–	5	10	–	–	–	–	2	40

as butchery, skinworking and boneworking and proposes that sites with a high percentage of scrapers can be linked to stock-raising. Again, morphologically similar sites occur in both of these groups (table 4.3). However, even within each of these two broad categories, there appears to be much further variability. For example, both Windmill Hill, Wiltshire (Whittle et al. in press), and Arreton Down, Isle of Wight (Alexander et al. 1960), fall into the group of sites with fewer scrapers (table 4.3). Yet, in contrast to Arreton Down, Windmill Hill produced an unusually high percentage of knives (table 4.4). Further variability between different assemblages is also demonstrated in table 4.4, with other kinds of specialist roles perhaps being indicated by differing proportions of tools types. For example, Arreton Down produced a very high percentage of notched flakes as well as a relatively large number of arrowheads and core tools (table 4.4). The number of serrated flakes and retouched blades found at Mount Pleasant is also noteworthy.

This degree of variability in finds assemblages makes it extremely difficult to identify functionally distinct categories of site. Although there may be some degree of task specificity, this is cross-cut at other levels, and most sites share several artefact types, including cooking and serving vessels, flint knives and the like. Yet, the difficulty of ascribing a single function to these common objects and the fact that they do not appear in specific combinations but are found together with a wide variety of other artefact types (see tables 4.1 and 4.4) makes it unlikely that such finds can be considered as components of a repeated package of domestic artefacts. In summary, it is not possible to demonstrate the existence of a functionally or spatially distinct category of domestic sites during the Early Bronze Age.

A critique of the concept of 'the settlement'

At this point, let us move away from the Early Bronze Age evidence itself and consider the concept of 'the settlement' in theoretical terms. The aim of the following three sections is to enable us to judge whether the implicit definition of settlement operationalized within British Bronze Age archaeology is necessarily applicable to the data.

Domestic practice

I begin by arguing that this definition of settlement depends on an historically specific conceptualization of the domestic as an arena of practice distinct from other areas of life (see also Lane 1986: 182; Thomas 1996: 3). In modern Western society, economic, political, domestic and ritual activities are identified as distinct and mutually exclusive spheres of practice, each with its own circumscribed locale, for example the house, church, workplace or parliament buildings. The imposition of this atomized and disarticulated notion of practice on the past has resulted in considerable interpretative confusion. Archaeologists expect to be able to identify equivalent categories of space and practice in the archaeological record, when in fact these may never have existed.

The development of a functionally and spatially distinct domestic sphere in modern British society is the result of a combination of processes. These include industrialization, the secularization of society and the development of the nation state. At a more fundamental level, this compartmentalization of space and practice is the product of an historically specific set of gender and age relations. In the modern Western world, the domestic sphere is separated and marginalized from other areas of practice (Strathern 1984: 24–6, 30–31; Moore 1988: 21–4). Traditionally, the home is characterized as private and passive, the locus of reproduction and consumption, and as a 'woman's place'. This is contrasted with the active, public world of men, a realm of production and politics located firmly outside of the domestic sphere (Tiffany 1978: 42–3, 46; La Fontaine 1981; Waterson 1990: 169–71). Thus, British archaeologists' notion of the domestic is the product of a set of values, economic practices and sociopolitical relations specific to the modern Western world.

These issues have been discussed by anthropologists studying gender relations in non-Western societies. They point out that in many societies, domestic practices are not spatially segregated from economic, ritual or informal political activities (Tiffany 1978: 42–3; Yanagisako 1979: 190–91; La Fontaine 1981; Waterson 1990: 169–71). Where the co-residential group is the main socioeconomic unit, settlements are often the focus for a whole range of such activities. Taking an example close to home, most British medieval and early modern households were not simply loci for consumption and reproduction, but constituted the mechanism through which agricultural production was organized. At the same time, these households (especially those of high status) often acted as political units. In such a context, the modern conception of the home as private, passive space did not exist (cf. Johnson 1993). A similar point can be made concerning ritual practice. For example, in eastern Indonesia, the elaborate houses of Sumbanese islanders symbolize descent groups and are therefore an important arena for ritual activities (Waterson 1990: 43–4). The notion that particular types of practice are restricted to certain categories of place is also problematic. For example, amongst hunter–gatherers, short-term, task-specific sites may act as temporary foci for daily maintenance activities such as food consumption and child-rearing.

The assumption made by many British prehistorians that a functionally and spatially distinct category of domestic sites should be identifiable for the Early Bronze Age is therefore not borne out by the historical or ethnographic evidence. Other societies do not appear to categorize space and practice in the same way as we do. This is not surprising when we remember that such factors as the organization of production and gender relations take very different forms among non-Western peoples. In other words, there is nothing to suggest that our concept of the domestic is universally shared by other societies. The existence of a distinct domestic sphere in British society today is the result of a set of social and material conditions peculiar to the modern world. If so, then we cannot make the *a priori* assumption that the category 'domestic' was articulated by past societies.

Returning to the Early Bronze Age evidence, we have seen above that it is difficult to demonstrate the existence of a functionally and/or spatially discrete domestic arena. The variability of the finds assemblages recovered from Early Bronze Age sites and the lack of a specialized and distinctive repertoire of domestic artefacts makes it hard to uphold the notion that the same relationship between types of practice and categories of place existed in the Early Bronze Age as in modern British society. This suggests that the modern concept of the 'domestic' did not exist during this period.

Ritual practice

These observations can help us to understand why the finds recovered from 'ritual' sites such as henges and barrows often provoke interpretative dilemmas. We have noted that some of the material found at these sites (e.g. flint-knapping debris) is difficult to accommodate within an interpretative framework that treats ritual and non-ritual activities as mutually exclusive categories of human practice. Such evidence appears ambiguous and contradictory according to a classificatory scheme in which ritual and secular practice are treated as distinct and bounded categories, fundamentally opposed to one another. The preceding section suggests that many other peoples do not consider ritual, domestic, economic and political activities as spatially and functionally distinct spheres of practice. Let us consider what further insights ethnographic studies may offer us into this problem.

I argue that the category 'ritual practice' is not something that exists in and of itself but is created through our own engagement with the data (Goody 1961: 157; Bell 1992: 13–14, 114–15). Our characterization of ritual is a product of post-Enlightenment thought wherein ritual comprises those implausible symbolic acts that are not easily accommodated by a contemporary 'practical' rationale (ibid.; Leach 1968: 521; see also discussion by Lane 1986: 182; Lewis 1980: 13–17). It therefore becomes identified as something separate from other aspects of day-to-day life. However, we have already seen that Western categorizations are not always applicable to other societies and that those activities that we deem to be mutually exclusive (e.g. domestic/economic/ritual activities) may not be conceived of as such. Among many peoples, ritual is an integrated part of day-to-day existence, not least because those cosmological principles that underlie ritual practice also constitute the logic of everyday activities (Bourdieu 1977: 96–158). For example, the rituals that accompany house-building in northern Thailand are as fundamental to the whole process as felling the trees that the house will be built from (Waterson 1990: 122). In other words, what we identify as 'ritual' acts are in fact essentially practical activities that enable people to deal with the world in an effective way. Thus, ritual practice is not always spatially, temporally or conceptually distinct from day-to-day activities. Rather, both arise from an underlying logic quite different to our own way of understanding the world. The dualism sacred: profane is therefore not always as strongly articulated as it is in modern Western society (Goody 1961: 151). For example, Bantu thinking describes a 'vital force' as inherent in all aspects of being (Tempels 1959). This force invests the world with a spirituality that affects day-to-day practice and endows much of it with a ritual significance. The Atoni of Timor have no concept of a 'profane' category at all and have no word to express it (Schulte Nordholt 1980: 247).

This discussion suggests that rather than despairing at our apparent inability to distinguish the ritual from the secular in the archaeological record of the Early Bronze Age, we should take the opportunity to critically consider whether contemporary ways of categorizing social practice might perhaps be inapplicable in this context. During the Early Bronze Age, it does not appear to have been considered contradictory for activities that modern Western people might characterize as 'domestic' or 'economic' (for example, working leather or processing grain) to be carried at locations such as round barrows or henge monuments. Similarly, vessels such as Collared Urns were used both for storing food and as containers for the cremated remains of the dead. Thus, there is little to suggest that ritual practice and those activities that formed part of daily maintenance routines were perceived as incompatible. I therefore argue that the dichotomy sacred–profane was less pronounced than it is in the modern Western world. Indeed, it seems likely that Early Bronze Age people did not recognize a major conceptual disjunction between ritual and habitual practice at all.

This is not to suppose that Early Bronze Age people did not distinguish different kinds of places. The substantial banks and ditches surrounding henge monuments, for example, certainly indicate that these were considered different from other locales. However, the point here is that there is little to suggest that Early Bronze Age people employed the same classificatory frameworks as we do today. As we have seen, it is difficult to neatly categorize Early Bronze Age sites as 'ritual' or 'secular'. This suggests that sites such as henges were not identified as 'sacred' spaces, set apart from the 'profane' world beyond their boundaries, but were distinguished from other locales according to a very different set of criteria (Brück 1997).

Houses

The notion that settlements should possess recognizable houses is deep-seated within British archaeology. This assumption can, for example, be seen at work in Simpson's paper on Beaker settlements (1971): because of his concern to identify 'houses', Simpson was able to list only seven Beaker settlements for the entirety of Britain, many of them in the far north of the country. Certainly, recognizable houses are notably absent from the archaeological record in the study area. Where structural evidence is unearthed, this frequently takes the form of clusters of stakeholes, often in no interpretable pattern (e.g. Snail Down, Wiltshire: N. Thomas, pers. comm.).

However, the presupposition that a settlement site should boast an identifiable house is problematic (cf. Hayden, Chapter 7, this volume; Lane 1986; Thomas 1996). In the contemporary Western world, houses tend to be substantial, permanent and elaborate structures not simply for functional reasons but, more fundamentally, because of their ideological and ontological significance. This may appear to contradict what has been said in the preceding paragraphs concerning the marginalization of the domestic sphere. However, the European concept of the 'home' has a much longer pedigree than the notion 'domestic' which is largely a product of post-Enlightenment classifications of practice. The house and the hearth hold a particular place in European social history (cf. Hodder 1990), and the rural idyll of the agricultural 'homestead' easily becomes projected into the past (Thomas 1991: 10). In modern society, houses serve as important points of reference in day-to-day existence; through them, wealth, status and taste are expressed. Our houses also constitute an essential part of our personal identity, as the ambiguous status of 'homeless' people illustrates.

It would clearly be a mistake to take it for granted that the kinds of houses with which we are familiar existed during the Early Bronze Age. The lack of substantial and easily identifiable houses implies that Early Bronze Age buildings were generally not a focus for the same level of material investment as houses in the modern Western world. It also suggests that they did not play the same ideological role as our own homes.

Reinterpreting the Early Bronze Age data

The preceding sections suggest that our own historically particular experience of settlement shapes what we look for in the archaeological record. To sum up, we have seen that there is nothing to suggest the existence of a functionally and/or spatially distinct category of domestic sites during the Early Bronze Age. Similarly, houses cannot be identified. The challenge is to use these observations in a positive way, as a means of understanding the essential difference of Early Bronze Age society. I argue that the evidence strongly suggests that settlements of the kind described in the definition discussed at the beginning of this chapter *actually did not exist* during the Early Bronze Age. This is because Early Bronze Age people did not categorize social practice in the same way as we do today.

What can this tell us about Early Bronze Age society?

If our concept of 'the settlement' is not an appropriate analytical category with which to understand the range and variability of Early Bronze Age sites, then we must start at the other end and consider what the Early Bronze Age data can tell us.

To begin with, the above discussion throws doubt on the widespread notion that settled agriculture formed the basis of the Early Bronze Age subsistence economy. It has long been realized that certain areas of the landscape were used on a intermittent, perhaps seasonal basis (e.g. Case 1963: 51; Bradley 1978b: 55–7, 59–60, 68–9, 1978c: 100). Examples include the floodplain of the River Thames and the wetlands of East Anglia, both of which would have been waterlogged during the winter and spring. Similar models of seasonal occupation have been proposed for upland areas, for example Dartmoor, although in these cases the evidence for seasonality is not so clear-cut. Some authors (e.g. Green 1974: 129–30; Bradley 1978b: 56–7, 1978c: 100; Fleming 1988: 100–3) have tried to accommodate the evidence for short-term and/or intermittent occupation of certain sites with the more generally accepted model of settled agriculture by arguing that there was a transhumant element to the Early Bronze Age economy. In other words, the settlement pattern was one of permanently occupied farmsteads but with sub-sections of the population forming temporary task-groups that moved to other specialized sites at particular times of the year. Specifically, Bradley (Holden & Bradley 1975: 101–3; Bradley 1978b: 56) has suggested that sites that produce many flint-scrapers may relate to seasonal patterns of stock movement between different parts of the landscape.

However, this model of settled agriculture with a transhumant element is prob-lematic because it presumes the existence, somewhere, of largely sedentary com-munities living in substantial, permanently occupied farmsteads. As we have seen, settlements of this kind cannot be documented in the archaeological record. Early Bronze Age sites do not provide evidence for long-term, continuous occupation of a single location. The absence of substantial, permanent architecture is an impor-tant initial point. Where unusual conditions of preservation occur, for example under Snail Down barrows X–XIV, Wiltshire (Annable 1958; N. Thomas, pers. comm.), scattered and shallow stakeholes testify to the ephemeral nature of most Early Bronze Age structures. Many sites appear to be the result of single, short-term episodes of activity. For example, at North Marden, West Sussex (Drewett 1986), excavations recovered a small deposit of Beaker pottery (11 sherds) and hearth debris from the ditch of an earlier oval barrow. At Dean Bottom, Wiltshire (Gingell 1992: 27), a pit had been filled with a series of dumps of refuse. The presence of conjoining sherds, flint refits and the generally good condition of both animal bone and pottery suggest that this material accumulated over a short period of time, most probably several months (Cleal 1992a: 62, 1992b: 133). The presence of neonatal lamb bones and a single hazelnut shell fragment may indicate an episode of occupation from spring to early autumn (Cleal 1992c: 152), although if the hazelnuts had been stored elsewhere since the previous autumn, a shorter term period of springtime occupation could be envisaged.

On the other hand, the ceramic assemblage recovered from some sites indicates that these may have been utilized over a period of several centuries. Examples include the artefact scatters sealed beneath round barrows on Ashey Down, Isle of Wight (Drewett 1970; Tomalin 1973), and Overton Hill, Wiltshire (Smith & Simpson 1966). The ceramic assemblages from these sites include both Late Neolithic and Early Bronze Age styles. However, the lack of substantial buildings is more suggestive of intermittent than continuous occupation. At Belle Tout, East Sussex (Bradley 1970a), for example, several separate foci of activity have been identified within an earthwork enclosure of c. 65 m × 35 m. The ceramics associated with these foci suggest that they were probably not contemporaneous and they may therefore have replaced one another over the course of time (Bradley 1982: 66–7). Within the framework of the model to be developed here, we may suggest that a group or groups returned to this site intermittently, certainly over a period of several years and perhaps longer. Such a model of short-term, discontinuous periods of occupation is already well accepted for certain types of site. For exam-ple, it has frequently been argued that henges were not permanently occupied but acted as centres at which dispersed groups periodically came together for short periods of time (e.g. Wainwright & Longworth 1971: 193–234; Bradley 1984: 76–9), perhaps for such events as feasts, marriages or gift exchanges. I argue that such a notion of short-lived, episodic usage can reasonably be extended to other Early Bronze Age sites.

Various other strands of evidence also suggest a considerable degree of residential mobility. As we have seen above, the artefactual inventories of Early Bronze Age sites indicate marked variability in the combination of activities undertaken at different sites. For example, the flint assemblages from many sites suggest that these possessed a task-specific element (see above; Holden & Bradley 1975: 101–3; Bradley 1978b: 56). Hence, different activities may have been carried out at different locations within the landscape (cf. Thomas 1996: 4). At the same time, finds such as cooking vessels, flint knives and burnt flint are common to most Early Bronze Age sites. This suggests that some tasks, including the preparation and consumption of food, were not confined to any one category of site but took place at many different locations in combination with a range of more specialized activities. This is certainly suggestive of some degree of mobility. The extensive but often sparse distribution of artefact scatters across the landscape (e.g. Richards 1990: fig. 159) also supports this proposal.

Thus, rather than finding a pattern in which seasonally occupied sites such as those on the Thames floodplain are complemented by permanent farmsteads in other parts of the landscape, it seems that most sites were occupied on a short-term or intermittent basis. Contrary to expectations, task-specific sites (such as those that produce high numbers of scrapers) are not confined to those parts of the landscape that might have been uninhabitable at certain times of the year (for example wetlands), but also occur in most other areas. These observations suggest that we need a new model that incorporates a higher degree of residential mobility than previously thought, with many, if not most sites being occupied for periods of months rather than years at a time.

What, then, was the pattern of this mobility? We have already seen that there is good evidence for cereal cultivation during the Early Bronze Age and that the notion of nomadic pastoralism has therefore been rejected (Bradley 1972). Yet, how can such a model of short-term, perhaps seasonal occupation accommodate evidence for cereal cultivation? An initial problem lies in the assumption that cereal cultivation implies a subsistence regime largely dependent on agriculture (e.g. Burgess 1980: 111–12, 193; see critique by Thomas 1991: 21) and that it requires a fully sedentary settlement pattern (see critique by Bradley 1972; Thomas 1996: 1–2). A first step will be to consider what evidence exists for the nature of the Early Bronze Age subsistence economy. It has long been realized that, alongside cereal cultivation and stock-raising, a diverse range of other resources were utilized. For example, Bradley (1978b: 79–95) has documented evidence for such activities as hunting, fishing and fowling as well as the use of a variety of wild plants. Despite this subsistence diversity, these resources have generally been considered marginal to the Early Bronze Age economy and most archaeologists have continued to envisage cereal agriculture as the main element of the subsistence base.

However, over the past ten years, it has become more and more difficult to sustain this view. Palaeobotanical samples of Later Bronze Age and Iron Age date are dominated by cultivated crops. In contrast, those from Later Neolithic and Early Bronze Age sites provide as much if not more evidence for the use of wild resources such as nuts, fruits and possibly also tubers (Entwistle & Grant 1989; Moffett et al. 1989; Bradley 1991: 55; Palmer and Jones 1991: 138). As Palmer and Jones (1991: 138) put it, palaeobotanical samples from the Neolithic and Early Bronze Age 'yield "muesli-like" mixtures of grains, nuts, fruits and edible wild plants in small quantities', indicating 'small volume collection and consumption of a range of cultivars and non-cultivars'. They contrast this with the Later Bronze Age and Iron Age data which comprise 'monotonous, but plentiful assemblages of grain crops, chaff and arable weeds' indicative of 'a large-scale arable "industry"' (ibid.). Bradley's assertion (1978b: 88) that 'until the Middle Bronze Age, "storage pits" are more likely to yield nuts than grain' has thus been borne out by more recent research. It has therefore been suggested that cereal-growing formed only one component of a broad-based subsistence economy (Entwistle & Grant 1989).[3] The possibility that cereals did not play such a central role in the Early Bronze Age economy may help us to understand why contemporary sites produce such variable finds assemblages. Where there is considerable subsistence diversity, we may expect to find a variety of different task-specific sites.

The lack of evidence for permanently occupied farmsteads and the broad-based nature of the subsistence economy are together suggestive of considerable mobility for most if not all members of the community, perhaps throughout the year (Barrett 1994: 136–46). Within such a context, how was the cultivation of cereals carried out? Thomas (1991: 21) has considered this same question with reference to the Neolithic and it is possible to apply a similar argument to the Early Bronze Age evidence. The perception that crops need tending throughout the year perhaps relates to the importance of cereals to the subsistence economy in recent European history. However, it is well known that some agriculturists do not watch their crops year round. For example, until the nineteenth century, the Cheyenne Indians grew maize, beans and squash in fields that they left unattended during the hunting season (Hodges 1957: 143). Indeed, the Early Bronze Age definition of a 'good' or 'sufficient' yield is likely to have been quite different to that of modern British farmers, and constant tending may not have been seen as necessary if cereals were not the mainstay of the subsistence economy, as Thomas also argues for the Neolithic (1991: 20–21). Together, these points suggest that the locations where cereals were grown were not occupied year-round but comprised only one of several resource locales utilized over the annual cycle. The evidence also hints at other patterns of mobility. The absence of field systems and the extreme rarity of lynchets dating to the Early Bronze Age is generally taken to indicate that plots of land were not cultivated for long periods of time but may have been abandoned after only a few seasons (e.g. Barrett 1994: 143–5; Entwistle & Grant 1989: 208).

Barrett (1994: 143–5) argues that this agricultural regime was probably a long fallow system. Again, this contributes to the overall picture of Early Bronze Age groups as relatively mobile.

However, I should emphasize that this notion of inbuilt mobility does not imply a return to the kind of nomadic pastoralist model favoured until the 1960s. Although stock-raising was undoubtedly important, it formed only one element of a set of diverse subsistence strategies. Certainly, formative critiques of the nomadic pastoralist model (e.g. Bradley 1972) still stand, yet similarly it remains difficult to conclusively identify an alternative ethnographic analogy for the kind of mobile residence pattern proposed above. At present, all too little is known of the Early Bronze Age subsistence economy to move beyond the most tentative generalizations. Clearly, there are a number of possible patterns of movement that might have characterized Early Bronze Age residential mobility (Whittle 1997). Future research will need to focus more closely on the definition and understanding of these patterns.

Finally, if we agree that the Early Bronze Age lifestyle incorporated a considerable degree of residential mobility, then this may help us to understand why finds such as quern fragments, cooking vessels and hearth-sweepings are frequently recovered from sites such as henges, ring-ditches and barrows. It has already been argued that Early Bronze Age people did not draw a sharp distinction between ritual and secular practice. Similarly, they do not appear to have considered it contradictory for what would be characterized today as 'ritual' and 'secular' activities to be carried out at the same location. As Early Bronze Age communities moved from one locale to the next over the course of each year, periodic visits to sites such as henges and ring-ditches (for such events as burials, initiation ceremonies, feasts or exchanges) would no doubt have formed part of the annual round. Within such a context, groups coming together at these sites for the duration of particular events will have produced refuse over the course of their stay.

The implications of residential mobility

The above discussions indicate that we can no longer envisage the kinds of permanent settlements that archaeologists so often assume to have existed during the Early Bronze Age. One important issue raised by this observation is that we must investigate anew the set of territorial and social practices through which Early Bronze Age groups defined and maintained their place in the landscape (cf. Barrett 1994: 137–41; Pollard, Chapter 5, this volume). With this aim in mind, even such apparently intractable sites as isolated pits or spreads of burnt flint have a role to play because these constitute some of the elements through which Early Bronze Age people articulated their relationship with the landscape. Such an approach is beginning to be developed by several British prehistorians. For example, recent studies of lithic scatters have underlined the need to investigate the nature of these sites more closely (e.g. Richards 1990; Schofield 1991).

On the basis of the evidence discussed above, we may make some tentative suggestions concerning the nature of Early Bronze Age territoriality. The degree of movement around the landscape that is implied by the data suggests that local family/household groups were not tied to specific areas of land, but rather had rights of access to a large area of the landscape as part of a wider community, lineage or group of lineages. Barrett (1994: 144) argues that if long fallow agriculture was practised during this period, access to land would have formed part of generalized rights arising from kinship relations and alliances between members of a wider community. He therefore suggests that during the Early Bronze Age, tenurial rights were probably held by extended kin or community groups such as lineages rather than by individual households. In such a context, resources including land might be periodically reallocated. Barrett's proposal is substantiated by the lack of identifiable houses at Early Bronze Age sites. During the Early Bronze Age, individual households did not employ substantial domestic architecture to establish and legitimate an enduring relationship to place. The ideology of possession and permanence that is created through the elaboration of the home in modern Western society does not seem to have existed. This suggests that long-term tenurial rights were not invested in the household, but in wider social groupings such as lineages. Furthermore, it is evident that different groups shared access to certain places or parts of the landscape. For example, the nature and scale of henge monuments, and the quantity of finds recovered from some of these sites, suggests that large numbers of people periodically gathered together at these locales (e.g. Clark 1936: 25–7; Wainwright & Longworth 1971: 193–234; Bradley 1984: 76–9). A similar argument has been proposed for flint mines, which appear to have been seasonally worked and may have acted as foci for large gatherings (Edmonds 1995: 117–20). Again, this is suggestive of a situation in which residentially mobile households shared access to particular re-sources as members of wider communities linked by networks of kinship and exchange relations.

The mobile lifestyle described above will also have resulted in very different models of space and time to those of later periods. From the Middle Bronze Age, settled agriculture appears to have become a major element of subsistence production. At this point, a class of substantial and permanent 'settlement sites' appears in the archaeological record (e.g. Barrett et al. 1991: 184–211). These are often surrounded by field systems and appear to have acted as centres for the annual subsistence cycle (Barrett 1989); as such, it is possible to suggest that the Middle Bronze Age conception of space was essentially centripetal (Barrett 1994: 147). This forms an interesting contrast with the Early Bronze Age when movement through the landscape (whether linear or cyclical) must have been influential in creating very different concepts of space (ibid.: 136–46). Similarly, the temporalities created by this pattern of residential mobility must have been quite different to the rhythms of later settled agriculture (ibid.: 147).

The social implications of mobility are particularly important. Individual and group identity was constituted through patterns of movement around a meaningful landscape rather than through a bond with a specific place, as may have been the case during the Middle Bronze Age. Inter-group relations must therefore have differed substantially to those of later periods, when sedentary household groups each had their own permanent and securely defined place in the landscape. The fluid settlement system proposed above also hints that the size and composition of groups may have changed markedly throughout the year (cf. Thomas 1996: 4), with larger groups congregating periodically at places such as henges or flint mines. Indeed, the existence of task-specific sites suggests that the occupants of certain locations may have been members of particular age or gender groups (ibid.). Patterns of mobility may therefore have played a vital role in reproducing the historically particular structure of Early Bronze Age society (Barrett 1994: 145; Thomas 1996: 4). On the other hand, the very varied combination of activities that were carried out at different Early Bronze Age sites hints at a fluidity in social practice that casts doubt on the existence of inflexible categories of social persona.[4] Finally, the lack of a discrete class of domestic sites has important implications for gender roles. The gender inequalities characteristic of the twentieth-century Western world are in part predicated on the reproduction of a separate and under-valued domestic sphere (Strathern 1984). No such domestic sphere can be identified in the Early Bronze Age, suggesting that gender relations were articulated quite differently. Tasks such as the preparation of food appear to have been carried out alongside many other kinds of activities. This makes it difficult for us to imagine Early Bronze Age women as passive, cloistered individuals who played no role in productive, political or ritual activities.

Conclusion

The discussion presented in this chapter suggests that the kinds of settlements that archaeologists have spent so long searching for did not exist during the Early Bronze Age. Domestic space does not appear to have been distinguished (either physically or conceptually) and a class of settlement sites cannot be recognized. There was no equivalent to the home in modern Western society. Rather, the Early Bronze Age evidence suggests the existence of a culturally specific set of 'occupation practices' in which the relationships between people and places were defined not through permanent attachment to a single locale but through traditions of movement around the landscape. These practices were fundamentally different to those of the modern Western world in that they did not involve the construction of substantial, permanent 'houses', or a definition of 'dwelling' that identified or prioritized domestic activities. Importantly, such a shift in perspective allows the incorporation of sites that have confounded the classificatory and inter-pretative frameworks applied to them. A critical re-evaluation of such sites in fact casts light on the ways in which Early Bronze Age people categorized human practice: for example, it seems likely that what might today be characterized as 'ritual' and 'secular' activities were not regarded as mutually exclusive or antagonistic during the Early Bronze Age. To conclude, the archaeological evidence has much to reveal concerning Early Bronze Age social practice but this requires us to question our own categories and conventions. However, by doing so, it may be possible to write a new and more sensitive account of Early Bronze Age society.

Appendix: references for sites listed in tables 4.1–4.4

1 Arreton Down, Isle of Wight: Alexander et al. 1960
2 Ashey Down, Isle of Wight: Drewett 1970; Tomalin 1973
3 Avebury G55, Wiltshire: Smith 1965a
4 Belle Tout, East Sussex: Bradley 1970a, 1982
5 Bullock Down, East Sussex: Holgate 1988
6 Church Hill, Findon, West Sussex: Pull 1953
7 Coneybury henge, Wiltshire: Richards 1990
8 Cowleaze, Dorset: Woodward 1991
9 Dean Bottom, Wiltshire: Gingell 1992
10 Downton, Wiltshire: Rahtz 1962
11 Durrington Walls, Wiltshire: Wainwright & Longworth 1971
12 Firtree Field, Dorset: Barrett et al. 1991: 118
13 Hengistbury Head, Dorset: Chadburn 1987
14 Holdenhurst, Hampshire: Piggott 1937
15 Lamb Down, Codford St. Mary, Wiltshire: Vatcher 1963
16 Mount Pleasant, Dorset: Wainwright 1979
17 North Marden, West Sussex: Drewett 1986
18 Overton Hill, Wiltshire: Smith & Simpson 1966
19 Playden, East Sussex: Cheyney 1935; Bradley 1978a; Cleal 1982
20 Rackham, West Sussex: Holden & Bradley 1975
21 Snail Down, Wiltshire: Thomas & Thomas 1956; Annable 1958; Trump 1958
22 Stockbridge, Hampshire: Stone & Hill 1938
23 West Kennet Avenue, Avebury, Wiltshire: Smith 1965b
24 Wilsford Down, Wiltshire: Richards 1990
25 Windmill Hill, Wiltshire: Smith 1965b; Whittle et al. in press.

Notes

1. For the purposes of this paper, I shall consider the classic archaeological heartlands of Wessex, that is the counties of Wiltshire, Dorset and Hampshire, along with sites in the Thames Valley, Kent and Sussex. The sites discussed date from *c.* 2500–1500 BC, that is from the first appearance of Beaker pottery and metalwork until the beginning of the main period of use of Deverel-Rimbury ceramics.
2. Round barrows are circular mounds of chalk rubble, earth or turves, raised over one or more inhumation or cremation burials; they are often surrounded by a ditch. Henges are roughly circular enclosures, usually delimited by an earthen bank and ditch; some of these contain stone or timber circles and alignments.
3. It is worth noting, however, that preservational factors are likely to bias palaeobotanical samples (Jones 1991). Jones has argued that hazelnut shell is likely to survive better in the

archaeological record than cereal remains such as chaff and straw. This is not only because of the density and hardness of nut shells but also because chaff and straw are likely to have been used as fodder for animals. There are few uses for nut shell except as fuel; charring would, of course, facilitate survival. Nonetheless, the contrast between Neolithic/Early Bronze Age palaeobotanical assemblages and those of later periods remains a clear indication of changes in subsistence strategy.

4. Although the evidence from graves suggests otherwise.

References

Alexander, J., P. C. Ozanne, A. Ozanne 1960. Report on the investigation of a round barrow on Arreton Down, Isle of Wight. *Proceedings of the Prehistoric Society* **26**, 263–302.

Annable, F. K. 1958. Excavation and fieldwork in Wiltshire: 1957. *Wiltshire Archaeological and Natural History Magazine* **57**, 2–17.

Ashbee, P. 1960. *The Bronze Age round barrow in Britain: an introduction to the study of the funerary practice and culture of the British and Irish single-grave people of the second millennium BC*. London: Phoenix House.

Barrett, J. C. 1989. Time and tradition: the rituals of everyday life. In *Bronze Age studies: transactions of the British – Scandinavian Colloquium in Stockholm, May 10–11, 1985*, H.-A. Nordström & A. Knape (eds), 113–26. Stockholm: The National Museum of Antiquities Studies 6.

Barrett, J. C. 1994. *Fragments from antiquity: an archaeology of social life in Britain, 2900–1200 BC* Oxford: Blackwell.

Barrett, J. C., R. Bradley, M. Green 1991. *Landscape, monuments and society: the prehistory of Cranborne Chase*. Cambridge: Cambridge University Press.

Bell, C. 1992. *Ritual theory, ritual practice*. Oxford: Oxford University Press.

Bourdieu, P. 1977. *Outline of a theory of practice*. Cambridge: Cambridge University Press.

Bradley, R. 1970a. The excavation of a Beaker settlement at Belle Tout, East Sussex, England. *Proceedings of the Prehistoric Society* **36**, 312–79.

Bradley, R. 1970b. Where have all the houses gone? Some approaches to Beaker settlement. *Current Archaeology* **21**, 264–6.

Bradley, R. 1972. Prehistorians and pastoralists in Neolithic and Bronze Age England. *World Archaeology* **4**, 192–204.

Bradley, R. 1978a. A reconsideration of the Late Neolithic site at Playden, East Sussex. In *Excavations at Fengate: second report*, F. Pryor, 219–23. Toronto: Royal Ontario Museum.

Bradley, R. 1978b. *The prehistoric settlement of Britain*. London: Routledge & Kegan Paul.

Bradley, R. 1978c. Colonisation and land-use in the Late Neolithic and Early Bronze Age. In *The effect of man on the landscape: the lowland zone*, S. Limbrey & J. G. Evans (eds), 95–103. London: Council for British Archaeology Research Report 21.

Bradley, R. 1982. Belle Tout: revision and reassessment. In *The archaeology of Bullock Down, Eastbourne, East Sussex: the development of a landscape*, P. Drewett (ed.), 62–71. Lewes: Sussex Archaeological Society Monograph 1.

Bradley, R. 1984. *The social foundations of prehistoric Britain: themes and variations in the archaeology of power*. London: Longman.

Bradley, R. 1991. The pattern of change in British prehistory. In *Chiefdoms: power, economy and ideology*, T. Earle (ed.), 44–70. Cambridge: Cambridge University Press.

Brown, A. 1991. Structured deposition and technological change among the flaked stone artefacts from Cranborne Chase. In *Papers on the prehistoric archaeology of Cranborne Chase*, J. Barrett, R. Bradley, M. Hall, 102–33. Oxford: Oxbow Monograph 11.

Brück, J. 1997. *The Early-Middle Bronze Age transition in Wessex, Sussex and the Thames Valley*. PhD thesis, Department of Archaeology, University of Cambridge.

Burgess, C. 1980. *The age of Stonehenge*. London: J. M. Dent.

Burl, A. 1976. *The stone circles of the British Isles*. New Haven: Yale University Press.

Case, H. J. 1963. Notes on the finds and on ring-ditches in the Oxford region. *Oxoniensia* **28**, 19–52.

Case, H. 1977. The Beaker culture in Britain and Ireland. In *Beakers in Britain and Europe: four studies*, R. Mercer (ed.), 71–101. Oxford: British Archaeological Reports, British Series S26.

Chadburn, A. 1987. The excavations: site 6. In *Hengistbury Head, Dorset, vol. 1: the prehistoric and Roman settlement, 3500 BC–AD 500*, B. Cunliffe, 61–6. Oxford: Oxford University Committee for Archaeology Monograph 13.

Cheyney, H. J. 1935. An Aeneolithic site at Playden, near Rye. *Antiquaries' Journal* **15**, 152–64.

Childe, V. G. 1940. *Prehistoric communities of the British Isles*. London: Chambers.

Clark, J. G. D. 1936. The timber monument at Arminghall and its affinities. *Proceedings of the Prehistoric Society* **2**, 1–51.

Cleal, R. J. 1982. A re-analysis of the ring-ditch site at Playden, East Sussex. *Sussex Archaeological Collections* **120**, 1–17.

Cleal, R. J. 1992a. The Neolithic and Beaker pottery. See Gingell (1992), 61–70.

Cleal, R. J. 1992b. Dean Bottom: the assemblage from the Beaker pit. See Gingell (1992), 133–5.

Cleal, R. J. 1992c. Summary. See Gingell (1992), 151–3.

Colt Hoare, R. 1812. *The ancient history of south Wiltshire*. London: William Millar.

Darvill, T. 1987. *Prehistoric Britain*. London: Batsford.

Drewett, P. 1970. The excavation of two round barrows and associated fieldwork on Ashey Down, Isle of Wight, 1969. *Proceedings of the Hampshire Field Club and Archaeological Society* **27**, 33–56.

Drewett, P. 1986. The excavation of a Neolithic oval barrow at North Marden, West Sussex, 1982. *Proceedings of the Prehistoric Society* **52**, 31–51.

Edmonds, M. 1995. *Stone tools and society: working stone in Neolithic and Bronze Age Britain*. London: Batsford.

Entwistle, R. & A. Grant 1989. The evidence for cereal cultivation and animal husbandry in the southern British Neolithic and Bronze Age. In *The beginnings of agriculture*, A. Milles, D. Williams, N. Gardner (eds), 203–15. Oxford: British Archaeological Reports, International Series 496.

Fleming, A. 1988. *The Dartmoor Reaves: investigating prehistoric land divisions*. London: Batsford.

Fox, C. 1941. Stake-circles in turf barrows: a record of excavation in Glamorgan 1939–40. *Antiquaries' Journal* **21**, 92–127.

Gibson, A. 1980. A re-interpretation of Chippenham Barrow 5, with a discussion of the Beaker-associated pottery. *Proceedings of the Cambridge Antiquarian Society* **70**, 47–60.

Gibson, A. 1982. *Beaker domestic sites: a study of the domestic pottery of the late third and early second millennium BC in the British Isles*. Oxford: British Archaeological Reports, British Series 107.

Gibson, A. 1992. Approaches to the later Neolithic and Bronze Age settlement of Britain. In *L'habitat et l'occupation du sol à l'âge du Bronze en Europe*, C. Mordant & A. Richard (eds), 41–8. Paris: Comité des Travaux Historiques Scientifiques, documents préhistoriques 4.

Gingell, C. 1992. *The Marlborough Downs: a Later Bronze Age landscape and its origins*. Devizes: Wiltshire Archaeology and Natural History Society Monograph 1.

Goody, J. 1961. Religion and ritual: the definitional problem. *British Journal of Sociology* **12**, 142–64.

Green, H. S. 1974. Early Bronze Age burial, territory and population in Milton Keynes, Buckinghamshire, and the Great Ouse Valley. *Archaeological Journal* **131**, 75–139.

Hodder, I. 1990. *The domestication of Europe: structure and contingency in Neolithic societies*. Oxford: Blackwell.

Hodges, H. W. M. 1957. Braves, Beakers and battle-axes. *Antiquity* **31**, 142–6.

Holden, E. W. & R. J. Bradley 1975. A late Neolithic site at Rackham. *Sussex Archaeological Collections* **113**, 85–103.

Holgate, R. 1988. Further investigations at the later Neolithic domestic site and Napoleonic 'camp' at Bullock Down, near Eastbourne, East Sussex. *Sussex Archaeological Collections* **126**, 21–30.

Hughes, G. 1996. Lockington. *Current Archaeology* **146**, 44–9.

Johnson, M. 1993. *Housing culture: traditional architecture in an English landscape*. London: UCL Press.

Jones, G. 1991. Cultivation and gathering in Neolithic Britain. Paper presented at the winter meeting of the Neolithic Studies Group, London.

La Fontaine, J. 1981. The domestication of the savage male. *Man* **16**, 333–49.

Lane, P. 1986. Past practices in the ritual present: examples from the Welsh Bronze Age. *Archaeological Review from Cambridge* **5**, 181–92.

Leach, E. 1968. Ritual. In *International Encyclopaedia of the Social Sciences*, 520–26. New York: Macmillan and Free Press.

Lewis, G. 1980. *Day of shining red: an essay on understanding ritual*. Cambridge: Cambridge University Press.

Moffett, L., M. A. Robinson, V. Straker 1989. Cereals, fruit and nuts: charred plant remains from Neolithic sites in England and Wales and the Neolithic economy. In *The beginnings of agriculture*, A. Milles, D. Williams, N. Gardner (eds), 243–61. Oxford: British Archaeological Reports, International Series 496.

Moore, H. 1988. *Feminism and anthropology*. Cambridge: Polity Press.

Palmer, C. & M. Jones 1991. The plant remains. In *Maiden Castle: excavations and field survey 1985–6*, N. M. Sharples, 129–39. London: English Heritage Archaeology Report 19.

Piggott, S. 1937. The excavation of a long barrow in Holdenhurst parish, near Christchurch, Hampshire. *Proceedings of the Prehistoric Society* **3**, 1–14.

Piggott, S. 1940. Timber circles: a re-examination. *Archaeological Journal* **96**, 192–222.

Pull, J. H. 1953. Further discoveries at Church Hill, Findon. *Sussex County Magazine* **27**, 15–21.

Rahtz, P. A. 1962. Neolithic and Beaker sites at Downton, near Salisbury, Wiltshire. *Wiltshire Archaeological and Natural History Magazine* **58**, 116–42.

Richards, J. 1990. *The Stonehenge environs project*. London: English Heritage Archaeological Report 16.

Ruggles, C. L. N. & A. W. R. Whittle (eds) 1981. *Astronomy and society in Britain during the period 4000–1500 BC*. Oxford: British Archaeological Reports, British Series 88.

Schofield, A. J. 1991. Interpreting artefact scatters: an introduction. In *Interpreting artefact scatters: contributions to ploughzone archaeology*, A. J. Schofield (ed.), 3–8. Oxford: Oxbow Books.

Schulte Nordholt, H. G. 1980. The symbolic classification of the Atoni of Timor. In *The flow of life: essays on eastern Indonesia*, J. J. Fox (ed.), 231–47. Cambridge, Mass.: Harvard University Press.

Simpson, D. D. A. 1971. Beaker houses and settlements in Britain. In *Economy and settlement in Neolithic and Early Bronze Age Britain and Europe*, D. D. A. Simpson (ed.), 131–52. Leicester: Leicester University Press.

Smith, I. F. 1965a. Excavation of a bell barrow, Avebury G55. *Wiltshire Archaeological and Natural History Magazine* **60**, 24–46.

Smith, I. F. 1965b. *Windmill Hill and Avebury: excavations by Alexander Keiller, 1925–1939*. Oxford: Clarendon Press.

Smith, I. F. & D. D. A. Simpson 1966. Excavation of a round barrow on Overton Hill, north Wiltshire, England. *Proceedings of the Prehistoric Society* **32**, 122–55.

Stone, J. F. S. & N. G. Hill 1938. A Middle Bronze Age site at Stockbridge, Hampshire. *Proceedings of the Prehistoric Society* **4**, 249–57.

Strathern, M. 1984. Domesticity and the denigration of women. In *Rethinking women's roles: perspectives from the Pacific*, D. O'Brien & S. Tiffany (eds), 13–31. Berkeley: University of California Press.

Tempels, P. 1959. *Bantu philosophy*. Paris: Présence Africaine.

Thomas, J. 1991. *Rethinking the Neolithic*. Cambridge: Cambridge University Press.

Thomas, J. 1996. Neolithic houses in mainland Britain and Ireland – a sceptical view. In *Neolithic houses in northwest Europe and beyond*, T. Darvill & J. Thomas (eds), 1–12. Oxford: Oxbow.

Thomas, N. & C. Thomas 1956. Excavations at Snail Down, Everleigh: 1953, 1955. An interim report. *Wiltshire Archaeological and Natural History Magazine* **56**, 127–48.

Tiffany, S. 1978. Models and the social anthropology of women. *Man* **13**, 34–51.

Tomalin, D. J. 1973. Reappraisal of a Collared Urn and other pottery from barrow 8, Ashey Down, Isle of Wight. *Proceedings of the Hampshire Field Club and Archaeological Society* **30**, 31–4.

Trump, D. 1958. Notes on excavations in the British Isles. *Proceedings of the Prehistoric Society* **24**, 211–20.

Vatcher, F. de M. 1963. The excavation of the barrows on Lamb Down, Codford St Mary. *Wiltshire Archaeological and Natural History Magazine* **58**, 417–41.

Wainwright, G. J. 1979. *Mount Pleasant, Dorset: excavations 1970–1971*. Reports of the Research Committee of the Society of Antiquaries of London 37.

Wainwright, G. J. 1989. *The henge monuments: ceremony and society in prehistoric Britain*. London: Thames & Hudson.

Wainwright, G. J. & I. H. Longworth 1971. *Durrington Walls: excavations 1966–1968*. Reports of the Research Committee of the Society of Antiquaries of London 29.

Waterson, R. 1990. *The living house: an anthropology of architecture in south-east Asia*. Oxford: Oxford University Press.

Whittle, A. 1981. Later Neolithic society in Britain – a realignment. In *Astronomy and society in Britain during the period 4000–1500 BC*, C. L. N. Ruggles & A. W. R. Whittle (eds), 297–342. Oxford: British Archaeological Reports, British Series 88.

Whittle, A. 1997. Moving on and moving around: Neolithic settlement mobility. In *Neolithic landscapes*, P. Topping (ed.), 15–22. Oxford: Oxbow Monograph 86.

Whittle, A., J. Pollard, C. Grigson in press. *The harmony of symbols: the Windmill Hill causewayed enclosure, Wiltshire*. Oxford: Oxford University Press.

Woodward, P. J. 1991. *The South Dorset Ridgeway: survey and excavations 1977–1984*. Dorchester: Dorset Natural History and Archaeological Society monograph 8.

Yanagisako, S. J. 1979. Family and household: the analysis of domestic groups. *Annual Review of Anthropology* **8**, 161–205.

CHAPTER FIVE

'These places have their moments': thoughts on settlement practices in the British Neolithic

Joshua Pollard

Introduction

Each of us, through the process of living in the world, has an intimate experience of the act of settlement. We hold mental biographies of relationships with people, memories and events, these being associated with particular lived places and times. Those relationships will have varied in intensity and favourability according to circumstance and to personal and group experience. Living in any location that does not involve complete social isolation embroils us in networks of power, dependency and reciprocity with other people. The experience of dwelling is conceptually complex. It goes beyond the basic needs of survival and constitutes much of our understanding of cultural order and value.

What is curious is that as archaeologists we rarely reflect on this sense of personal experience when engaged in studying settlement.[1] Settlement is often abstracted as a category of analysis, although this is infrequently acknowledged. The consequence is that the act and process of settlement are often approached, at one level, through the analysis of regional patterns and, at another, through the structural and economic detail of particular 'sites'. Such approaches have proved invaluable at a basic level of data collection and analysis, but it can be argued that their success is predicated on a particular functionalist conceptualization of settlement involving permanent bounded spaces and sedentism. Whether for good or ill, this formal and particularistic presentation of spatial relationships also operates within an abstracted time-frame, that of millennium and century divisions, periods, phases and subphases. Like any form of social practice, archaeology is an act of continual interpretation that necessarily involves such forms of categorization in order to make sense of the information we encounter. However, if we are to construct meaningful social archaeologies of settlement, we should acknowledge the necessity of moving beyond formal analysis to constructing narratives within which the interpretation of the grounded values of past lived experience come to the fore. Social time, place as an arena of action rather than neutral space, and settlement as a realization of relationships, not just with people, but with landscape and history, are essential ingredients. This represents a move away from concerns with settlement *pattern* and long-term process to an understanding of settlement as social *practice*.

The act of settlement is a skilled practice involving intimate experiential knowledge, social and ontological risk, decisions about where and how to live, with whom and at what cost or benefit. Such decisions are themselves mediated in relation to the values of historically constituted structure. I would like to suggest that these are issues that archaeology can address, arguably as successfully as current approaches to prehistoric 'economy' or long-term settlement pattern, by focusing on the detail of contextually situated action. To an extent, direction is provided by approaches to prehistoric landscapes and monuments that borrow much of their theoretical outlook from phenomenological and ontological theory (e.g. Richards 1993; Thomas 1993a; Barrett 1994; Tilley 1994). In this chapter, I should like to explore some of these themes under the banner of 'settlement as practice', considering issues of temporality, mobility, scale, tenure and remembrance in the Neolithic (and to a lesser extent Mesolithic) of the British Isles. Central to this is the idea that 'where and how people chose to settle, and for how long, is at least as interesting as the variety of crop they cultivated or the age at which they slaughtered cattle' (Whittle 1988: 38).

Understanding settlement in the British Neolithic

For the British Neolithic,[2] we are faced with the record of very particular kinds of settlement practices that defy immediate understanding because of the lack of contemporary frames of analogy. Despite initial expectations, it is now generally acknowledged that, for the most part, Neolithic settlement did not involve the construction of permanent domestic structures nor the formal division of the landscape into field systems and areas of demarcated landholdings (Thomas 1991: 9–10). Settlement mobility is recognized as commonplace. Although domestic livestock was kept and cereals cultivated, perhaps on a small scale for either routine or special-event consumption (cf. Entwistle & Grant 1989), sedentary mixed farming was clearly not the norm. Ceremonial and funerary monuments dominate the archaeological record for the period, whereas houses and domestic settlement enclosures are rarely encountered (cf. Thomas 1996: 7–12). For much of southern Britain, the traces of settlement take the form of surface lithic scatters that can be interpreted as the ploughed-out remnants of erstwhile middens (Needham & Trott 1987). Excavation of such lithic scatters occasionally exposes loosely structured scatters of pits, stakeholes and shallow postholes (e.g. Spong Hill: Healy 1988). Faced with such sparse evidence, it is not surprising that so many narratives on the Neolithic are constructed around the archaeology of monuments, material culture, material practices and the relations of social power, rather than dwelling (e.g. Barrett et al. 1991; Thomas 1991; Barrett 1994).

The central problem with the archaeology of Neolithic settlement rests not with the nature of the information we recover, but with the way it is understood. Perceptions determine interpretation, yet these are always intimately linked to present conceptualizations of what the Neolithic was. The pit dwellings that littered the literature between the wars were tied into an archaeology whose dominant mode of discourse was social evolution (Evans 1988: 52–4). Similarly, notions of pastoralism led to the interpretation of causewayed enclosures as cattle corrals and seasonal meeting places (Piggott 1954: 29; Smith 1965: 19). The models of Neolithic sedentary mixed farming popular during the 1960s and 1970s convinced some people that permanent settlement sites lay buried under colluvium and alluvium in river valleys and were just waiting to be found (Thomas 1991: 8–9). Rather than coming to grips with the evidence of settlement as it presents itself, and working 'from the bottom up', recourse is often made to monothetic models and imposed rather than data-derived theorization.

In a sense, Neolithic studies are still caught in this trap. The evidence of lithic scatters, pits, the rare presence of isolated or small groups of houses, and the predominance of cattle in many faunal assemblages is amalgamated into simple models of settlement. For the earlier part of the sequence, this is one of small family or lineage groups engaged in fixed plot horticulture, but with seasonal or short-term movement based around the herding of cattle (Thomas 1991: 28). The more expedient use of lithic resources during the Later Neolithic, and the presence in some areas of extensive scatters dating to the third millennium BC, has been taken to suggest increased sedentism (Bradley 1987: 184; Edmonds 1987: 174). Holgate (1988: 109) goes further and sees the development of permanently occupied farmsteads with infield/outfield systems of agriculture as emerging during the third millennium BC. Significantly, the results of fieldwork in the southern English 'heartlands' of Wessex and the Thames Valley are often taken as models or the baseline for practices in the rest of the British Isles. Only the 'marginal' regions of Orkney, Shetland and the Western Isles, with their tradition of stone built houses (Clarke & Sharples 1985; Whittle et al. 1986; Armit 1992), are acknowledged to stand as something different. Here lies a fundamental contradiction: we use simple, all-embracing models, yet at the same time we think of the period as a fragmented tradition (Thomas 1993b: 383–90) within which values operated and were reproduced at the local level of the lineage group or region (Sharples 1992). The problem resides in reconciling a tension between understanding and writing about general process in the past, and at the same time acknowledging the centrality of the particular in shaping those processes.

I propose that Neolithic settlement practices varied widely in terms of mobility and scale; this is visible in the variety of 'sites' ranging from short-lived single households to seasonal or long-term aggregations (some associated with enclosures). Settlement should be seen as operating within different arenas of social value according to time and place, and within rather fluid and contingent systems of social relations and 'place relations'. Three key areas need to be addressed: 'temporality and mobility', 'scale', and 'remembrance and reference'.

Temporality and mobility

Temporality is experiential social time, the rhythms by which we go about life and their relationship to past and future states of being. Even though they are often bound up in cycles of resource procurement or production, such rhythms are not those of nature but of human practice (Gosden 1994: 7–10). Temporality is structured differently according to specific contexts of place or practice, whether these are the routines of domestic production, the working of the landscape, or ritual time (Bradley 1991: 210–12). Barrett sees temporality as a major structuring principle, and posits human existence within the Neolithic as organized around a conceptualization of 'becoming', which he defines as 'a movement towards a future state which was described by reference to ancestors or to gods and where life itself might be spoken of as ephemeral' (Barrett 1994: 136).

Organized movement within a landscape is inextricably linked to temporality. Physical movement presupposes the passage of time as much as space, and is equally constituted by and results from particular cultural values that determine the appropriateness of action. The idea of settlement mobility, or of sedentism, is not inherent in human nature, nor can it be said to be determined by economic practices, since those practices are themselves social constructs. It is evident that time and space/place (which movement and settlement imply) are intermeshed with biography.[3] These biographies exist not just in relation to people, but also to places, and indeed to times (Dietler & Herbich 1993: 255–8). In fact, there exists a reflexive relationship between land/place/time and personal or group identity to the extent that it would be meaningless to try to separate the biographies of people from those of the 'inanimate' physical context of their existence (Ingold 1986: 137).

Investigations of long-term changes in settlement patterns often have more to do with abstract, formalized time than that which is humanly centred (Shanks & Tilley 1987: 118–36). They are presentations of changing configurations of occupational practice within the framework of distanced chronometric time and Cartesian space. This is not to devalue such approaches, but rather to reinforce the idea that they do not constitute the only way of looking at settlement. It is perhaps because of the difficulty of constructing refined chronologies in prehistory – those that can be related to the level of human experience such as the decade or generation – and the desire to be able to piece together long-term change, that any analysis of occupation in relation to substantial time (Shanks & Tilley 1987: 128) has been largely avoided. However, there have been successful studies of the presentation of time within contemporary monumental contexts (Bradley 1991). The key to understanding temporality in an occupational setting rests in the interpretation of the rhythms of life seen, for example, in the practice of residential mobility and in the referencing of time.

In the 1990s, most interpretations have recognized an element of residential mobility in Neolithic settlement, often seen as being analogous to that practised by earlier (Mesolithic) hunter–gatherers (e.g. Edmonds 1995: 22), although its precise nature is usually ill-defined. There has been a tendency to produce extreme models of either permanent or shifting settlement that ignore potential variability (Whittle 1988: 59). With an appreciation of variability also goes the range of temporal/

spatial and tenurial relationships that mobility implies. Three types of temporal/ spatial relationships could be suggested: those of seasonal transhumance;[4] sedentism with periodic shift of locale and resettlement (encapsulated in the swidden model); and full sedentism (usually equated with intensive mixed farming). To the list can perhaps be added various irregular practices, for example involving an occasional shift between transhumance and full sedentism. No single form of temporal/spatial relationship encapsulates settlement practices in the British Neolithic, and in the following section examples of each will be offered.

Seasonal transhumance   Ideas of planned movement on a seasonal basis have been dominant in the study of Neolithic settlement practices for some time and indeed the concept of embedded movement does fit the evidence from many areas rather well. Taking the dominance of cattle remains in many fourth-millennium BC faunal assemblages, and the scarcity of permanent domestic structures, seasonal movement of people and livestock from lowland to upland regions or along river valleys is frequently argued to have been the rhythm of landscape dwelling (Pryor 1988: 67–9; Thomas 1991: 19; Barrett 1994: 141–6). However, 'seasonality, perhaps the most visible form of temporary absence, is notoriously hard to prove archaeologically' (Pryor 1995: 97). Only in exceptional circumstances might seasonal residential mobility be confidently identified, for example in relation to locations such as flood-prone river valleys where environmental conditions would have precluded year-round settlement.

Reference can be made to two small Later Neolithic stake-built structures excavated at Trelystan, Powys (Britnell 1982: 139–43), located at 370 m OD on a hill crest above the Severn valley (fig. 5.1). Occupation of this locale is likely only to have occurred during the climatically favourable seasons of spring and summer (Gibson 1996: 138–9), the main focus of occupation being in the valley itself where a series of earthwork and timber monuments were constructed between the fourth millennium BC and the second millennium BC (Gibson 1994). Neither structure at Trelystan was rebuilt, and given their flimsy construction it is unlikely that the life of each went beyond a decade or so. A cycle of construction, seasonal occupation over several years, abandonment and rebuilding elsewhere on the hill might have been followed (Britnell 1982: 185). On the one hand, the temporary nature of the structures and the absence of repeated rebuilding at this locale illustrates a rather fluid use of the landscape. However, although it was set within a routine of the short-term and seasonal, such activity took place in relation to wider frames of temporal reference. Within the space between the structures lay an isolated cairn-marked grave containing the cremated remains of an adult woman along with traces of an inhumation. A single radiocarbon determination suggests this may have predated the stake-built structures. Whatever its precise position within the sequence, the presence of the grave within the settlement, and its permanent marking-out through the construction of a cairn, would have served as a mnemonic of past lineage members, their relationship to the land, and earlier routines of occupation. Moving from the lowland of the Severn Valley to the upland, people would have been aware of an even deeper biography of time, orientation (physical,

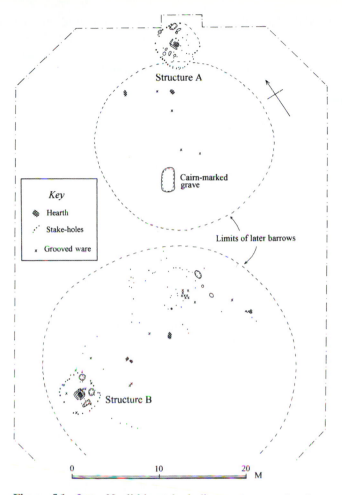

Figure 5.1 Late Neolithic stake-built structures and cairn-marked grave at Trelystan, Powys (after Britnell 1982).

cosmological and historical) and belonging, manifest in the Sarn-y-bryn-caled cursus (a linear, parallel-ditched monument) constructed several centuries earlier (Gibson 1994) that reinforced the dominant northeast–southwest axis of the landscape. This axis was itself reinstated by the orientation of both the grave at Trelystan and the hearths of the structures at this site.

The rather diminutive size of the Trelystan houses is also a reminder that not all members of a community may have made the journey to the uplands. Seasonal movement of livestock was probably managed by only a small section of the family or lineage, with the old, the very young, and those with the responsibility of looking after them remaining in other, semi-sedentary, occupation locales. Within the community, this would have contributed to differential experience and perceptions of time and place, that experience being structured by and serving to reproduce social roles of age, gender and task responsibility. The potential for a range of practices to co-exist within a single situation should also be acknowledged (Graham 1993: 25–9): for instance, both transhumant and semi-sedentary occupations may be co-existent, although with different or changing residential membership.

Periodic shift of settlement locale   Although seasonal movement of people and herds *may* have been a dominant mode of practice in the Neolithic, the difference between this and that practised by Mesolithic hunter–gatherers in following herds of wild ungulates needs emphasizing. It is important to situate seasonal movement within broader temporal trends that relate to the overall duration of occupation at particular locales. Significantly, distinctions are clearly manifest in the archaeological 'signature' of occupations between the two periods. The repeated return to particular locales on a seasonal/episodic basis over long periods of time, not simply decades but sometimes centuries or even millennia (Tilley 1994: 84), is a particular feature of Mesolithic occupation. This is seen most explicitly in Late Mesolithic coastal shell middens, such as those on Oronsay (Mellars 1987), and also in tightly defined, high-density lithic scatters such as those at Thatcham, Berkshire (Wymer & Churchill 1962), and Downton, Wiltshire (Higgs 1959) (fig. 5.2). These lithic scatters undoubtedly form the durable component of former middens. Such middens probably accumulated over successive occupations that might have spanned several generations. Mellars' figures of occupation of approximately 100 to 150 years at Cnoc Coig and 400 to 500 years at the Caisteal nan Gillean and Priory Middens on Oronsay (Mellars 1987: 191, 233) provide an apt illustration. These sites show a pronounced long-term commitment to particular locales, with middening potentially being employed as a visible statement of occupation and belonging, as well as serving to create a sense of place through a material linkage between the present and past.

It can be argued that there is little sense of such rigid long-term commitment to place *through settlement* during the Earlier Neolithic. Tightly defined, high-density lithic scatters of the sort that frequently define Mesolithic occupation sites are not common. The poor survival of Neolithic middens, even under the protection of alluvium or the mounds and banks of later monuments, suggests that these rarely had the chance to accumulate to any great extent. Where it is possible to gauge duration of occupation at particular locales, this seems to be measurable in years or a few decades, rather than centuries. Assemblages of pottery, lithics and animal bone from surface and pit deposits provide the best indicators of duration. The small material assemblages from settlements such as those at Hemp Knoll, Wiltshire (Robertson-Mackay 1980: 125–9), and Hazleton North, Gloucestershire (Saville 1990: 141–75), do not speak of occupation over more than a few years at most. The homogeneity of lithic and ceramic assemblages from large pit clusters such as those excavated at Hurst Fen, Cambridgeshire (Clark 1960: 241), and Broome Heath, Norfolk (Wainwright 1972: 70), is also more suggestive of aggregation than long-term settlement. Clearly, the spatial/temporal rhythms of

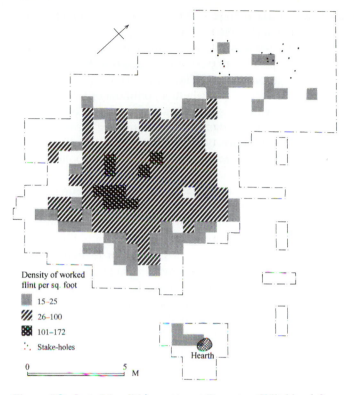

Figure 5.2 Late Mesolithic scatter at Downton, Wiltshire (after Higgs 1959).

settlement in operation during the Neolithic were different to those of the Mesolithic. In this respect, Ingold's observation regarding the frequent relocations of settlement made by pioneer cultivators, who have a 'pronounced "shiftiness", or impermanence in their ties to specific locales' (Ingold 1986: 180), is pertinent, although perhaps not wholly accurate. Unlike hunter–gatherers, such communities did not repeatedly retrace their steps year-in-year-out over generations. The dominant mode of landscape occupation practised in the southern British Earlier Neolithic appears to have involved a process of piecemeal clearance, settlement (seasonal movement accepted), periodic shift after a few years and resettlement. This can be described as a swidden process, but without the kind of cyclical agricultural system argued for parts of the Continental Early Neolithic *Bandkeramik* (Soudský 1962: 196).

Variability in the settlement record at both site and regional levels warns against too broad a generalization. Evidence for the rebuilding of wooden structures at the Earlier Neolithic settlement at Lismore Fields, Buxton (Garton 1987: 251), for example, is indicative of more sustained commitment to a locale *through settlement* than the rather event-like nature of the pre-cairn occupation at

Hazleton North, which was represented by a single-phase wooden structure and a small artefact assemblage (Saville 1990: 14–22). Another line of inquiry may also be fundamental in addressing such issues. Although rarely given much consideration, or written off as a product of postdepositional transformation (e.g. Schofield 1991: 163), density variations between lithic scatters also provide an illustration of the relative duration of occupation, whether continual or intermittent, at particular locales. Rather than viewing surface scatters simply as evidence of landscape exploitation, they should be recognized as constituting a record of place-values constructed through the practice of occupation; they were formed as part of a process by which the landscape was ascribed meaning, symbolic value and historical significance.

In the case of the Neolithic of southern Britain, the fleeting occupational ties to particular locales suggest that relationships to the landscape were often different to those of Mesolithic hunter–gatherers. During the Mesolithic, ontological stability may have been created through constant return to historically significant locales where occupation took place on a seasonal or regular basis over generations. Birth, death and other critical moments in human life-cycles are likely to have taken place within the arena of living sites; such places would therefore embody lengthy genealogies specific to a group. It is therefore possible to envisage how social identities may have been created through reference to these places. The rather impermanent nature of ties to locales over much of the Neolithic, as is reflected in a process of shifting settlement, was perhaps countered by the construction in many areas of earthen and chambered tombs and other monuments to an ancestral past (see below). Social identities and a sense of belonging to a region were created and embodied by monuments that stood as a testimony to group origins and a genealogy of occupation within a fluid social landscape. Within a mythical order, a monument might have constituted a proper place of belonging within what Barrett (1994: 136) has described as a state of 'becoming', where the ephemeral nature of human life was contrasted with a more stable and timeless world of ancestors.

The movement of settlements around the landscape, although socially embedded and probably considered necessary or desirable, would also have been effective as a social strategy. Mobility in settlement practices would have reduced the potential for particular interest groups within society to enact any form of lasting social control. It would have allowed individual households some freedom to dictate their own conditions of existence, perhaps shifting affiliation and alliances (cf. Bogucki 1988: 180–83). Furthermore, there is an argument that by following the system of extensive, swidden cultivation that residential mobility might imply, households were maximizing returns on the labour of food production by avoiding the repetitive task of maintaining the fertility of the fixed plots/fields typical of settled intensive agriculture.

Full sedentism   However, by focusing too much on settlement practices that embodied varying degrees of 'inbuilt' mobility, there is a danger of making recourse to general models for the period and consequently ignoring clear regional variations in practice. Nowhere is this seen more dramatically than by comparison between the rather ephemeral and impermanent character of settlements in southern England and the permanent or semi-permanent 'farmstead' and 'village'-scale sites of the Northern Isles of Scotland. Reference can be made to stone-built settlements of the late fourth and third millennium BC at Skara Brae, Barnhouse, Rinyo and the Links of Noltland on the Orkneys (Clarke & Sharples 1985), and the Scord of Brouster on the Shetlands (Whittle et al. 1986). These sites saw several generations of occupation, with phases of rebuilding being clearly evident. It has been argued that several were associated with organized, intensive infield systems of arable agriculture with manure amendment (Bond et al. 1995: 127). Whether or not the particular environmental conditions and spatial constraints imposed by the islands were instrumental in the creation of this distinctive mode of settlement (which appears to us deceptively familiar), its practice and maintenance were surely structured by a form of temporality and definition of space distinct from that embodied in the more mobile occupation practices characteristic of many other regions. Like the Mesolithic middens referred to above, these settlements embodied and served to create long-term commitment to particular places. The permanence of the architecture may itself have contributed to a perception of long-term social stability, even if the symbolism and values ascribed to domestic space were constantly renegotiated (Richards 1990, 1993).

Scale

The basic social unit in the British Neolithic is usually argued to be the household, operating in varying degrees of independence within segmentary lineage systems (e.g. Bogucki 1988: 10–11; see Thomas 1996: 5 for critical comment). However, as the 'village'-scale settlements of the Orkneys aptly illustrate, individual occupations did not always equate with individual households. Tremendous variation in settlement scale is immediately evident throughout the period, even contemporaneously within single regions. The Fen edge of East Anglia[5] during the mid-fourth millennium BC provides a case in point. From surface and excavated evidence, it is possible to identify a range of different settlement forms, from small, single household occupations, such as that represented by the Fengate house (Pryor 1974: 6–14), to larger sites indicative of the aggregation of several households, for example at Hurst Fen (Clark 1960).[6] Further afield, occupation sites such as that of the late fourth–early third millennium BC at Bharpa Carinish, North Uist, with its series of three hearth complexes distributed in a linear arrangement over several metres (Crone 1993: 362–7), are suggestive of a segmented social group (fig. 5.3).

Aggregation is seen most clearly in the context of certain fourth-millennium BC enclosures where the quantity and range of excavated material indicates occupation by large numbers of people over at least part of the year (e.g. Robertson-Mackay 1987: 125; Sharples 1991: 254). Seasonal aggregation, allowing exchange and the formation and maintenance of social networks through marriage, feasting, deposition and other activities, remains a favoured interpretation (e.g. Thomas 1991: 35–6; Edmonds 1993: 125), although there is nothing in the evidence to suggest that *some* people were not living at *some* enclosures all year round. The

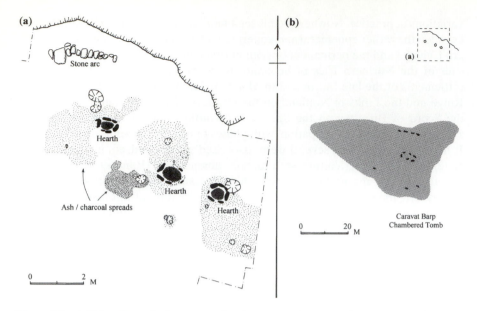

Figure 5.3   (a) Hearths and other occupation features under peat at Bharpa Carinish, North Uist; and (b) their relationship to the chambered tomb of Caravat Barp (after Crone 1993).

idea of seasonal gathering illustrates the potential fluidity of settlement practices during the period, with people coming together and dispersing at appropriate times. That few of the enclosures associated with occupation show evidence for uninterrupted use over more than a few generations is also a reminder of the contingent nature both of social values surrounding the desirability of aggregation and of the sacred tradition embodied within these monuments that served to provide social cohesion (Whittle & Pollard 1998).

Aggregation on a seasonal or longer-term basis is not a feature restricted to enclosures. Unenclosed Early Neolithic occupation sites of comparable overall scale are known from East Anglia and the Fen edge, such as Hurst Fen, Cambridgeshire (Clark 1960), Broome Heath, Norfolk (Wainwright 1972), and Tattershall Thorpe, Lincolnshire (Bradley et al. 1993). Investigation of these unenclosed sites provides a context for understanding aggregation as a social strategy. Excavation at Hurst Fen revealed a spread of lithic artefacts and associated subsoil features (principally, over 200 pits containing pottery, flint and worked stone) covering an area of approximately 50 m by 70 m on a low Breckland hillock (Clark 1960) (fig. 5.4). Typically, for sites of this type, traces of domestic buildings were not present and it is the pits that really provide the key to understanding the site. The distribution of pits was not uniform, but formed a series of distinct clusters, more easily definable around the periphery of the site where they occurred in groups of 10 to 15. Clark equated individual pit clusters with the presence of separate households (Clark 1960: 241): the implication is that several

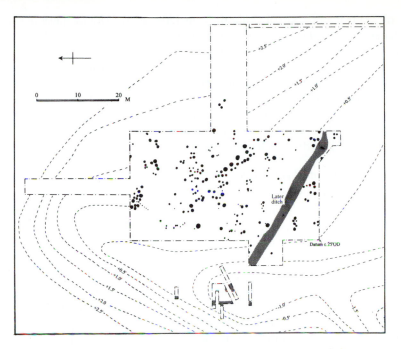

Figure 5.4   The early Neolithic pit group at Hurst Fen, Cambridgeshire (after Clark 1960).

groups were present on the site all or some of the time. The dense concentration of pits within the central area implies more protracted activity here than around the edges of the site, perhaps to be associated with a single 'long-lived' household. That the central area may have been regarded as somehow special or different is also indicated by deposits of complete pottery vessels in pits on its eastern and western sides.[7] Taking this evidence together, we could envisage a model wherein the central area marked the location of a senior group and the peripheral pit clusters indicate the arrival of other groups at a subsequent date. Here, it could be that settlement aggregation was cumulative, with a primary household associated with a successful or pre-eminent individual or family attracting others. This may illustrate the formation, and ultimate demise, of alliances between individual households. Perhaps here we are also seeing how the value of living in a community may have been constituted as desirable, or was even socially prescribed. Elsewhere, circumstances could have led to the creation of an ethos that valued household independence and the avoidance of imposed political control.

Scale of residence should be viewed as dynamic (Bogucki 1988: 181) and as a product of social strategy surrounding the maintenance and transformation of particular conditions of existence. Both dispersal and aggregation create their own opportunities and disadvantages. Dispersed settlement would offer individuals and households the possibility to dictate their own conditions to a greater degree than if they lived within larger communities (Whittle 1988: 87–8). However, the risks of 'going it alone' are obvious: these include coping with the periodic 'failure' of domestic and wild resources, vulnerability from raiding and other forms of conflict, as perhaps seen with the Fengate multiple burial (Pryor 1984: 19–22), and the like. Conversely, aggregation may have offered the advantages of shared risk, political affiliation and advancement, and wider marriage networks (Whittle 1988: 88). However, even large enclosures occupied by many people may not have been safe from attack, as is dramatically illustrated by the evidence for conflict and violent deaths at several Earlier Neolithic enclosures in southwestern England (Mercer 1980: 51, 1981: 69; Dixon 1988: 82).

Remembrance and reference

The act of settlement implies the creation of relationships to place(s) that in turn are reflected in the way that these relationships are marked and remembered. Houses, for example, frequently become intimately associated with the lives of their owners, and indeed can come to symbolize and structure present and future social relations (e.g. Carsten & Hugh-Jones 1995). Since the act of settlement serves to situate the identities of occupants, their biographies, values and relations with other people and places within particular locales in the landscape (Ingold 1993: 152–3), it is not surprising that the memory and commemoration of acts of settlement can take on an importance in their own right. As Pryor (1995: 97) has pointed out, it is essential that we should not confuse abandonment with the end of a relationship to place. The remembrance of previous events in relation to particular places may be seen to constitute another form of temporality concerned with a past state of being that is objectified through the physicality of the landscape and locales within it. Remembering plays an important role in social reproduction (Barth 1987: 24–7; Connerton 1989: 6–40), providing context and meaning for contemporary action.

To judge from the evidence of monuments commemorating the dead and a generalized ancestral past, Neolithic communities possessed an active concern with past belonging and origins, and the marking of these in the landscape (Tilley 1994: 117). This seems to have been a particular feature of the fourth millennium BC as is witnessed in the construction of earthen and chambered tombs in many regions. The tombs often contain the remains of many individuals (e.g. Kinnes 1992: 98); their disarticulated state has led some authors to suggest that mortuary rites transformed these bodies from individuals to generalized ancestors (e.g. Thomas 1991: 112). A concern with genealogy and the relationship of past kin to particular places is also manifest in special activities that referenced occupation events. This was essentially done in two ways: through acts of formal deposition on or after the abandonment of a settlement and by the construction of monuments over former occupation sites as permanent embodiments of place-values.

Within the first category are settlement-related pit deposits of the fourth millennium BC. The classic discussion of these features (Field et al. 1964: 367–75) argues that they are nothing more than disused storage pits casually backfilled with rubbish. However, Thomas (1991: 76) has proposed that the digging and filling of these features was a formal affair intended to symbolically situate meaning and reference within particular locales. Many deposits comprise selected collections of domestic refuse that must have accumulated on surface middens prior to redeposition in the pits. The quantity of artefactual and faunal material contained within individual pit deposits implies that they do not represent *ad hoc* events, but took the form of temporally and locationally specific acts that may have been associated with the 'closing' of settlements (Pollard 1993: Chap. 4.2). The *act* of settlement abandonment and movement, like any state of social transition, was probably perceived as threatening to the social order and in need of mediation through ritual practice. Pit deposits may have served to counter this by evoking a continuity between past and present, as well as presencing 'the evidence of domesticity in the landscape' (Thomas 1991: 76). They thereby embodied the identities and histories of communities in relation to particular locales.

The frequency with which earthen and chambered long barrows were built over pre-existing occupation sites during the fourth millennium BC (Hodder 1994: 77) suggests that the construction of monuments may have deliberately made reference to acts of earlier settlement. The places selected for the location of monuments were never arbitrary, but were situated in a landscape redolent with social value and reference that was structured by the routines of occupancy (Barrett 1988: 32). By locating ancestral tombs and other monuments on locales that had witnessed earlier activity, a link could be established between several states of being: that of the present, a generalized ancestral past, and the specific social biography of a particular place. What is of interest is that in some instances the architecture of a monument, albeit working within a received format, seems to have been designed to mimic the spatial organization of earlier settlement features. At Hazleton North, Gloucestershire, a stone longcairn was placed on the site of a short-lived single-household settlement. The centre of the cairn was situated over an earlier midden and the lateral chambers of the tomb followed an axis defined by the postholes of a pre-existing wooden structure (Saville 1990: 15). This degree of spatial reference between two arenas of practice – a process of homology that has been illustrated by Richards' work (1993) on the Orcadian Later Neolithic – is apparent in other contexts, for instance in the parallel alignments of hearths at the occupation site at Bharpa Carinish, North Uist, and the axis of an adjacent chambered tomb (fig. 5.3). The segmentary structure of the hearth arrangement at this site is also curiously reminiscent of the divided linear arrangement of space within wooden and megalithic mortuary chambers (Kinnes 1992: 81–6). Although similarities in format could be taken to indicate that tombs did 'mean houses' (Hodder 1994: 75), it may be more productive to think of the way in which the construction of space in different contexts served to reproduce social categorization, both within and beyond life.

In summary

The rather intractable nature of the data relating to settlement in the British Neolithic has had the unfortunate effect of relegating its study to a second place in narratives of the period. The high archaeological visibility of monuments and of the practices that produced and sustained them has contributed to an archaeology where it would seem that structures of symbolic order and relations of power were constructed in arenas of practice divorced from the everyday routines of living. It is all too easy to see settlement as a passive backdrop to other 'more meaningful' forms of practice, yet it is within the context of occupation that most of the 'social action' would have taken place. The domestic arena is, after all, where people would have spent most of their lives. Through domestic routine, the practical skills and social values that constitute the structure of culture were transmitted, creating the *habitus* of individuals (Bourdieu 1990: 52–65). It is through the rhythms of dwelling and movement that the landscape came to be acculturated and places invested with meaning.

At a more general level, a call is made for studies that accept the possibility of diversity in practice within defined time periods and across regions. Single models are rarely appropriate and their abstraction only serves to hinder understanding of the humanly centred experience of settlement. We should be aware that settlement constituted a form of social practice that required knowledge, skill and strategy, acted out in relation to contextual and historically created cultural values. This should be reflected in the way we write about prehistoric settlement.

Notes

1. The definition and characterization of 'settlement' and the concomitant concept of the 'domestic' are themselves problematic, as papers by Brück and Carman (Chapters 4 and 2, this volume) have illustrated. In part because of the particular and highly variable nature of occupation practices in the British Neolithic, only a broad working definition can be offered here. Settlement is both a noun and refers to an action (Carman, Chapter 2, this volume). As action, it relates to the occupation of a particular locale by a group of people for more than an immediate period of time, providing the context within which the daily routines of life were enacted. As noun, it refers to the locations within which such practices and processes took place.

2. A conventional date range for the British Neolithic would span *c.* 4000–2400 cal BC. It has been variously defined on the basis of economy (the period that witnessed the introduction of horticulture and the husbandry of domestic livestock), new material technologies (the widespread use of ceramics and ground stone tools), and novel ideologies (seen in the construction of elaborate funerary and ceremonial monuments). Rather than representing a uniform cultural tradition imposed by incoming groups, the Northwest European Neolithic might best be understood as the outcome of indigenous (hunter–gatherer) adoptions of a flexible set of novel material and symbolic resources (Thomas 1993b).

3. Recollection of the passage of time, and the relation of events to particular people and locales, necessarily produces a narrative. Such narratives constitute biographies that have a formative role in the construction of human and place-centred identities. (See Kovacik, Chapter 10, this volume for consideration of the role of memory in such processes.)

4. The distinction between transhumance and other forms of mobility should be made clear. Transhumance involves the seasonal movement of livestock from one climatic zone to another, often between lowland and upland, and as such possesses specific ecological correlates (Salzman 1996: 553). The practice may involve only one element of a social group being

engaged in livestock movement, and does not entail a total dependence upon domestic animals for subsistence; as such, it can operate alongside semi- and full sedentism.

5. The Fens comprise a large expanse of former wetlands bordering the Midlands and East Anglia, reclaimed through drainage between the seventeenth and nineteenth centuries AD.

6. An alternative interpretation of these sites views their formation as resulting not from aggregation, but from the repeated, intermittent use of the same location for settlement (e.g. Healy 1988: 108–9). The argument presented here for aggregation rests on the homogeneity of the associated artefact assemblages (indicating activity over a relatively short duration of time) and the spatial respect often displayed in the distribution of features (re-cutting pits are rare).

7. The digging and filling of pits during the Neolithic is generally recognised to have constituted a special form of activity. The contents of these features often comprise deliberately selected collections of artefactual and faunal material (Thomas 1991: 59–63).

References

Armit, I. 1992. The Hebridean Neolithic. In *Vessels for the ancestors: essays on the Neolithic of Britain and Ireland*, N. Sharples & A. Sheridan (eds), 307–21. Edinburgh: Edinburgh University Press.

Barrett, J. C. 1988. The living, the dead and the ancestors: Neolithic and Early Bronze Age mortuary practices. See Barrett & Kinnes (1988), 30–41.

Barrett, J. C. 1994. *Fragments from antiquity: an archaeology of social life in Britain, 2900–1200 BC*. Oxford: Blackwell.

Barrett, J. C. & I. A. Kinnes (eds) 1988. *The archaeology of context in the Neolithic and Bronze Age: recent trends*. Sheffield: Department of Archaeology and Prehistory, University of Sheffield.

Barrett, J. C., R. Bradley, M. Green 1991. *Landscape, monuments and society: the prehistory of Cranborne Chase*. Cambridge: Cambridge University Press.

Barth, F. 1987. *Cosmologies in the making*. Cambridge: Cambridge University Press.

Bogucki, P. I. 1988. *Forest farmers and stockherders: early agriculture and its consequences in north-central Europe*. Cambridge: Cambridge University Press.

Bond, J. M., A. R. Braby, S. J. Dockrill, J. Downes, C. C. Richards 1995. Stove Bay: a new Orcadian Grooved Ware settlement. *Scottish Archaeological Review* **9–10**, 125–30.

Bourdieu, P. 1990. *The logic of practice*. Oxford: Polity Press.

Bradley, R. J. 1987. Flint technology and the character of Neolithic settlement. In *Lithic analysis and later British prehistory*, A. G. Brown & M. R. Edmonds (eds), 181–5. Oxford: British Archaeological Reports, British Series 162.

Bradley, R. J. 1991. Ritual, time and history. *World Archaeology* **23**, 209–19.

Bradley, R., P. Chowne, R. M. J. Cleal, F. Healy, I. Kinnes 1993. *Excavations on Redgate Hill, Hunstanton, Norfolk and at Tattershall Thorpe, Lincolnshire*. Gressenhall: East Anglian Archaeology Report 57.

Britnell, W. 1982. The excavation of two round barrows at Trelystan, Powys. *Proceedings of the Prehistoric Society* **48**, 133–201.

Carsten, J. & S. Hugh-Jones 1995. Introduction. In *About the house: Lévi-Strauss and beyond*, J. Carsten & S. Hugh-Jones (eds), 1–46. Cambridge: Cambridge University Press.

Clark, J. G. D. 1960. Excavations at the Neolithic Site at Hurst Fen, Mildenhall, Suffolk (1954, 1957 and 1958). *Proceedings of the Prehistoric Society* **26**, 202–45.

Clarke, D. V. & N. M. Sharples 1985. Settlements and subsistence in the third millennium BC. In *The prehistory of Orkney*, C. Renfrew (ed.), 54–82. Edinburgh: Edinburgh University Press.

Connerton, P. 1989. *How societies remember*. Cambridge: Cambridge University Press.

Crone, A. 1993. Excavation and survey of sub-peat features of Neolithic, Bronze and Iron Age date at Bharpa Carinish, North Uist, Scotland. *Proceedings of the Prehistoric Society* **59**, 361–82.

Dietler, M. & I. Herbich 1993. Living on Luo time: reckoning sequence, duration, history and biography in a rural African society. *World Archaeology* **25**, 248–60.

Dixon, P. 1988. The Neolithic settlement on Crickley Hill. In *Enclosures and defences in the Neolithic of western Europe*, C. Burgess, P. Topping, C. Mordant, M. Maddison (eds), 75–87. Oxford: British Archaeological Reports, International Series S403.

Edmonds, M. 1987. Rocks and risk: problems with lithic procurement strategies. In *Lithic analysis and later British prehistory*, A. G. Brown & M. R. Edmonds (eds), 155–81. Oxford: British Archaeological Reports, British Series 162.

Edmonds, M. 1993. Interpreting causewayed enclosures in the past and the present. See Tilley (1993), 99–142.

Edmonds, M. 1995. *Stone tools and society: working stone in Neolithic and Bronze Age Britain*. London: Batsford.

Entwistle, R. & A. Grant 1989. The evidence for cereal cultivation and animal husbandry in the southern British Neolithic and Bronze Age. In *The beginnings of agriculture*, A. Milles, D. Williams, N. Gardner (eds), 203–15. Oxford: British Archaeological Reports, International Series S496.

Evans, C. 1988. Monuments and analogy: the interpretation of causewayed enclosures. In *Enclosures and defences in the Neolithic of western Europe*, C. Burgess, P. Topping, C. Mordant, M. Maddison (eds), 47–73. Oxford: British Archaeological Reports, International Series S403.

Field, N., C. L. Matthews, I. F. Smith 1964. New Neolithic sites in Dorset and Bedfordshire, with a note on the distribution of Neolithic storage pits in Britain. *Proceedings of the Prehistoric Society* **30**, 352–81.

Garton, D. 1987. Buxton. *Current Archaeology* **103**, 250–53.

Gibson, A. 1994. Excavations at the Sarn-y-bryn-caled cursus complex, Welshpool, Powys, and the timber circles of Great Britain and Ireland. *Proceedings of the Prehistoric Society* **60**, 143–223.

Gibson, A. 1996. The later Neolithic structures at Trelystan, Powys, Wales: ten years on. In *Neolithic houses in northwest Europe and beyond*, T. Darvill & J. Thomas (eds), 133–41. Oxford: Oxbow.

Gosden, C. 1994. *Social being and time*. Oxford: Blackwell.

Graham, M. 1993. Settlement organization and residential variability among the Rarámuri. In *Abandonment of settlements and regions: ethnoarchaeological and archaeological approaches*, C. M. Cameron & S. A. Tomka (eds), 25–42. Cambridge: Cambridge University Press.

Healy, F. 1988. *The Anglo-Saxon cemetery at Spong Hill, North Elmham, part IV: occupation during the seventh to second millennia BC*. Gressenhall: East Anglian Archaeology Report 39.

Higgs, E. S. 1959. The excavation of a late Mesolithic site at Downton, near Salisbury, Wilts. *Proceedings of the Prehistoric Society* **25**, 209–32.

Hodder, I. 1994. Architecture and meaning: the example of Neolithic houses and tombs. In *Architecture and order: approaches to social space*, M. Parker Pearson & C. Richards (eds), 73–86. London: Routledge.

Holgate, R. 1988. A review of Neolithic domestic activity in southern Britain. See Barrett & Kinnes (1988), 104–12.

Ingold, T. 1986. *The appropriation of nature*. Manchester: Manchester University Press.

Ingold, T. 1993. The temporality of the landscape. *World Archaeology* **25**, 152–74.

Kinnes, I. 1992. *Non-megalithic long barrows and allied structures in the British Neolithic*. London: British Museum Publications.

Mellars, P. 1987. *Excavations on Oronsay*. Edinburgh: Edinburgh University Press.

Mercer, R. J. 1980. *Hambledon Hill: a Neolithic landscape*. Edinburgh: Edinburgh University Press.

Mercer, R. J. 1981. Excavations at Carn Brea, Illogan, Cornwall, 1970–73. *Cornish Archaeology* **20**.

Needham, S. P. & M. R. Trott 1987. Structure and sequence in the Neolithic deposits at Runnymede. *Proceedings of the Prehistoric Society* **53**, 479–82.

Piggott, S. 1954. *The Neolithic cultures of the British Isles*. Cambridge: Cambridge University Press.

Pollard, J. 1993. *Traditions of deposition in the Neolithic of Wessex*. PhD thesis, School of History and Archaeology, University of Wales at Cardiff.

Pryor, F. 1974. *Excavation at Fengate, Peterborough, England: the first report*. Toronto: Royal Ontario Museum.

Pryor, F. 1984. *Excavation at Fengate, Peterborough, England: the fourth report*. Toronto and Northampton: Royal Ontario Museum and Northamptonshire Archaeological Society.

Pryor, F. 1988. Earlier Neolithic organised landscapes and ceremonial in lowland Britain. See Barrett & Kinnes (1988), 63–72.

Pryor, F. 1995. Abandonment and the role of ritual sites in the landscape. *Scottish Archaeological Review* **9–10**, 96–109.

Richards, C. 1990. The Late Neolithic house in Orkney. In *The social archaeology of houses*, R. Samson (ed.), 112–24. Edinburgh: Edinburgh University Press.

Richards, C. 1993. Monumental choreography: architecture and spatial representation in Late Neolithic Orkney. See Tilley (1993), 143–78.

Robertson-Mackay, M. E. 1980. A 'head and hoofs' burial beneath a round barrow, with other Neolithic and Bronze Age sites, on Hemp Knoll, near Avebury, Wiltshire. *Proceedings of the Prehistoric Society* **46**, 123–76.

Robertson-Mackay, R. 1987. The neolithic enclosure at Staines, Surrey: excavations 1961–63. *Proceedings of the Prehistoric Society* **53**, 23–128.

Salzman, P. C. 1996. Transhumance. In *Encyclopedia of Social and Cultural Anthropology*, A. Barnard & J. Spencer (eds), 553. London: Routledge.

Saville, A. 1990. *Hazleton North: the excavation of a Neolithic long cairn of the Cotswold-Severn group*. London: English Heritage.

Schofield, A. J. 1991. Lithic distributions in the Upper Meon Valley: behavioural response and human adaptation on the Hampshire chalklands. *Proceedings of the Prehistoric Society* **57**, 159–78.

Shanks, M. & C. Tilley 1987. *Social theory and archaeology*. Cambridge: Polity Press.

Sharples, N. M. 1991. *Maiden Castle: excavations and field survey 1985–6*. London: English Heritage.

Sharples, N. M. 1992. Aspects of regionalisation in the Scottish Neolithic. In *Vessels for the ancestors: essays on the Neolithic of Britain and Ireland*, N. Sharples & A. Sheridan (eds), 322–32. Edinburgh: Edinburgh University Press.

Smith, I. F. 1965. *Windmill Hill and Avebury: excavations by Alexander Keiller 1925–1939*. Oxford: Clarendon Press.

Soudský, B. 1962. The Neolithic site of Bylany. *Antiquity* **36**, 190–200.

Thomas, J. 1991. *Rethinking the Neolithic*. Cambridge: Cambridge University Press.

Thomas, J. 1993a. The hermeneutics of megalithic space. See Tilley (1993), 73–97.

Thomas, J. 1993b. Discourse, totalization and 'the Neolithic'. See Tilley (1993), 357–94.

Thomas, J. 1996. Neolithic houses in mainland Britain and Ireland – a sceptical view. In *Neolithic houses in northwest Europe and beyond*, T. Darvill & J. Thomas (eds), 1–12. Oxford: Oxbow.

Tilley, C. (ed.) 1993. *Interpretative archaeology*. Oxford: Berg.

Tilley, C. 1994. *A phenomenology of landscape: places, paths and monuments*. Oxford: Berg.

Wainwright, G. J. 1972. The excavation of a Neolithic settlement on Broome Heath, Ditchingham, Norfolk, England. *Proceedings of the Prehistoric Society* **38**, 1–97.

Whittle, A. 1988. *Problems in Neolithic archaeology*. Cambridge: Cambridge University Press.

Whittle, A, M. Keith-Lucas, A. Milles, S. Rees, J. C. C. Romans 1986. *Scord of Brouster: an early agricultural settlement on Shetland*. Oxford: Oxford University Committee for Archaeology.

Whittle, A. & J. Pollard 1998. Windmill Hill causewayed enclosure: the harmony of symbols. In *Understanding the Neolithic of north-western Europe*, M. Edmonds & C. Richards (eds), 231–47. Glasgow: Cruithne Press.

Wymer, J. J. & D. M. Churchill 1962. Excavations at the Maglemosian sites at Thatcham, Berkshire, England. *Proceedings of the Prehistoric Society* **28**, 329–70.

CHAPTER SIX

What is a tell? Settlement in fifth millennium Bulgaria

Douglass W. Bailey

Introduction

Prehistoric tells dominate the archaeology of Neolithic, Eneolithic and Early Bronze Age southeastern Europe.[1] They are the centres of major fieldwork projects (e.g. Yunatsite), they provide the chronocultural yardsticks of Balkan prehistory (e.g. Karanovo, Ezero) and they serve, almost exclusively, as the material for reconstructing contemporary community activity and behaviour (e.g. Ovcharovo, Golyamo Delchevo).

Traditional interpretations read tells as permanent settlements, stable in function and dimension (e.g. Todorova 1978, 1982, 1986); places where people lived and carried out the various tasks of their daily existence. As such, they are seen as the passive locations for dwelling. They provided shelter from the elements and a geographic context for village living. This reconstruction is naïve and inaccurate. It results from the implicit acceptance of five ill-founded assumptions.

First, traditional research assumes that the activities carried out on tells covered a wide range of the daily needs of the sites' occupants (e.g. eating, sleeping, hunting, farming). This is misguided. I contend that the activities carried out on southeast European tells were narrowly restricted to the processes of cereal agriculture.

Second, traditional tell interpretations rest on the assumption that tells were continuously occupied. This view is mistaken. I argue in this chapter, as I have argued elsewhere (Bailey 1990, 1993, 1997), that the character and demands of tell use in agricultural production favour long-running cycles of occupation, abandonment and reoccupation. I review recent sedimentological research around the Podgoritsa Tell in northeastern Bulgaria that supplements and refines the long-held link between tell location and floodplain agriculture (e.g. Sherratt 1980). The Podgoritsa evidence illuminates the importance of changes in water table level for modeling vacillations in tell use over the long-term (Bailey et al. 1998).

Third, traditional interpretations assume that the demography of tell communities was static in size and composition. This assumption is unsupportable. I suggest that the nature of the activities that dominated tell use (i.e. large-scale cereal cultivation in a temperate environment) required a pool of workers that, although well controlled and organized, was flexible in size and various in skill and knowledge. These labour pools expanded and contracted, dispersed and reformed as was required by the labour demands of the sequential stages of cultivating and processing cereal plants.

Fourth, traditional research assumes that the buildings making up the tell, and indeed the tell itself, formed a passive backdrop against which social life occurred. This is naïve and ignores the substantial research on the social archaeology of buildings (e.g. Samson 1990; Parker Pearson & Richards 1994) and the wider tradition that recognizes the complexity of the relationship between people and the built environment (e.g. Rapoport 1982, 1990). I suggest below that tells were active expressive components within the productive and sociopolitical strategies of fifth-millennium BC southeastern Europe.

Fifth, most traditional tell research assumes that the spatial (and thus the social and functional) limits of a tell coincided with the visible, topographic circumference of the mound of the tell.[2] This is incorrect. Recent geophysical investigations of off-tell areas around the Podgoritsa and Tutrakan tells in northeastern Bulgaria as well as test-trenches and soil cores from the former site have documented off-tell activity areas and fired clay structures contemporary with the Eneolithic use of the tells (Bailey et al. 1998).

Thus, to answer the question 'what is a tell?' is to counter traditional assumptions. The answer I propose is a redefinition of southeast European tells in terms of the activities that took place at them, their temporal and spatial dimensions, the flexibility of their demography, and the active role played by the built environment in contemporary social and political agendas.

Redefinition

In contesting the traditional perception of tells, I propose a redefinition of the Chalcolithic tells of northeastern Bulgaria (e.g. Ovcharovo, Golyamo Delchevo, Turgovishte, Radingrad) (fig. 6.1). I demonstrate here that these tells represent specialized components in larger transregional networks of agricultural production and exchange. These networks linked the communities of the Black Sea Coast to the tells of the inland regions of northeastern Bulgaria. The successful operation of these networks rested on a sociopolitical system in which people and other resources were authoritatively managed. Management was by confederation of individuals, distinguished from the majority of their consociates and bound together, not only by their ability to acquire and consume exotic materials such as the marine mollusc *Spondylus gaederopus*, copper and gold, but consequently by their success in controlling and organizing human and natural resources and agricultural produce.

Tells are best defined and understood within these elite-managed systems of agricultural production. They are small but critical tools in the management of

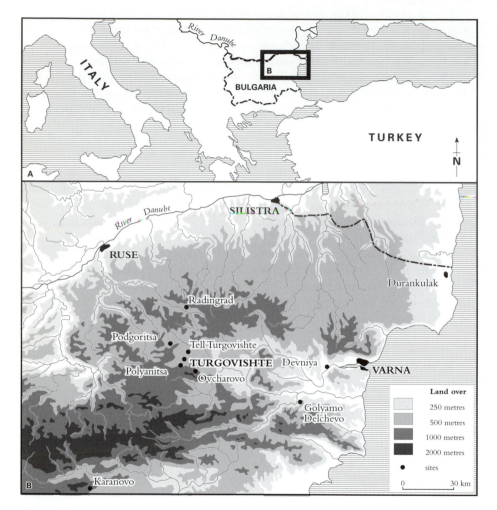

Figure 6.1   Map of northeastern Bulgaria showing key excavated Copper Age tells.

labour and resources. As such, tells were employed to alter and control the spatial and temporal boundaries of activity and existence. With respect to time, they were visible statements alluding to a permanence of place that did not in reality exist. Spatially, they acted as tangible claims to local resources and they were the physical containers of agricultural produce. Furthermore, they delineated physically produce from producer. With respect to demography, they were foci for the sequential congregations of people required for successful high-yield cereal agriculture. In sum, tells were expressive, monumental agents in the creation and manipulation of the sociopolitical and productive reality of fifth-millennium BC life.

The landscapes of northeastern Bulgaria during the fifth millennium BC provide an excellent laboratory to investigate the dimensions of prehistoric tells. In the first place, this region is well populated with tells from this period. Todorova's (1986: 277–8) seminal synthesis of Copper Age Bulgaria records 39 tells in the region of Turgovishte, a modern administrative region of 2500 km.[2] Some of these sites have also been excavated and published and thus their inventories are accessible for post-excavation analysis and interpretation (Todorova et al. 1975, 1983; Raduncheva 1976; Angelova 1982, 1986; Ivanov 1982; Todorova 1982). Furthermore, excavation of these sites was complete: the entire surfaces of the tells were excavated and thus we are presented with much wider bodies of data than those available from programmes of sondage work carried out at tells in other regions. The tells of the fifth millennium BC occupy a curious slot in the longer-term trends in the settlement activity of northeastern Bulgaria. The preceding Neolithic period (6300–4900 BC) and the succeeding transitional period and Early Bronze Age (3850–2000 BC) are without any substantial remains of built settlement: both periods are marked by small-scale, relatively impermanent habitations (Todorova 1995; Bailey 1996c). For all of these reasons, the Copper Age tells of northeast Bulgaria provide a well-documented context in which to begin the redefinition of prehistoric tells.

In the main, the arguments advanced in this chapter are based on two northeast Bulgarian tells: Ovcharovo and Podgoritsa (fig. 6.1). Both are in the Turgovishte region. Ovcharovo was excavated in the early 1970s under the direction of Professor-Dr Henrietta Todorova of the Archaeological Institute of the Bulgarian Academy of Sciences. The site was published soon afterwards (Todorova et al. 1983) and I made a detailed study of the site's inventories in 1988 (Bailey 1991). In making the latter study, I became concerned with the limitations to the traditional definition of tell settlements in the region. Were they really self-contained units? Were they continuously occupied throughout their long existence? Did they contain evidence of the full range of activities that we might expect in a prehistoric village? The more I investigated the published and archive records of Ovcharovo and the more I reconstructed the patterns of the tell's existence, both in terms of architectural building trends (Bailey 1990) and the prehistoric activities carried out on the tell (Bailey 1996a), the more I was convinced that previous research strategies that isolated the tell outside of its landscape context were in error (Bailey 1997).

These emerging concerns that traditional perceptions of tells were fatally limited led to the Podgoritsa Archaeology Project co-directed by myself, Professor Ruth Tringham (University of California at Berkeley), Ilka Angelova (Turgovishte Regional Museum) and Ana Raduncheva (Archaeological Institute of the Bulgarian Academy of Sciences).[3] The primary goals of the project were to redefine the dimensions of prehistoric tells of northeastern Bulgaria. As noted below and as detailed in the excavation report, the work at Podgoritsa succeeded in documenting the dynamic, vacillating dimensions of tells in this region (Bailey et al. 1998). Taken together, work on the Ovcharovo archives and the fieldwork at Podgoritsa suggest a redefinition of tells along five critical dimensions: the range of activities carried out on these sites, the continuity of their occupation, the stability of tell-based demographies, the geographic limits of tell space and the internal division of space within a tell.

Tell-based activities

Although most discussions on tells have focused on their place in regional and chronological sequences or in pan-European conceptual traditions (Hodder 1990), little effort has been directed towards understanding what went on at these sites.[4] It has been assumed that a tell was a permanent, year-round settlement and that as such it can be read as the place of a wide range of domestic and productive activities. Indeed, the density of material from tells is impressive. However, without a detailed study of the material inventories of buildings within a tell, it is easy to overlook the limited range of artefacts present. The large concentration of tools and facilities for agricultural crop-processing and the absence of evidence for other major activities (e.g. potting, simple metal-working) suggest that tells were contexts not for a wide range of activities but were primarily centres for agricultural activities (Bailey 1996a).

The case of the Ovcharovo tell serves as an example. Ovcharovo was occupied over the second half of the fifth millennium BC, that is the Early, Middle and Late Eneolithic, corresponding to Polyanitsa III, IV and Kodzhaderman–Gumelnitsa–Karanovo VI respectively in terms of the local regional cultural traditions.

With respect to activities performed on site, two important trends emerged from my analysis. First, it appears that two particular activities were dominant at Ovcharovo: animal management and cereal production. Activities in the earlier horizons (I–VII) appear to have been focused on exploiting primary and secondary products of animals (especially sheep/goat and cattle) and on growing and processing cereals (wheat and barley). The high numbers of loomweights and spindle whorls and the erection of animal pens in the early sequence illuminate the management of animals for secondary products (especially for textile production). Activity in the later horizons of the site (VIII–X) appears to have been directed much more intensively towards the exploitation of cereal grain. Grinding stones and grain silos appear in horizons VIII–X. At the same time, the frequency of loomweights decreases (from an average of 24.57 to 4.17 per horizon)[5] and the site comes to be dominated by objects and facilities primarily employed in agricultural production. Most obvious among these were the grinding stones (from horizons VIII–X), antler digging sticks and large concentrations (up to 4 kg) of carbonized einkorn, emmer wheat and barley (*Triticum monococcum, Triticum dicoccum, Triticum durum, Hordeum vulgare*).

Further evidence of the increased scale of agricultural production during the site's later phases are the increasingly large ceramic vessels made during this time (up to 29 l). The appearance of large pots and grain silos suggests that storage of large quantities of grain was increasing in importance. The concentrations of carbonized cereal grain in the silos confirm the scale of the site's use in the agricultural process. The proposed contents of the large vessels is difficult to confirm, although their shapes suggest that they were made to hold dry goods.[6] The large pots were concentrated in selected buildings in the later horizons, buildings that may have served as storage or distribution places.

Another feature of the later horizons at Ovcharovo that may complement the shift in site use and the increase in agricultural yield is the partial or complete destructions of buildings by fire (horizons VII and VIII–X, XII respectively). Tringham has suggested that house fires may have been either an unwanted consequence of a drive to increase the processing, mainly parching, of cereal grain (Tringham & Krstic 1990) or a planned destruction that may have served as resolution of engendered political tension (Tringham 1991a, b, 1994). I read house fires as the consequence of intensified agricultural activity and thus their occurrence in the later horizons of Ovcharovo complements the contemporary appearance of silos, grinding stones and large storage pots.

A second important trend to emerge from the Ovcharovo analysis is the absence of non-agricultural activities. There are no recognizable centres for ceramic production at the site, nor is there any evidence of copper-working. The large number of pots and the presence of copper objects in some graves make the absence of traces of these activities all the more remarkable.

As far as can be inferred from excavated examples, the tells from the region follow the Ovcharovo pattern of relatively narrow purpose: animal and cereal exploitation (Bailey 1996a). Furthermore, the range of activities taking place at Ovcharovo during the second half of its life was restricted, in the main, to intense processing and storage of cereals. From the Ovcharovo study, tells emerge as centres for intensified production and not, as has often been assumed, simply as centres for a wide range of domestic activities.

Occupational impermanence

It has long been assumed that tell settlements represent a long-term continuity of permanent occupation. The tells of Eneolithic northeast Bulgaria do indeed produce substantial ranges of radiocarbon dates (Kohl and Quitta 1966; Quitta and Kohl 1969; Quitta 1978; Boyadzhiev 1995). However, little attention has been directed to refining the internal chronology of sites such as Ovcharovo.[7] All of the

mud, clay and timber buildings in each layer are assumed to have been contemporaneous. The entire plan of each horizon is assumed to have been a coherent
whole, built, used and destroyed over an uninterrupted span of time. Further, it
has been assumed that horizons were built one on top of another with very few
breaks in a site's occupation. In the traditional scheme, a temporal hiatus of
occupation is recognized only in a physical break in stratigraphy. Thus, at
Ovcharovo the only break in occupation accompanies the stratigraphic hiatus
between horizons X and XI.

The stratigraphy of tells is notoriously complex and the coarse methodology
that continues to be applied to excavation (as at Ovcharovo) is of a scale too gross
to produce precise data on intra- (or even inter-) horizon temporal relationships.[8]
With little data available on the micro-stratigraphy of horizon interfaces, we are
forced to employ indirect evidence in order to study the temporal character of tell
occupation. Primary among this material is the hydrology of tells' micro-regions
and the evidence for changes in local water table levels.

It is widely agreed that a major factor in the location and use of Balkan tells was
the agricultural advantage of seasonally replenished soil fertility in small river
flood plains (Sherratt 1980). Van Andel's work on north Greek tells in the
Thessalian river plains demonstrates the differences between modern and prehistoric hydrology and geomorphology and suggests that tells in that area were in use
during times when river plains were actively being flooded (Van Andel et al. 1995).
Recent work at the Podgoritsa tell in northeast Bulgaria has refined our understanding of the relationship between river-plain flooding and tell occupation and
suggests that variations in the level of the water table affected the amount of
circum-tell land available for use (Bailey et al. 1998).

At Podgoritsa, a series of soil cores and test-trenches demonstrated that the
water table around the site had not remained constant throughout the life of the
tell (Bailey et al. 1998). Before the first prehistoric use of the tell, the site's micro-
region was dominated initially by dry conditions in the early Holocene. In some
areas around the tell (i.e. away from the edge of the tell on the west), the Holocene
deposits were covered by a marsh of standing water. Eneolithic deposits appear
in these areas only after a subsequent build-up of organic silty clays (indicating
drier conditions) had taken place. In other areas (i.e. those closer to the tell and
to the north), there is no pre-Eneolithic evidence of inundation. In these areas,
Eneolithic deposits are present on the siltier soils that reflect the loessic parent
material.

Significantly, the level of the water table did not remain constant throughout
the tell's existence. It rose and fell in a series of vacillations. During episodes of low
water table, the land around the tell was dry and usable for agriculture, grazing or
other purposes. Soil cores taken from these zones identified activity areas and built
structures in use during the dry episodes. During wetter phases, activity areas and
structures are not recognized around the site.

To the northwest of the tell and in some other places, the dry deposits containing Eneolithic material are overlain by a layer of dense silty clay representing a
second episode of marshy conditions. The wet deposit, in turn, is followed by a
second concentration of cultural material found on well-drained, dry deposits. This

last dry deposit was overlain by a final episode of wetter conditions that has continued until recent times.

Although the preliminary nature of the data from Podgoritsa does not allow suggestions as to the length of each of the wet and dry episodes, the sequence from the original wet to dry conditions followed by a shift to the second wet and then to the second dry and then to the third and final wet episode is secure. The present evidence suggests that the vacillations in water table would have affected the agricultural utility of the land around the tell. If the main focus of tell activity was large-scale cereal agriculture, then the long episodes of inundation would have made large parts of the circum-tell land unusable for planting. Periods of inundation may mark periods of the tell's life in which it was less heavily used and only partially occupied, if not abandoned completely.

Elsewhere, I have detailed the building sequence at Ovcharovo (Bailey 1990, 1991). The off-tell hydrology at Podgoritsa helps our understanding of other data on tell occupation in this region. The succession of building horizons (e.g. 13 in all at Ovcharovo (Todorova et al. 1983)) that make up the main elements of tell stratigraphies may represent episodes of building and rebuilding of structures at times of major tell reoccupation that took place after periods of inundation and abandonment. The patterns of house rebuilding (Bailey 1990) that were part of contemporary strategies to legitimate the continuity of occupation thus found a stimulus in the inundation-driven abandonments of tells. The long-running patterns of building repair, replastering and repainting may reflect patterns of abandonment and reoccupation over shorter periods, perhaps of annual or even seasonal duration. This may be the case for a floor in an Early Eneolithic house at Ovcharovo that had been replastered 47 times (Todorova et al. 1983: 30).

In the light of the episodes of tell use and abandonment that are suggested by the hydrology, stratigraphy and plastering sequences, the occupation of tells appears less permanent than previously assumed. Indeed, there is less evidence to support arguments for the continuous occupation of the tell than there is to support a reconstruction marked by episodes of abandonment and reoccupation. In the light of this reconstruction it is perhaps more accurate to think in terms of people moving to and from the tells in temporary, seasonal and longer-term, multi-year sequences.

Demographic flexibility

If people were moving to and from tells at different times of the year (as well as over longer periods) and if the late Eneolithic tells were primarily used for high-yield cereal agriculture, then the assumption that the demographies of tell communities were stable in size and organization needs rethinking. The sequence of events inherent in high-yield cereal production, processing and consumption and their particular requirements of skill, labour size and labour organization suggests that the demographies of tell communities were not stable but flexible in size, ability and duration. Furthermore, a reconstruction of the agricultural cycle for the tells of northeast Bulgaria suggests a concrete model for variation in tell occupation throughout the cycle.

The process of tell-based cereal cultivation in fifth-millennium BC northeastern Bulgaria consisted of five main categories of sequential events: soil preparation, planting, tending, harvesting, processing and storage or consumption. Furthermore, different events required different numbers of labourers (with varying skills) who would have been required to carry out particular tasks at a range of speeds for different durations of time. For example, soil preparation, planting and harvesting would have required relatively high numbers of moderate- and low-skilled labour to work quickly for a short period of time. Other events in the agriculture cycle would have required different labour groups of different sizes and skills to work over longer periods of time at a more relaxed pace (e.g. tending the crop as it grows or post-harvest processing).

Barker (1985) has suggested that the cereal-based communities of temperate Europe sowed their wheat in the spring after the mid-fifth millennium BC. He proposes that spring planting eliminated the problem of winter cold inherent in autumn planting and thus should be seen as an adaptation to the temperate climate that took advantage of the heavy spring rainfall (Barker 1985).[9] The floral evidence from northeast Bulgarian sites supports this as both einkorn and emmer can be sown in the summer and the latter prefers spring planting in temperate climates (Gregg 1988). Barley can also be planted in the spring. Furthermore, wild buckwheat (*Polygonum convolvulus L.*), an annual spring weed that favours damp soils along stream banks, appears in four of the Eneolithic horizons at the Golyamo Delchevo tell (Hopf 1975).

By reconstructing the agricultural cycle for spring-sown cereals, a clearer image emerges of the seasonal use of the north Bulgarian tells (table 6.1). From March through August the tell would have served as the aggregation point for changing densities of people and as the focus for activities carried out over diverse periods of time and that required work of various speeds. Thus, during late July and August large numbers of people would have been at the tell working quickly to carry out the harvest and initial processing – a series of activities that may only have lasted for several weeks. From late September through late February the tell may very well have been the focus for very few people and limited activities (perhaps nothing more than sporadic processing of grain and tending grain stores).[10]

In reconstructing the character of tell communities with respect to their agricultural activities, it is therefore perhaps better to think in terms of demographic flexibility rather than demographic stasis. It was through the control of such flexibility that success in agriculture could be achieved.

Beyond the tell

The models of demographic flexibility and settlement impermanence proposed above suggest that both occupants and occupational history of the tell varied over the multi-century duration of the tells' lives. It remains for us to examine the

Table 6.1 Suggested labour, skill and time requirements in cereal-based agricultural cycle in early agricultural tell communities in the Balkans during the fifth millennium BC for spring-sown crops (after Dennell 1974, Barker 1985, Gregg 1988, de Garine 1994, Ellen 1994).

	Autumn			Winter			Spring			Summer		
	Oct	Nov	Dec	Jan	Feb	Mar	Apr	May	Jun	Jul	Aug	Sept
Events												
Soil prep.				*******								
Tilling					**							
Planting						****						
Growing						***						
Weeding							*************					
Harvesting											********	
Processing										****************		
Labour required												
Numbers			----NONE----		----HIGH----		-LOW- -MODERATE--		-----LOW-----		-HIGH- -MODERATE	
Skill						-MODERATE-		-----LOW-----			----HIGH----	
Duration of activity						--SHORT-		----LONG----			-----SHORT-----	
Speed						--FAST--		-----SLOW-----			--FAST-- ---SLOW---	
Tell occupation			----EMPTY----		---FULL---		----PARTIALLY OCCUPIED----				--FULL-- -PARTOCC-	

spatial dimensions of tells. The traditional assumption holds that tells were spatially coherent and static entities, that is to say both that the geographic limits of a tell (and thus the limits of its community) did not extend beyond the mound of the tell's protuberance above the ground[11] and that this limit did not change through time. The research at Podgoritsa, noted above, concerning variation in availability of usable land around the site, suggests not only that activities took place beyond the topographic limits of the tell, but also that changes in water table level affected the area available.

One of the most important results of the geophysical work around the Podgoritsa tell was the location and identification of activity areas and built structures outside of the topographic limits of the tell's mound (Bailey et al. 1998). At Podgoritsa, magnetometry identified ten off-tell structures (fig. 6.2). Structure size ranged from 36–168 m^2, orientation was either north–south by east–west or northwest–southeast by northeast–southwest, and shape varied between rectilinear and amorphous-double (or double) structures. The magnetometry survey was supplemented by a coring and test-trenching programme. Test-trenches confirmed the shape, orientation and contemporaneity of several of the structures with the tell. The cores (originally intended to recover soils for analysis) revealed that traces of off-tell activity and building were widespread around the tell (fig. 6.3): of the 70 cores, 80 per cent contained cultural material. Although the four small test-trenches did not provide any material to suggest the type of activity taking place off-tell at Podgoritsa, the number of structures identified and the spatial range of material provide clear proof that the limit of activity was not restricted to the visible topography of the tell.

The work at Podgoritsa confirmed the presence of activities and structures immediately surrounding the tell and other, less proximate, areas can be added to the emerging, increasingly deep picture of tell landscapes in northeastern Bulgaria. I have suggested elsewhere (Bailey 1997) that it is useful to consider early agricultural tells as only one of many geographic and social zones in a shifting composition of local, meso-local and extra-local landscapes. Other zones included not only those that are within reach (visually, tangibly or both) of the tell (e.g. rubbish middens, animal pens and corrals, extramural cemeteries, some hunting, farming and grazing land) but also those less obviously connected (e.g. more distant grazing and hunting lands, ore and clay sources) as well as those that may have had no relation to the tell (e.g. other settlements and perhaps independent markets and cemeteries) (Bailey 1997).

By setting tells into these landscapes, it becomes easier to see tells as one of many components within complex and dynamic social and physical landscapes. Thus, from one season to the next, over successive years and through longer periods of time, the identity of the landscapes of fifth-millennium BC northeastern Bulgaria undoubtedly shifted and varied (see Bailey 1996d). As circum-tell land became inundated and unusable, the focus of people and activities would have shifted away from the tell and towards other parts of the landscape and region (perhaps to the drier uplands) and energy would have been directed towards other non-agricultural activities. Similarly, when considered over the longer-term (e.g.

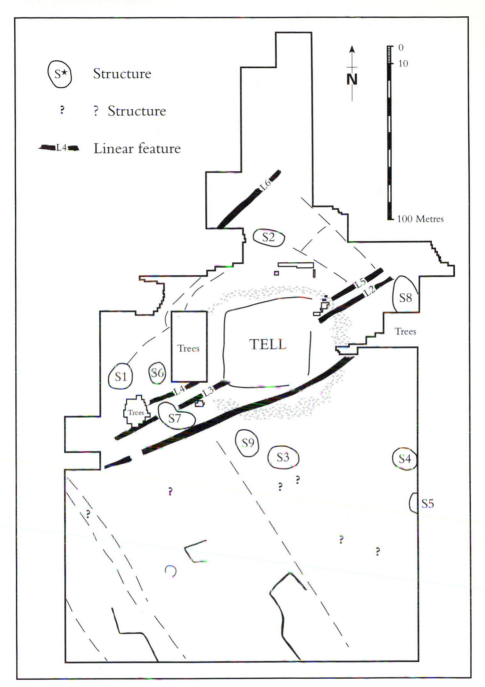

Figure 6.2 Plan of off-tell structures identified by magnetometry at Podgoritsa.

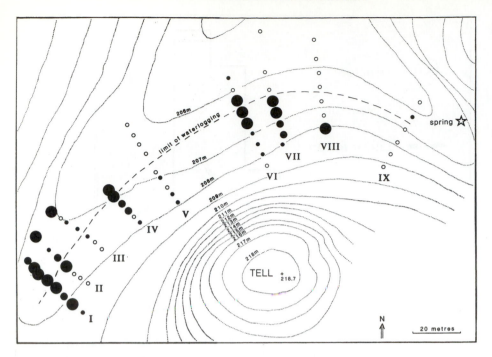

Figure 6.3 Plan of soil cores and density of cultural material to the north and west of Podgoritsa tell. Clear circles: no material; small black circles: trace of cultural material; medium black circles: moderate amounts of cultural material; large black circles: dense concentrations of cultural material.

from the Neolithic through the Eneolithic), the focus of people and activity may well have shifted from small-scale agriculture and animal management with limited need for permanent structures (as appears to be the case for the Neolithic of northeast Bulgaria) to the large-scale agriculture of the Eneolithic (as documented by the appearance of the floodplain tells). Clearly, these different social and productive strategies were based on different configurations of the landscape and of people. I will suggest below that in their ability to demarcate space, tells played a significant role in imposing these configurations.

Spatial demarcation

Tells served as potent, durable tools that demarcated space on two levels. On the one hand, tells contained powerful demarcations of internal space. The buildings and structures of a tell's interior served to limit and control the visual and physical access to particular parts of the tell. The mud, clay and timber media of the buildings provided visual concealment. The layout of floorplans controlled access via room depth (Chapman 1990). Thus, the people, activities, products, tools and other material within the tell were organized into separate units, marked off from one another.[12]

On the other hand, the internal space was dominated by the visual and physical concealment of people, activities, materials and produce and as such was made distinct and bounded from that which existed beyond the tell. As noted above, outside of the topographic boundaries of the tell lie both proximate structures and areas and the more distant zones of landscapes. Demarcation of tell from off-tell took the form of boundary walls and banks as well as the topographic rise of the mound itself.

Physical demarcation of space, both internal and external, served to separate or to aggregate people, activities, resources and products. Thus, the tell and its physical and visual boundaries separated the people, things and activities of the tell interior from the people, things and activities of off-tell areas of the landscape. The processing, storage and, perhaps, distribution (for food, trade, or planting) of cereal grain was contained and controlled within the physical boundaries of the tell. These activities and the people who engaged in them were separate from the activities and contexts beyond the tell (e.g. the location of middens and non-agricultural activities such as pot-making). Perhaps most significantly, the physical demarcation of tells may well have separated the products of agricultural activity from those who had produced them. Thus the parching, grinding and storing of cereals within the tell buildings can be read as a politically powerful component of tell-based agriculture.

Although the ability of the tell to separate is clear, tells also served as a focus for the aggregation of people and activities. As a physically imposing, visible, durable and seemingly permanent monument, a tell was a claim for immobility and permanence in a contemporary landscape and demography that were both mobile and impermanent. The tell retained an identity through time, an identity based on agricultural production. Furthermore, it anchored that identity through the vacillations of demography and the vacillations of land availability occasioned by changes in water table. As such, a tell provided a durable focus for episodic labour aggregation.

In serving to separate or to aggregate, spatial demarcation imposed and maintained an order on the relationships among people, activities, resources and products. The powerful physical and visible authority of tells regulated this order not only through space but also through time. The imposition and maintenance of such order were the foundations of sociopolitical power in fifth-millennium BC Bulgaria.

Conclusions: sociopolitics and active tells

The redefinition of tells proposed above contains many elements of social, temporal and spatial variability and flexibility. It is these contexts of instability and flux that provide the stimulus for the creation and continued use of tells in early agricultural southeastern Europe. Success in high-yield cereal agriculture relied on the authoritative control of people, by people, through time and space. Tells were a fundamental tool in expressing and realizing this control of people and resources through time and through space.

The fifth millennium in southeastern Europe was a time of social divisions and ongoing negotiations and claims to status (Renfrew 1986; Chapman 1990; Bailey 1996b). This is seen not only in the dramatic burials on the Bulgarian Black Sea coast (e.g. Varna, Durankulak) where gold, copper and *spondylus* combine in striking examples of mortuary claims to status and hierarchy. Less sensational, but equally informative are the inland cemeteries (e.g. Devniya), which produce fewer objects of metal than do the coastal sites, but that also provide evidence for the practice of social negotiation through mortuary display. Similar practices appear, in their least dramatic form, in the cemeteries of the inland tells (e.g. Golyamo Delchevo, Tell Turgovishte and Ovcharovo) where shell ornaments (e.g. bracelets, pendants, rings) are found with little if any metal. Equally important, although less often noted, expressions of interpersonal identity and claims to status, are the anthropomorphic figurine assemblages that become increasingly rich and diverse during this period (Bailey 1991, 1994, 1995, 1996b).

Burials and anthropomorphic imagery illustrate a social reality in which people actively expressed their relationships with each other in both the public sphere of burial and the more private sphere of buildings[13] (Bailey 1995). The fifth millennium was a time of interpersonal power legitimation. It was very much a political time. To the categories of burial and figurine evidence, I suggest we can add the control of resources of time and space as facilitated by tells.

Tells objectified land and time and the relationships between time, space and resources. They provided a context for control and stood simultaneously as a symbol of that control and of the order thus imposed. Through them, resources and output became possessible. Most importantly, tells were the productive backbone of the transregional patterns of status maintenance and negotiation. Tells were the critical pivot between the benefits of high-yield cereal agriculture (i.e. the creation of a relatively durable product, perhaps even possessing some characteristics of a commodity) and the human and other resources required for such production. Perhaps most importantly, tells provided a means by which resource and produce could be physically appropriated by a few and separated from the many.

Notes

1. In using the term tell, I refer to sites physically formed by the successive building, destruction or perishing and rebuilding of mud, clay and wooden buildings that, in sum, represent the repeated use of a particular place over long periods of time. The present paper addresses Chalcolithic tells in northeastern Bulgaria (e.g. Ovcharovo, Golyamo Delchevo, Turgovishte, Radingrad) and their position in contemporary productive and social contexts.

However, the parameters investigated here (the creation of permanence from imperma-nence, the structure and division of place, and the use of monumental expressive architecture as a point of aggregation) should prove informative when applied to other periods (e.g. Neolithic or Bronze Age southern Bulgaria) and other regions (e.g. Hungary or Anatolia) where tells refer to sites of different scale altogether and that may be parts of very different productive and political contexts.

2. A praiseworthy exception is the work at the Chalcolithic–Bronze Age tell in southcentral Bulgaria at Yunatsite where off-tell investigations have located activity areas contemporary with the middle Bronze Age use of the site (Bailey 1996c; Katincharov et al. 1995).

3. The project was funded by the National Science Foundation, the British Academy, the Society of Antiquaries of London, the University of California at Berkeley and the University of Wales at Cardiff.

4. But see Chapman 1990 for an attempt to reconstruct the dynamics of life within a tell.

5. The decrease in loomweight numbers occurs despite the better level of postdepositional preservation in these later horizons.

6. The majority of the large vessels were neutral or open in form and would not have been suitable for storing liquids. In addition, their shape (and the use of lids) would have made them ideal containers for dry-good storage over short and medium periods of time (i.e. within one agricultural cycle).

7. But see Boyadzhiev's attempts to calculate duration of horizon life (Boyadzhiev 1995).

8. The dogmatic defence of the Balkan tradition of using one central stratigraphic profile to represent the stratigraphy of the entire site adds to the problem of refining the inter-horizon stratigraphy of these sites.

9. This is counter to Sherratt's proposal for autumn sowing (Sherratt 1980). I favour Barker's model as it addresses agricultural communities in temperate regions of southeastern Europe, and as such applies best to northeastern Bulgaria.

10. This brief analysis has concentrated on cereal-cropping and has disregarded other cycles of activity, such as those based on animal exploitation and management. Two of the three key animal species at these sites would have been most likely to birth in the early spring (i.e. sheep/goat and pig; cattle have no special breeding season) (Gregg 1988:103, 111, 119). This may suggest a greater degree of human attention to animals at the times of conception and birth (i.e. in autumn and spring respectively). Gregg has suggested that there may have existed the need to overwinter animals in the shelter of buildings. The questions of whether or not this occurred at the tells or at other places in the landscape, and what would have been the concomitant requirements of human labour (in terms of numbers and skills), remain unanswered.

11. An exception to this is the association of extra-mural cemeteries to the northeast Bulgarian tells.

12. Perhaps the absence of any potentially communal areas (i.e. areas without buildings but with evidence of activities) within tells is best understood in parallel to the rigid demarcation of space. See Chapman (1990) for an analysis and interpretation of internal tell space in northeastern Bulgaria.

13. Anthropomorphic figurines are found only in buildings.

References

Angelova, I. 1982. Tell Targovishte. In *Kupferzeitliche siedlungen in Nordostbulgarien,* H. Todorova (ed.), 175–180. Munich: C. H. Beck.

Angelova, I. 1986. Eneolitna selishtnata mogila Turgovishte. *Interdistsiplinaria Izsledvaniya* **14**(A), 33–44.

Bailey, D. W. 1990. The living house: signifying continuity. In *The social archaeology of houses,* R. Samson (ed.), 19–48. Edinburgh: Edinburgh University Press.

Bailey, D. W. 1991. *The social reality of figurines from the Chalcolithic of northeastern Bulgaria.* Ph.D. thesis, Department of Archaeology, Cambridge University.

Bailey, D. W. 1993. Chronotypic tension in Bulgarian prehistory: 6500–3500. *World Archaeology* **25**, 204–22.

Bailey, D. W. 1994. Reading prehistoric figurines as individuals. *World Archaeology* **25**, 321–31.

Bailey, D. W. 1995. The representation of gender: homology or propaganda. *Journal of European Archaeology* **2**, 193–202.

Bailey, D. W. 1996a. The life, time and works of house 59, Tell Ovcharovo, Bulgaria. In *Neolithic houses of northwest Europe and beyond*, T. Darvill & J. Thomas (eds), 143–56. Oxford: Oxbow.

Bailey, D. W. 1996b. Interpreting figurines: the emergence of illusion and news ways of seeing. *Cambridge Archaeological Journal* **6**, 291–5.

Bailey, D. W. 1996c. The interpretation of settlement: an exercise from Bronze Age Thrace. In *Early Bronze Age settlement patterns in the Balkans (c. 3500–2000 BC)*, part 2, L. Nikolova (ed.), 201–13. Sofia: Agato.

Bailey, D. W. 1996d. The analysis of tells in northeastern Bulgaria: settlement behaviour in the context of time, space and place. In *Early Bronze Age settlement patterns in the Balkans (c. 3500–2000 BC)*, part 2, L. Nikolova (ed.), 289–308. Sofia: Agato.

Bailey, D. W. 1997. Impermanence and flux in the landscape of early agricultural southeastern Europe. In *Landscapes in flux*, J. Chapman & P. Dolukhanov (eds), 39–56. Oxford: Oxbow.

Bailey, D. W., R. E. Tringham, J. Bass, M. Hamilton, H. Neumann, M. Stevanović, I. Angelova, A. Raduncheva 1998. Expanding the dimensions of early agricultural tells: the Podgoritsa Archaeological Project, Bulgaria. *Journal of Field Archaeology* **25**(4), 1–24.

Barker, C. 1985. *Prehistoric farming in Europe.* Cambridge: Cambridge University Press.

Boyadzhiev, Y. 1995. The chronology of Bulgarian prehistoric cultures. In *Prehistoric Bulgaria*, D. W. Bailey & I. Panayotov (eds), 149–92. Madison, Wisconsin: Prehistory Press.

Chapman, J. 1990. Social inequality on Bulgarian tells and the Varna problem. In *The social archaeology of houses*, R. Samson (ed.), 49–92. Edinburgh: Edinburgh University Press.

Dennell, R. W. 1974. Botanical evidence for prehistoric crop processing activities. *Journal of Archaeological Science* **1**, 275–84.

Ellen, R. 1994. Modes of subsistence: hunting and gathering to agriculture and pastoralism. In *Companion encyclopedia of anthropology*, T. Ingold (ed.), 197–225. London: Routledge.

de Garine, I. 1994. The diet and nutrition of human populations. In *Companion encyclopedia of anthropology*, T. Ingold (ed.), 226–64. London: Routledge.

Gregg, S. A. 1988. *Foragers and farmers: population interaction and agricultural expansion in prehistoric Europe.* Chicago: University of Chicago Press.

Hodder, I. 1990. *The domestication of Europe.* Oxford: Blackwell.

Hopf, M. 1975. Razitelni nakhodki ot selishtnata mogila pri Golyamo Delchevo. In *Selishtnata mogila pri Golyamo Delchevo*, H. Todorova, S. Ivanov, V. Vasilev, M. Hopf, H. Quitta, G. Kohl, 303–24. Sofia: BAN.

Ivanov, T. 1982. Tell Radingrad. In *Kupferzeitliche siedlungen in Nordostbulgarien*, H. Todorova (ed.), 166–74. Munich: C. H. Beck.

Katincharov, R., N. Ya. Merpert, V. S. Titov, V. X. Matsanova, L. I. Avilova 1995. *Selishte mogila pri selo Yunatsite (Pazardzhishko)*, Tom 1. Sofia: Agato.

Kohl, G. & H. Quitta 1966. Berlin radiocarbon measurements 2. *Radiocarbon* **80**(1), 27–45.

Parker Pearson, M. & C. Richards (eds), 1994. *Architecture and order: approaches to social space.* London: Routledge.

Quitta, H. 1978. Radiovuglerodnite dati i tri khronologicheski sistemi. *Interdistsiplinarni Izsledvaniya* **1**, 12–24.

Quitta, H., G. Kohl 1969. Neue radiocarbondaten zum Neolitikum und zur frühen Bronzezeit Südosteuropas und der Sowjetunion. *Zeitschrift für Archäologie* **3**, 233–55.

Raduncheva, A. 1976. *Vinitsa. Eneolitno selishte i necropol.* Sofia: BAN.

Rapoport, A. 1982. *The meaning of the built environment: a non-verbal communication approach.* Beverly Hills: Sage.

Rapoport, A. 1990. Systems of activities and systems of settings. In *Domestic architecture and the use of space*, S. Kent (ed.), 9–20. Cambridge: Cambridge University Press.

Renfrew, C. 1986. Varna and the emergence of wealth in prehistoric Europe. In *The social life of things*, A. Appadurai (ed.), 141–68. Cambridge: Cambridge University Press.

Samson, R. (ed.), 1990. *The social archaeology of houses*. Edinburgh: Edinburgh University Press.

Sherratt, A. G. 1980. Water, soil and seasonality in early cereal cultivation. *World Archaeology* **11**, 313–30.

Todorova, H. 1978. *The Eneolithic in Bulgaria*. Oxford: British Archaeological Reports, International Series 49.

Todorova, H. 1982. *Kupferzeitliche siedlungen in Nordostbulgarien*. Munich: C. H. Beck.

Todorova, H. 1986. *Kammeno-mednata epokha v Bulgariya*. Sofia: Nauka i Izkustvo.

Todorova, H. 1995. The Neolithic, Eneolithic and Transitional period in Bulgarian prehistory. In *Prehistoric Bulgaria*, D. W. Bailey & I. Panayotov (eds), 79–98. Madison, Wisconsin: Prehistory Press.

Todorova, H., V. Vasilev, Z. Yanushevich, M. Kovacheva, P. Vulev 1983. *Ovcharovo*. Razkopki i Prouchvaniya 8. Sofia: BAN.

Todorova, H., S. Ivanov, V. Vasilev, M. Hopf, H. Quitta, G. Kohl 1975. *Selishtnata mogila pri Golyamo Delchevo*. Sofia: BAN.

Tringham, R. E. 1991a. Houses with faces: the challenge of gender in prehistoric and architectural remains. In *Engendering archaeology: women and prehistory*, J. M. Gero & M. W. Conkey (eds), 93–131. Oxford: Blackwell.

Tringham, R. E. 1991b. Men and women in prehistoric architecture. *Traditional Dwellings and Settlements Review* **3**(1), 9–28.

Tringham, R. E. 1994. Engendered places in prehistory. *Gender, Place and Culture* **1**(2), 169–203.

Tringham, R. & D. Krstić 1990. *Selevac: a Neolithic village in Yugoslavia*. Los Angeles: University of California Press.

Van Andel, T. H., K. Gallis, G. Toufexis, 1995. Early Neolithic farming in a Thessalian river landscape. In *Mediterranean Quaternary river environments*, J. Lewin, M. G. Macklin, J. C. Woodward (eds), 131–44. Rotterdam: Balkema.

CHAPTER SEVEN

Houses and monuments: two aspects of settlements in Neolithic and Copper Age Sardinia

Christopher Hayden

Introduction

Settlements, of course, are the places where people live. However, although everyone must live somewhere, at different times and in different places people have lived in very different ways. Although settlement may be universal, in their particular historical contexts settlements always and everywhere assume particular forms.

It is not surprising, then, that both of Childe's great revolutions (1981) involve significant changes in settlements. Although it has become ever clearer that the transition from relatively mobile patterns of settlement to sedentary village life is not inevitably associated with the onset of farming (ibid.: 71; Zvelebil 1986), in much of Europe a tradition of settled life in villages began in the Neolithic. The notion of the urban revolution makes explicit the equally profound changes in the size, economic relations and social and political constitution of settlements that followed. But although the settlements of modern Europe are very different from those of the first farmers, there is, nevertheless, continuity between them: the houses in which many of us live are still recognizably similar in some respects to those of the first farmers (Lichardus & Lichardus-Itten 1987: fig. 32).

Here I want to consider two aspects of the very varied range of settlements of the Neolithic and Early Metal Ages in Europe, lying between the first villages and the first cities. The first is how sites are recognized as settlements. The second is how, once recognized, we may define their particular character more closely. Of the many ways in which this last issue could be approached, I concentrate here on the variation in the constitution of settlements as social groups and in the role of settlements in constituting those groups. Both issues will be addressed through the analysis of activities, in the first case focusing on the identification of different kinds of activities and in the second on the spatial relationships between differing kinds of activities.

My examples are drawn from the Late Neolithic and Copper Age of Sardinia (Atzeni 1981; Atzeni et al. 1988; Lilliu 1988: chs 2–4) and Malta (Trump 1966: 30–35; Evans 1971). This period in Sardinia is divided into three phases: the Late Neolithic or Ozieri phase (*c.* 4000–3600 BC), the Early Copper Age or Abealzu-Filigosa phase (*c.* 3600–3100 BC) and the Late Copper Age or Monte Claro phase (*c.* 3100–2300 BC). In Malta only the Late Neolithic or Red Skorba phase (*c.* 4000–3900 BC)[1] will be examined. Although any body of evidence raises questions particular to itself, the Sardinian and Maltese evidence exemplifies, in particularly striking ways, issues that I believe are of much wider relevance to the inter preta-tion of the range of settlements that fall between the first villages and the first cities.

Recognizing settlements

'Settlement' is one of several terms, such as 'ritual site' or 'tomb', that are used to interpret and classify archaeological sites in terms of the kinds of activities that occurred upon them: ritual upon ritual sites, burial in tombs and domestic activities on settlements. The definition of what a settlement is thus depends on a prior definition of kinds of activities. However, like similar terms, the 'domestic' is difficult to define. Although there are some activities that we might regard as typically domestic, there is no established, universal set of domestic activities, still less a set that is exclusively domestic. The term refers, rather, to a set of activities that are united by their spatial and social context. As its etymology suggests, the notion of the house and its social correlate – the household – are the defining elements of that context: domestic activities are the quotidian activities related to the household carried out in and around the house.

Difficulties with the term remain. There may be no clear distinction between domestic and other kinds of activities; some domestic activities, for example, may be ritual in character. The argument that settlements are defined as the location of domestic activities in no way implies that settlements were not also the location of other activities, merely that these are secondary to the site's status as a settlement. Furthermore, the importance attached to the notion of domestic activities and houses in the definition of settlements is a product, in part, of our own experience. It thus belongs to a particular historical tradition and is hence poten-tially anachronistic. However, it is not an uninformed notion: the remote continu-ity we may perceive between the first villages of the Neolithic and modern European towns and cities has been revealed only by decades of archaeological research. Nor, might it therefore be argued, is it a notion, in some parts of the world, without any connection to the past: the historical tradition at the end of which it stands is itself derived from the Neolithic. In interpreting prehistoric settlements, we thus face the difficult task of appreciating the difference of the apparently familiar.

If settlements are defined as the sites on which domestic activities occurred, it might be thought that they could be recognized simply by the identification of the remains – the tools and rubbish – of domestic activities. However, a comparison of the way in which two kinds of sites from the Late Neolithic of Sardinia – settlements and tombs – have been interpreted as such reveals that the process of interpretation is very much more complex.

Although there is no universal set of domestic activities, the kinds of artefacts found on the Sardinian settlements (fig. 7.1) could easily be regarded as having been related to a typical set of domestic activities. Although we cannot be entirely sure what they were used for, the querns, blades, scrapers, animal bones, arrows, axes, spindle whorls and loom-weights can easily be seen as the tools for and waste generated by the acquisition, preparation and consumption of food and a range of simple craft activities. It might, then, be thought that the interpretation of these sites as settlements depends on the recognition of these artefacts as the remains of domestic activities.

A comparison of the artefacts occurring on the settlements with those occurring in tombs shows that this is not the case. Although the proportions differ slightly and a few types are missing from the tombs, the range of artefacts occurring in tombs is in general very similar to that occurring on settlements (fig. 7.1). It is not, then, simply the recognition of the artefactual remains of domestic activity that has led to the recognition of some sites as settlements. If this were the case, the tombs too would have been interpreted as settlements. Nor are the different interpretations of the two kinds of sites based on the presence of human remains. Burials have been found in only a very small proportion of the sites interpreted as tombs and they occur occasionally on settlements too.[2]

The distinction between the two kinds of sites rests, in fact, purely on the differences in the structural evidence. The tombs, or *domus de janas* (Lilliu 1988: 199–221), are underground structures consisting of between one and 20 chambers cut into the rock, whereas the settlements are open sites on which the commonest features are pits (ibid.: 76–80). Some of these form wells and storage pits (e.g. Ugas et al. 1985), but more commonly they take the form of shallower pits, around 50 cm deep and between 1 m and 7 m in width, and of varied, often irregular, rounded shapes in plan. Sardinian archaeologists have interpreted these features as *fondi di capanne* – the bases or foundations of houses.

The contrast between these two contexts is particularly striking in Sardinia for two reasons. First, it is in fact highly unlikely that the *fondi di capanne* are actually the remains of *grubenhäuser* (Childe 1949). In ethnographic studies (Guidoni 1987; Oliver 1987) and in well-documented archaeological cases (e.g. Lichardus & Lichardus-Itten 1987: figs 11 and 16), houses always assume forms much more regular than those of the *fondi de capanne*. In Sardinia itself, there is evidence, albeit mostly from slightly later periods, that houses were constructed in more regular forms (fig. 7.2). The *fondi di capanne* are more plausibly interpreted as the pits from which the daub for the actual houses was dug.

The second striking feature of the Sardinian evidence is that it is the tombs that provide the best evidence for the form of houses. Eighty-two of the *domus de janas* mimic, in stone, the form of huts with wooden beams and posts supporting semi-circular, circular and rectangular gabled roofs (Demartis 1984). Other tombs have

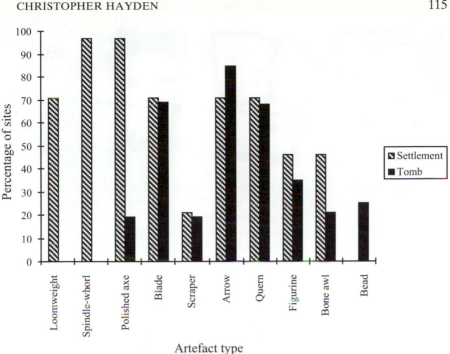

Figure 7.1 Comparison of artefacts deposited on settlements and in tombs in the Sardinian Late Neolithic. Settlements: San Michele (Lilliu 1981), Cuccuru s'Arriu (Depalmas 1990–1; Santoni 1977, 1982), Su Coddu (Ugas et al. 1985, 1989), Terramaini (Usai 1984, 1986). Tombs: Monte Crobu 1 (Atzeni 1987; Cocco 1988b; Frau 1985), San Benedetto 2 (Atzeni 1987; Maxia & Atzeni 1964), Perda Lada 2, layer 3 (Ugas 1990), Serra Crabiles 4 (Foschi 1981, Foschi Nieddu 1984), Su Avagliu (Desantis 1987–8), Cannas di Sotto 12 (Cocco & Usai 1988b).

circular features in their floors that have been interpreted as mimicking hearths (Tanda 1984). It is an irony peculiar to the Sardinian evidence that the tombs look more like houses than do the mistakenly interpreted 'houses' on settlements but it does give some indication of the importance of our preconceptions about houses in the recognition of settlements and thus of the significance of the continuity in the form of houses from the Neolithic.

However, the important point here is not simply that the recognition of settlements depends on the recognition of houses but that the interpretation of the artefactual evidence through which we might identify domestic activities is not independent of the context in which it occurs. The same artefacts have been interpreted in different ways when found on settlements and in tombs: on settlements they are the remains of domestic activities whereas in tombs they are grave goods, a use regarded as derivative of and secondary to their primary use in the domestic context. Rather than evidence for domestic activities identifying a site as

Figure 7.2   Houses from the Late Neolithic and Copper Age in Sardinia. From left: Serra Linta (Late Neolithic?: after Tanda 1990: fig. 9), Monte d'Accodi (Early Copper Age: after Contu 1966: fig. 3), Biriai (Late Copper Age: after Castaldi 1981: fig. 13). Far right: imitation of wooden-framed huts in rock cut tombs at Sant' Andrea Priu (Late Neolithic: after Contu 1966: fig. 4; Taramelli 1918). (Scales = 1 m)

a settlement, activities have been interpreted as domestic because they occur on sites that are presumed to be settlements.

It would, nevertheless, be wrong to think that artefactual evidence has no role to play in the recognition of settlements. Although artefacts are often interpreted in the light of assumptions concerning the contexts in which they are found, it is equally true that, using a different set of assumptions, artefacts can be interpreted independently of the contexts in which they occur. Artefactual evidence therefore has the potential to challenge or support interpretations based on its structural context. However, rather than being used to indicate the presence of domestic activities, artefactual evidence has more often been used to suggest that house-like structures were not in fact houses.

The Late Neolithic structures at Skorba in Malta (Trump 1966: 11–14, figs 11 and 12) provide a typical example in which artefactual evidence has been used to argue that house-like structures actually served a ritual purpose. The two adjacent structures consist of hollows, one oval and one D-shaped, surrounded by the rubble-filled stone footings of walls that were continued in mud brick. Initially, the structures have the appearance of houses but several features militate against such an interpretation: 'domestic use is made unlikely by the irregularity of the floor, the absence of hearths and the unnecessarily large southern wall' (ibid.: 14). However, it is the artefacts that suggest an alternative interpretation. The figurines, bovine tarsals (the lower surfaces of which are ground down) and goat skulls (the facial bones of which have been removed) found within the structures suggested to the excavator a religious purpose. Although acknowledging that the case is not proven, he therefore concluded that 'the interpretation that the building was some sort of shrine for votive offerings rather than a temple for public worship seems to meet more of the difficulties than any alternative theory' (ibid.: 14).

Although this interpretation begins with discussion of the structural features, it ultimately rests on assumptions about the functions of some of the artefacts that are independent of their context. However, the structures also contained artefacts – pottery, chert flakes and domestic animal bones – that would support a domestic interpretation. It could also be argued that the irregularity of the floor does not support a ritual any more than a domestic interpretation.

The difficulty of interpreting these structures may stem from a false opposition. There is no reason to assume that domestic and ritual interpretations are exclusive. There are many cases where ritual activity has been documented in houses (e.g. Humphrey & Laidlaw 1994: 29); domestic activities may include ritual. One way to resolve this issue would be to compare the supposed shrines with other structures and to ask whether the structural elements and artefacts of the shrines really stand out as exceptional (cf. Mellaart 1967; Hodder 1987). Unfortunately, the structures at Skorba are the only examples known from this period in Malta and the interpretation therefore remains open. Nonetheless, the difficulty in resolving this issue clearly indicates the complexities of interplaying interpretations of structural and artefactual evidence in the recognition of domestic activities, houses and thus of settlements.

Although each period and place has its own peculiarities, the two foregoing cases exemplify some aspects of the way in which settlements have been recognized that are of wider relevance. They suggest that two sets of preconceptions have influenced our interpretations of sites as settlements. The first set concerns the character of domestic activities, the presence of which is the defining feature of settlements. The second concerns the context of those activities that is crucial in defining them as domestic: the character of houses.

The interpretation of the evidence related to these two elements – artefacts and structures – are not ultimately independent. The interpretation of artefacts is strongly influenced by the interpretation of their structural context: the same artefacts may be interpreted in quite different ways when found in different contexts. The recognition of domestic activities and hence of settlements may thus depend on the recognition of structures that look like the remains of houses. In their absence, it may be impossible to unambiguously identify the remains of domestic activities. However, the two sets of preconceptions are sufficiently distinct to be able to challenge each other. When house-like structures contain artefacts that deviate strongly from our expectations about domestic activities, the structures have often been interpreted in other ways.

It is easier to point out problems than to provide remedies, and given the possible variation in settlement, it is impossible to give prescriptions for their identification that are valid in all contexts. The best, I think, that can be offered is that in attempting to overcome the apparent familiarity of what must have been very different, it is important to allow the evidence to challenge our preconceptions. One way in which this can be achieved is to allow our interpretations of differing kinds of evidence, for example artefacts and their structural context (each of which relates to differing preconceptions), to confront one another.

The social character of settlements

However, merely recognizing settlements is just a beginning. As the chapters in this book demonstrate, settlements have assumed many different forms at different times and in different places. I now look at one important aspect of this variation: the constitution of settlements as social groups and the role of settlements in constituting those groups.

Although dispersed settlement patterns exist in which each house stands on its own, more often settlements consist of groups of houses and thus form social

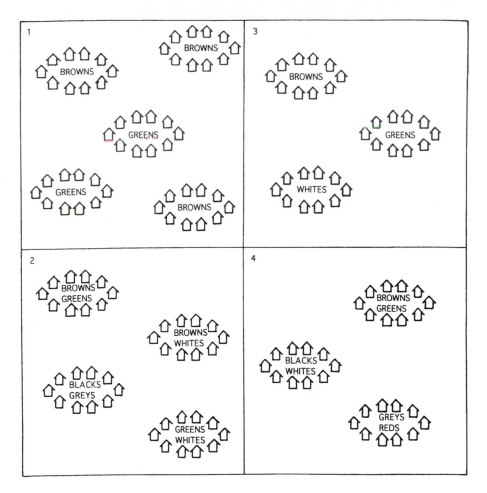

Figure 7.3   The possible distribution of descent-based groups among settlements. Descent groups may reside in one settlement (cases 3 and 4) or be divided among several (cases 1 and 2) and each settlement may be home to only one descent group (cases 1 and 3) or to several (cases 2 and 4) (after Keesing 1975: figs 14–17, following Hogbin & Wedgewood 1953).

groups greater than individual households. These social groups may be of many different kinds. Keesing (1975: 39–41, figs 14–17, following Hogbin & Wedgewood 1953), for example, has summarized the possible relationships between descent groups and settlements for patrilineal societies (fig. 7.3). Among this possible variation, an important distinction falls between cases where individuals reside together because they are related by, for example, descent (in such cases, the settlements form descent-based local groups) and others where 'the ties of community . . . transcend in everyday affairs the ties of common descent' (Keesing 1975: 41) (in this case, co-residence or local contiguity (Maine 1861: 128) within settlements forms the basis of the community). The hypothesis I want to explore here is that this variation in the social constitution of settlements is related to the way in which societies distribute their activities through space.

So far, it has been argued that settlements are defined by the occurrence of domestic activities. However, they may also be the location of many other kinds of activities, some of which may be related, not to households, but to the wider social group from which the settlement is constituted. Among these other activities, the importance of ritual in promoting the solidarity of social groups has long been recognized (e.g. Fustel de Coulanges 1980: book 3). However, as well as occurring on settlements, these other activities, for example communal ritual, may be distributed across the landscape at other locations.

We have already seen that settlement is just one of a set of terms, such as ritual site and tomb, used to interpret sites in terms of the kinds of activities occurring on them. In interpreting sites in these terms, we are also describing the way in which societies distribute their activities through space. Differing kinds of activities are related to differing kinds of social relationships and by viewing settlements in relation to the distribution of other kinds of sites we may, therefore, be able to reach some understanding of their social constitution. As an example of such an interpretation, I review the development of the character and spatial distribution of different kinds of sites in Sardinia from the Late Neolithic to the end of the Copper Age.

The Late Neolithic

Where Late Neolithic settlements have been extensively investigated they have sometimes been found to consist of very large numbers of *fondi di capanne*: 267 at Puisteris, for example (Puxeddu 1959–61; Lilliu 1988: 79). Although they are not themselves the remains of huts, their number may well be related in some way to the number of houses built at each site. Houses were probably constructed out of wood and daub (fragments of daub have been found at San Gemiliano (Atzeni 1959–61) and Barbusi (Atzeni 1972, 1987; Cocco 1988a)), and their lifespan would therefore have been limited. Given that many settlements were quite long-lived – Puisteris, for example, is typical in being occupied from the late Neolithic into the Late Copper Age – the number of houses in existence at any one time may have been quite small.

The discovery of figurines on settlements hints that these sites may have been the location of some ritual activity (although the interpretation of figurines is always problematical: Ucko 1968; Tallalay 1993). The character of this activity is obscure, but in the absence of any distinctive structures that might be interpreted as 'shrines', it can plausibly be suggested that the figurines were used for household rituals and can thus be regarded as domestic.

The main foci of ritual activity in this period were the elaborate rock-cut tombs, the *domus de janas*. Around 2500 of these tombs occur throughout almost all of the Sardinia (Lilliu 1988: 81). Most are quite simple, single-chambered structures (Santoni 1976). However, many of the larger tombs contain a range of painted and carved motifs, many of which represent, more or less schematically, bulls' heads or horns (Tanda 1977a, 1984). Larger tombs sometimes also contain features imitating huts. The elaboration of these tombs reveals the importance that was attached to funerary ritual. The limited evidence available (e.g. Maxia & Atzeni 1964; Ugas 1990) shows that they were used for collective burials, ultimately containing, in the case of average-sized tombs, tens of individuals. Each tomb, therefore, must have been related to a small social group of some kind. However, they were not located in or near to settlements and thus formed ritual foci, distinct from the settlements, for social groups that may have been based on descent.

The Early Copper Age

Alongside the smaller number of *domus de janas* used in the Early Copper Age, the new kinds of tombs constructed in this phase – *allées couvertes* and megalithic chamber tombs[3] – were also situated away from settlements (Atzeni 1979–80, 1982, 1987, 1988). These new kinds of tombs were much simpler, smaller structures than the *domus de janas*. They began a trend that continued in the Late Copper Age involving a reduction in the size and elaboration of tombs and, by implication, of the importance of funerary ritual and the dead.

One reason for this decline in the significance of funerary ritual was the development of new forms of ritual not directly connected with the dead, nor yet with settlements. The most spectacular example of these developments is provided by the site of Monte d'Accoddi (Contu 1966, 1984; Tiné 1987; Tiné & Traverso 1992). Here, on the site of an abandoned village, a large rectangular mound retained by cyclopean walls was constructed. On this mound stood a small, red-plastered building reached by a long ramp.

No similar sites of the same date have so far been found, but in other parts of the island there are further indications that ritual may have become dissociated from tombs. Many of the menhirs in Sardinia (Lilliu 1981: 63–82, 133–40) are difficult to date but several statue-menhirs – on the fronts of many of which are depicted a schematized face and trident and dagger motifs or breasts (Atzeni 1978, 1979–80, 1982; Arnal et al. 1983; Perra 1987–92; Lilliu 1988: 235–9; Cossu 1992–3) – can be more certainly dated to the Copper Age.[4] Their precise use is not clear. They may, for example, have acted as territorial markers but it is also possible that they formed the foci of ritual activities. Like Monte d'Accoddi, they are not associated spatially with either tombs or settlements.

In almost all cases, the evidence of excavation and surface survey provides no indication of any change in the form of settlements at the beginning of the Early Copper Age. However, two exceptional sites are worth noting because they presage developments more typical of the Late Copper Age. The settlement at the first site, San Giuseppe di Padria (Contu 1974; Lo Schiavo 1974; Tore 1975; Santoni 1976; Tanda 1976; Foschi 1980), was enclosed within a cyclopean wall. At the second site, Monte d'Accoddi, the first mound was subsequently buried beneath a new, larger structure of similar form around which a settlement of stone-footed houses grew up (fig. 7.2).

The Late Copper Age

Both these sites were abandoned before the Late Copper Age but their two distinctive features – specialized ritual structures within settlements and the enclosure of settlements within walls – exceptional in the Early Copper Age, are more characteristic of settlements of the Late Copper Age. Monte Baranta (Moravetti 1981, 1988) and Biriai (Castaldi 1979, 1981, 1984a,b, 1985, 1992), the two most thoroughly investigated of the ever-increasing numbers of these settlements[5] that are being recognized, will serve as examples. Monte Baranta (fig. 7.4) is situated on the end of a triangular promontory, two sides of which are defined by steep scarps.

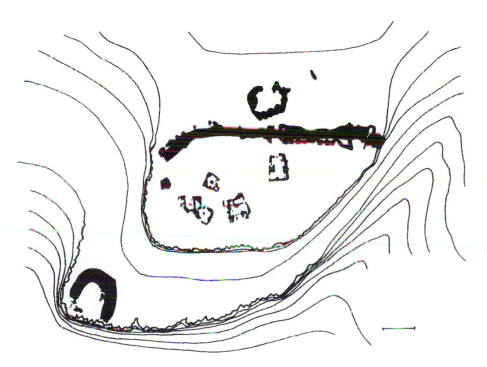

Figure 7.4   Monte Baranta (Late Copper Age: after Moravetti 1988).

On the third side, a large cyclopean wall delimits the edge of the settlement within which the remains of several huts were found. A second wall of similar construction cuts off a smaller area at the tip of the promontory. Just outside the walls lies the ritual area: a circle with a diameter of 10 m formed of 80 stones associated with several menhirs.

At the centre of the plateau on which the unwalled settlement of Biriai stands, rises the ritual area: a small hill or platform, partly natural, partly artificial, retained by cyclopean walls and terraces and entered by steps and a semi-circular ramp. Several menhirs were found on and around this platform.

The houses at both of these sites were more substantial than the wood and daub structures of earlier phases. At Monte Baranta, the footings of the walls of the quadrangular houses were of orthostatic stones, while at Biriai, the remains of stone footings revealed the plans of houses with apsidal ends (fig. 7.2). Like the ritual structures and the enclosure walls of the settlements of this period, they seem to have been designed for a more stable, permanent occupation than that which characterized earlier settlements.

Although older tombs continued to be reused, the trend towards smaller and less elaborate tombs continued during the Late Copper Age. The few tombs that were constructed during this phase are much slighter, simpler constructions: simple stone cists, trench graves and simple rock-cut tombs. However, most significantly, and in striking contrast to the tombs of earlier phases, they were built in or adjacent to settlements (Lilliu & Ferrarese Ceruti 1958–9; Atzeni 1959–61, 1967, 1986).

Thus, as the settlements took over the ritual role of the funerary and specialized ritual monuments of the earlier phases, the settlements themselves became monuments. Substantial and permanent structures were surrounded by cyclopean walls that differentiated residential from megalithic ritual spaces.

Discussion

My purpose is not to explain these changes in the distribution of activities and the form of settlements but to suggest that they can be understood in terms of changes in the constitution of the settlements as social groups and in the role of settlements in constituting those groups. The focusing of ritual on elaborate monumental tombs in the Late Neolithic suggests that descent was an important source of social solidarity that was reproduced partly through funerary rites at the tombs. That the tombs are sited away from the small, relatively slightly built settlements suggests that there was no simple relationship between the social groups related to the tombs (those buried in the tombs and their descendants who could expect to be buried there) and those occupying the settlements. The archaeological evidence gives no warrant for inferring kinship relationships in the detail available to social anthropologists, but it is easy to imagine a situation like Keesing's first model (fig. 7.3) in which wider descent groups, distributed widely through space in different settlements, were united by their common relationships with tombs. In contrast to the fixed, permanent tombs, the settlements may have been related to relatively small, fluctuating social groups.

The first signs of a change in this system appear in the Early Copper Age. Burial and hence social relationships conceived through the idiom of descent began to lose their importance. The shift in ritual to statue menhirs may indicate that a new significance was being attached to the demarcation of social territories (Perra 1987–92). However, these sites were still situated away from settlements (as was the first mound at Monte d'Accoddi). At the same time, the settlements them-selves retain their earlier form. Thus, although there may have been a decline in the relative importance of descent in the constitution of society, the spatial distri-bution of social relationships – and the social constitution of settlements – may have changed little. However, there are also indications of the changes that crys-tallized only in the Late Copper Age: the enclosure of settlements and the concen-tration of ritual and funerary activity within them.

Although it is clear that there were significant changes in the relationship between settlements and social groups in the Late Copper Age, the archaeological evidence again gives no indication of how the occupants of Late Copper Age settlements were related through kinship. It is perhaps easiest to imagine a situa-tion like Keesing's third or fourth models in which social groups are confined to particular settlements. However, although local contiguity may have grown in importance relative to descent as a principle of social organization, it may be going too far to suggest that, paraphrasing Keesing, the ties of community had come to transcend in everyday affairs the ties of common descent. Rather than replacing connection in blood as the condition of community in political functions (Maine 1861: 128), it is perhaps more likely that the two came to coincide.

It seems likely that there were also significant changes in the role of settlements in constituting communities. As much as excluding outsiders, the cyclopean walls created a political community out of the occupants within. This community was further bound together by the rituals now based in and on the settlements. As settlements became, in part, the basis of the community and of its religious and political institutions, the settlements themselves assumed monumental forms.

Conclusions

The Sardinian evidence is particular to that island and we should not expect the same developments to have occurred elsewhere. However, the general relation-ships that this evidence suggests may be of wider significance. In Sardinia, I have suggested that the settlements form parts of wider systems of sites of several different kinds.

It is only in the Late Copper Age that social groups and their religious and political institutions became based on settlements. This kind of relationship – between social groups, institutions and settlements – is much closer to that of modern European towns and cities than was that of the earlier settlements. It is striking, too, that almost all of the best evidence for recognizable houses comes from the settlements of this period. As the social character of the settlements approximates to that of our own, so too do the houses. Since the domestic sphere of the houses is defined partly in distinction from the wider political sphere of the settlements, it is perhaps not surprising that these two aspects of settlements are related.

In earlier phases, social groups and their religious and political institutions may have been constituted in quite different ways. The systems of sites, including settlements and the houses from which they were composed, may have had a significance quite different from that of their Late Copper Age successors and our own towns and cities. The settlements and houses, like the social groups to which they were related, may have been relatively ephemeral and other kinds of sites, such as tombs, may have had a much greater significance in reproducing social relationships.

There is no reason to think that settlements elsewhere should have developed in the same way as those in Sardinia. These are particular examples of ways in which the spatial constitution of social groups is related to the way in which they express their solidarity. Settlements are just one part of this relationship but the Sardinian examples do give some indication of how the spatial constitution of societies is reflected in the forms of their settlements and how this may influence our ability to recognize them.

Notes

1. Radiocarbon determinations for Sardinia are listed in Tykot 1994 and for Malta in Renfrew 1972 and Malone et al. 1995.
2. For example, burials have been found in pits at Cuccuru s'Arriu (Atzeni and Forresu in Santoni 1982: tav. XIX, 2), Conca Illonis, Santa Lucia (Atzeni 1981: XXXI) and Su Coddu (Ugas et al. 1985: 20).
3. However, it should be noted that the chronology of many of the megalithic tombs that may date from this phase (Lilliu 1988: 186–99; Santoni 1971–2) is very uncertain, even in the cases of the few that contain artefacts (Lilliu 1966–7; Ferrarese Ceruti 1980).
4. They have been found built into a Nuraghe and early Nuragic tombs (Atzeni 1979–80; Perra 1987–92). Thus, they predate the Nuragic period but cannot be earlier than the Copper Age since that was when copper daggers were first introduced. I place them in the Early Copper Age because the daggers depicted on the menhirs have sharp barbs that, although not identical, are more similar to the triangular blades of Early Copper Age daggers than to the foliate blades of Late Copper Age daggers. However, the discovery of a related but slightly different type of statue-menhir apparently placed in front of and therefore contemporary with a Nuragic *tombe di giganti* suggests that the use of statue-menhirs may have continued throughout the Copper Age (Moravetti 1984).
5. Others include Monte Ossoni (Moravetti 1979a, 1988), Punta S'Arroccu (Basoli et al. 1988; Moravetti 1984: note 60, 1988), Sa Urecci (Lilliu 1988: 134–5), Sos Settiles (Lo Schiavo et al. 1988), Bia Ebbas (Manunza 1985a,b), Cucché (Manunza 1985a,b), Mandra Comida (Moravetti 1979b), Sos Frontes (Moravetti 1979b), Sa Sillida 'e sa Cresia (Perra 1987–92), Lasasai (Manunza 1984), Marras (Manunza 1982), Pabude, Bolotano (Tanda 1977b) and Ortachis (Tanda 1977b). However, it should be noted that apart from Monte Ossoni, none of these sites have yet been investigated and their chronology and sometimes their form is thus very uncer-

tain. Some may date from other phases. The 'protonuraghi' of Brunku Màdugui (Lilliu 1982: 14–15) and Sa Corona, Villagreca (Atzeni 1966: 119–26), may also belong in this phase but their association with Monte Claro pottery may be purely fortuitous.

References

Arnal, J., L. Arnal, L. Demurtas, S. Demurtas 1983. Les statues-menhirs sardes. *Bulletin du Musée d'Anthropologie Préhistorique de Monaco* **27**, 123–50.

Atzeni, E. 1959–61. I villagi preistorici di San Gemiliano di Sestu e di Monte Ollàdiri di Monastir presso Cagliari e le ceramiche della facies di Monte Claro. *Studi Sardi* **17**, 3–216.

Atzeni, E. 1966. Il nuraghe Sa Corona di Villagreca. *Atti XIII Congresso di Storia del'Architettura*, 119–24.

Atzeni, E. 1967. Tombe a forno di cultura Monte Claro nella via Basilicata di Cagliari. *Rivista di Scienze Preistoriche* **22**, 157–79.

Atzeni, E. 1972. Notizario – Sardegna. *Rivista di Scienze Preistoriche* **27**, 475–7.

Atzeni, E. 1978. Le statue-menhirs di Laconi. In *Sardegna centro-settentrionale dal Neolitico alla fine del mondo antico*, 47–52. Sassari: Soprintendenza ai Beni Archeologici per le province di Sassari e Nuoro.

Atzeni, E. 1979–80. Menhirs antropomorfi e statue-menhirs della Sardegna. *Annali del Museo Civico della Spezia* **2**, 9–64.

Atzeni, E. 1981. Aspetti e svillupi culturali del Neolitico e della prima età dei metalli in Sardegna. In *Ichnussa: La Sardegna dalle origini all'età classica*, Anon (ed.), XIX–LI. Milano: Libri Scheiwiller.

Atzeni, E. 1982. Notizario – Sardegna. *Rivista di Scienze Preistoriche* **37**, 336–7.

Atzeni, E. 1986. *Cagliari preistorica (nota preliminare)*. Estratto da: S. Igia – Capitale Giudicale. Pisa: ETS.

Atzeni, E. 1987. *La preistoria del Sulcis-Iglesiente*. Cagliari: Stef.

Atzeni, E. 1988. Megalitismo e arte. Atti del Congresso Internazionale 'L'età del rame in Europa', Viareggio 15–18 Ottobre 1987. *Rassegna di Archeologia* **7**, 449–56.

Atzeni, E., E. Contu, M. L. Ferrarese Ceruti (eds) 1988. L'età del rame nell'Italia insulare: La Sardegna. Atti del Congresso Internazionale 'L'età del rame in Europa', Viareggio 15–18 Ottobre 1987. *Rassegna di Archeologia* **7**, 449–67.

Basoli, P., F. Lo Schiavo, L. D. Campus, F. Guido 1988. Ozieri. In *L'Antiquarium Arborense e i civici musei archeologici della Sardegana*, G. Lilliu (ed.), 71–92. Sassari: Amilcare Pizzi Editore.

Castaldi, E. 1979. Biriai (Oliena-Nuoro): il villaggio di cultura Monte Claro (nota preliminare). *Rivista di Scienze Preistoriche* **34**, 231–42.

Castaldi, E. 1981. Villaggio con santuario a Biriai (Oliena-Nuoro). *Rivista di Scienze Preistoriche* **36**, 153–221.

Castaldi, E. 1984a. L'architettura di Biriai. *Rivista di Scienze Preistoriche* **39**, 119–53.

Castaldi, E. 1984b. La cultura calcolitica di Monte Claro nel sito di Biriai (Oliena-Nuoro). See Waldren et al. (1984), 567–90.

Castaldi, E. 1985. Biriai e le fortezze prenuragiche: per una valutazzione socio-culturale. *Studi Urbinati* **58**, 29–54.

Castaldi, E. 1992. Il Santuario di Biriai. In *Monte d'Accoddi: 10 anni di nuovi scavi*, S. Tiné & A. Traverso (eds), 77–92. Genova: Istituto di Archeologia Sperimentale.

Childe, V. G. 1949. Neolithic house types in temperate Europe. *Proceedings of the Prehistoric Society* **15**, 77–86.

Childe, V. G. 1981. *Man makes himself*, 1st illustrated edn. Bradford on Avon: Moonraker.

Cocco, D. 1988a. Il villaggio preistorico di Barbusi (Carbonia-CA). See Cocco & Usai (1988a), 35–6.

Cocco, D. 1988b. La tomba 1 di Monte Crobu (Carbonia-CA). See Cocco & Usai (1988a), 27–30.

Cocco, D. & L. Usai (eds) 1988a. *Museo Villa Sulcis*. Cagliari: Soprintendeza Archeologica per le Province di Cagliari e Oristano.

Cocco, D. & L. Usai 1988b. Necropoli ipogeica in località Canas di Sotto (Carbonia-CA). See Cocco & Usai (1988a), 31–3.

Contu, E. 1966. Elementi di architettura prenuragica. *Atti del XII Congresso di Storia del'Architettura*, 93–124.

Contu, E. 1974. Notizario – Sardegna. *Rivista di Scienze Preistoriche* **29**, 262–7.

Contu, E. 1984. Monte d'Accoddi-Sassari – problematiche di studio e di ricerca di un singolare monumento preistorico. See Waldren et al. (1984), 591–610.

Cossu, A. M. 1992–3. Nuove statue-menhirs ed un inedito petroglifo nel territorio di Allai (Oristano). *Studi Sardi* **30**, 299–328.

Demartis, G. M. 1984. Alcune osservazioni sulle Domus de Janas riproducenti il tetto della casa dei vivi. *Nuovo Bulletino Archeologico Sardo* **1**, 9–19.

Depalmas, A. 1990–1. L'industria litica di Cuccuru is Arrius (Cabras – Or) nella collezione Falchi d'Oristano. *Studi Sardi* **29**, 55–91.

Desantis, P. 1987–8. La Domus de Janas di Su Avagliu. *Rivista di Scienze Preistoriche* **41**, 239–67.

Evans, J. D. 1971. *The prehistoric antiquities of the Maltese islands*. London: Athlone.

Ferrarese Ceruti, M. L. 1980. Le Domus de Janas di Mariughia e Canudedda e il dolmen di Motorra. In *Dorgali: documenti archeologici*, 57–65. Sassari: Soprintendenza Archeologica per le province di Sassari e Nuoro.

Foschi, A. 1980. La tomba I di Filigosa (Macomer). *Atti della XXII Riunione Scientifica del'Istituto Italiano di Preistoria e Protostoria 1978*, 289–303.

Foschi, A. 1981. Notizario   Sardegna. *Rivista di Scienze Preistoriche* **36**, 354–60.

Foschi Nieddu, A. 1984. I risulti degli scavi 1981 nella necropoli prenuragica di Serra Crabiles. See Waldren et al. (1984), 533–41.

Frau, M. 1985. Monte Crobu. *Archeologia Viva* **IV** (May), 16–27.

Fustel de Coulanges, N. M. 1980. *The ancient city*. Baltimore: Johns Hopkins University Press.

Guidoni, E. 1987. *Primitive architecture* (trans. Wolf, R. E.). London: Faber.

Hodder, I. 1987. Contextual archaeology: an interpretation of Çatal Hüyük and a discussion of the origins of agriculture. *Bulletin of the Institute of Archaeology, University College London* **24**, 43–56.

Hogbin, H. I. & C. Wedgewood 1953. Local groupings in Melanesia [published in two parts]. *Oceania* **23**, 241–76 and *Oceania* **24**, 58–76.

Humphrey, C. & J. Laidlaw 1994. *The archetypal actions of ritual*. Oxford: Clarendon Press.

Keesing, R. M. 1975. *Kin groups and social structure*. New York: Holt, Rinehart & Winston.

Lichardus, J. & M. Lichardus-Itten 1987. *La protohistoria de Europa* (trans. del Rincón Martínez, M. A.). Barcelona: Editorial Labor, Nueva Clio 1 bis.

Lilliu, G. 1966–7. Il dolmen di Motorra. *Studi Sardi* **20**, 74–128.

Lilliu, G. 1981. *Monumenti antichi bararacini*. Sassari: Ministero dei Beni Culturali e Ambientali, Quaderni 10.

Lilliu, G. 1982. *La civiltà nuragica*. Sassari: C. Delfino.

Lilliu, G. 1988. *La civiltà dei Sardi dal Paleolitico all'età dei nuraghi*, 3rd edn. Torino: Nuova ERI.

Lilliu, G. & M. L. Ferrarese Ceruti 1958–9. La facies nuragica di Monte Claro. *Studi Sardi* **16**, 3–266.

Lo Schiavo, F. 1974. Scavi e scoperte. *Studi Etruschi* **43** (ser. 3), 547–53.

Lo Schiavo, F., M. A. Fadda, A. Boninu 1988. Nuoro. In *L'Antiquarium Arborense e i civici musei archeologici della Sardegana*, G. Lilliu (ed.), 129–46. Sassari: Amilcare Pizzi Editore.

Maine, H. S. 1861. *Ancient law*. London: John Murray.

Malone, C., S. Stoddart, A. Bonnano, T. Gouder, D. Trump (eds) 1995. Mortuary ritual of the 4th millenium BC in Malta: the Zebbug period chambered tomb from the Brochtorff circle at Xaghra (Gozo). *Proceedings of the Prehistoric Society* **61**, 303–46.

Manunza, M. R. 1982. Notizario – Sardegna. *Rivista di Scienze Preistoriche* **37**, 334.

Manunza, M. R. 1984. Notizario – Sardegna. *Rivista di Scienze Preistoriche* **39**, 400–1.

Manunza, M. R. 1985a. Dorgali – censimento. *Nuovo Bulletino Archeologico Sardo* **1**, 371–85.

Manunza, M. R. 1985b. Il patrimonio archeologico del comune di Dorgali (Nu). In *10 anni di attivtà nel territorio della provincia di Nuoro 1975–85*, 14–16. Nuoro: Ministero per i Beni Culturali e Ambientali.

Maxia, C. & E. Atzeni 1964. La necropoli eneolitica di San Benedetto di Iglesias. *Atti VII & IX Riunione Scientifica dell'Istituto Italiano di Preistoria e Protostoria*, 123–35.

Mellaart, J. 1967. *Çatal Hüyük, a Neolithic town in Anatolia*. London: Thames & Hudson.

Moravetti, A. 1979a. Notizario – Sardegna. *Rivista di Scienze Preistoriche* **34**, 332–4.

Moravetti, A. 1979b. Monumenti, scavi e scoperte nel territorio di Ploaghe. In *Contributi su Giovanni Spano*, Ministero per i Beni Culturali e Ambientali, 11–46. Sassari: Chiarella (Soprintendenza ai Beni Archeologici per le province di Sassari e Nuoro).

Moravetti, A. 1981. Nota agli scavi nel complesso megalitico di Monte Baranta (Olmedo – Sassari). *Rivista di Scienze Preistoriche* **36**, 281–90.

Moravetti, A. 1984. Statue-menhirs in una tomba di giganti del Marghine. *Nuovo Bullettino Archeologico Sardo* **1**, 41–67.

Moravetti, A. 1988. La cultura di Monte Claro nella Sardegna settentrionale. Atti del Congresso Internazionale 'L'età del rame in Europa', Viareggio 15–18 Ottobre 1987. *Rassegna di Archeologia* **7**, 528–9.

Oliver, P. 1987. *Dwellings: the house across the world*. Oxford: Phaidon.

Perra, M. 1987–92. Statue-menhir in territorio di Samugheo (Oristano). *Nuovo Bullettino Archeologico Sardo* **4**, 17–42.

Puxeddu, C. 1959–61. Note preliminare sulla stazione prenuragica e nuragica di Puisteris – Mogoro. *Studi Sardi* **17**, 217–59.

Renfrew, C. 1972. Malta and the calibrated radiocarbon chronology. *Antiquity* **46**, 141–5.

Santoni, V. 1971–2. Il dolmen di Sculacacca – Oniferi Nuoro. *Studi Sardi* **22**, 3–37.

Santoni, V. 1976. Nota preliminare sulla tipologia delle grotticelle funerarie in Sardegna. *Archivio Storico Sardo* **30**, 3–49.

Santoni, V. 1977. Notizario – Sardegna. *Rivista di Scienze Preistoriche* **32**, 350–57.

Santoni, V. 1982. Cabras. Cuccuru s'Arriu. Nota preliminare di scavo 1978–80. *Rivista di Studi Fenici* **10**(1), 103–11.

Tallalay, L. E. 1993. *Deities, dolls and devices: Neolithic figurines from Franchthi cave, Greece*. Excavations at Franchthi Cave, Greece: fasc. 9. Bloomington: Indiana University Press.

Tanda, G. 1976. Notizario – Sardegna. *Rivista di Scienze Preistoriche* **31**, 322–9.

Tanda, G. 1977a. *Arte preistorica in Sardegna*, Quaderni 5. Sassari: Dessi (Ministero dei Beni Culturali e Ambientali).

Tanda, G. 1977b. Notizario – Sardegna. *Rivista di Scienze Preistoriche* **32**, 359–63.

Tanda, G. 1984. *Arte e religione della Sardegna preistorica nella necropoli di Sos Furrighesos*. Sassari: Chiarella.

Tanda, G. 1990. La tomba n. 2 di Sas Arzolas de Goi a Nughesu S. Vittoria (Oristano). In *Studi in onore di Pietro Meloni*, 75–95. Cagliari: Edizione della Torre.

Taramelli, A. 1918. Fortezze, recinti, fonti sacre e necropoli preromane nell'agro di Bonorva (Prov. di Sassari). *Monumenti Antichi dei Lincei* **25**, 767–903.

Tiné, S. 1987. Nuovi scavi nel santuario di Monte d'Accoddi (Sassari). *Annali Istituto Orientale, Napoli* **9**, 9–22.

Tiné, S. & A. Traverso (eds) 1992. *Monte d'Accoddi: 10 anni di nuovi scavi*. Genova: Istituto di Archeologia Sperimentale.

Tore, G. 1975. Notizario archeologico. *Studi Sardi* **23**, 12–15.

Trump, D. H. 1966. *Skorba*. Reports of the Research Committee of the Society of Antiquaries of London 22. Oxford: Oxford University Press.

Tykot, R. H. 1994. Radiocarbon dating and absolute chronology in Sardinia and Corsica. In *Radiocarbon dating and Italian prehistory*, R. Skeates & R. Whitehouse (eds), 115–46. Accordia specialist studies on Italy 3. Archaeological monographs of the British School at Rome 8.

Ucko, P. J. 1968. *Anthropomorphic figurines of predynastic Egypt and Neolithic Crete*. London: Andrew Szmidla.

Ugas, G. 1990. *La tomba dei guerrieri di Decimoputzu*. Norax 1. Cagliari: Edizione della Torre.

Ugas, G., G. Lai, L. Usai 1985. L'insediamento prenuragico di Su Coddu (Selargius-Ca). *Nuovo Bullettino Archeologico Sardo* **2**, 7–41.

Ugas, G., L. Usai, M. P. Nuvoli, G. Lai, M. G. Marras 1989. Nuovi dati sull'insediamento di Su Coddu – Selargius. In *La cultura di Ozieri*, L. D. Campus (ed.), 217–78. Ozieri: Il Torchietto.

Usai, L. 1984. Il villaggio di età eneolitica di Terramaini presso Pirri (Cagliari). *Atti del IV Convegno Nazionale di Preistoria e Protostoria*, 175–96.

Usai, L. 1986. Il villaggio di Terramaini presso Cagliari. *Studi di Archeologia e Antichità* **1**, 5–17. Soprintendenza Archeologica per le Province di Cagliari e Oristano. Quaderni 3.

Waldren, W. H., R. Chapman, J. Lewthwaite, R-C. Kennard (eds) 1984. *The Deya conference of prehistory: early settlement in the western Mediterranean islands and their peripheral areas*. Oxford: British Archaeological Reports, international series 219.

Zvelebil, M. (ed.) 1986. *Hunters in transition: mesolithic societies of temperate Eurasia and their transition to farming*. Cambridge: Cambridge University Press.

CHAPTER EIGHT

Kinship, tradition and settlement pattern: an archaeology of prehistoric Middle Missouri community life

Richard A. Krause

Introduction

Despite early pleas for flexibility (Vogt 1956: 173–82), an ecological approach has dominated Americanist settlement pattern studies. It appears to be based on the assumption that a settlement pattern is determined by the interaction of two sets of variables: environment and technology as these were understood and used by human beings seeking to maximize the efficiency of their economic and reproductive efforts (Gibbon 1984: 220–64). The practitioners of this approach have called it processual but it has become primarily an investigation of how a given settlement pattern represents the efficiency a prehistoric society has achieved in its adjustment to its environment. While a devotion to efficiency may be central to contemporary American thought (if not to American action), I doubt that it is universal. However, commitment to kin is universal and an allegiance to tradition is, I suspect, more widespread than an emphasis on efficiency. I therefore prefer to focus on kinship and tradition when studying the behaviour of prehistoric people. Here, I will use these variables and settlement-pattern data to wring from the archaeological record a mere fraction of the information it contains on the social, economic and political life of the prehistoric farming peoples of North and South Dakota's Missouri River trough.

For Native American farmers the natural resources of the North and South Dakota stretch of the Missouri River trough required subsistence and community strategies that mediated the tension between the centripetal pull of a linear distribution of tillable soils and the centrifugal force of dispersed reserves of huntable and harvestable natural foods. The valley of the Missouri proper hosted Native American farming communities for the greater part of a millennium (Cooper 1949, 1953; Wedel 1947) but the tough sod cover, scant surface water and unpredictable rainfall restricted farming to the river's alluvial bottomlands, and farming commu-

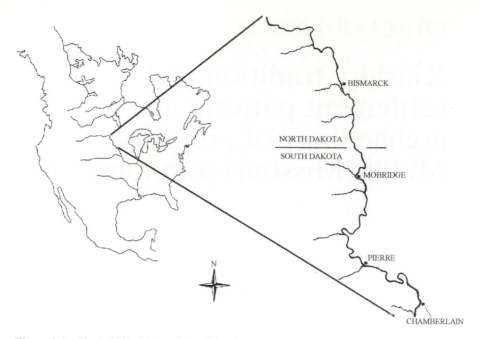

Figure 8.1   The Middle Missouri Tradition in North America.

nities to the immediately adjacent strip of terrace and plain. However, Native American farmers did utilize the full range of the region's dispersed floral and faunal resources in a mixed economy, emphasizing both hunting–harvesting and crop-growing (Krause 1972: 12–14). In other words, the region's prehistoric inhabitants struck a balance between extractive practices that treated the natural environment as an instrument of labour and those that treated it as an object of labour (Marx 1977 [1867]: 284–5).

However, the region's prehistoric farming populations did spread themselves over the same landscape in different ways at different times. These have been expressed in taxonomic terms as time and/or space-ordered variations on common developmental themes. Lehmer (1971: 25–9), for example, classified the region's archaeological remains into two Traditions, Middle Missouri (*c.* AD 1000 to AD 1675) and Coalescent (*c.* AD 1300 to AD 1850), that were divided into seven Variants: Initial, Extended and Terminal Variants of the Middle Missouri Tradition and Initial, Extended, Post-Contact and Disorganized Variants of the Coalescent Tradition. He described a Variant as:

> a unique and reasonably uniform expression of a cultural tradition which has a greater order of magnitude than a [Willey and Phillips] phase, and which is distinguished from other variants of the same tradition by its geographic distribution, age, and/or cultural content (Lehmer 1971: 32). Here, I

will restrict myself to the Initial (*c.* AD 1000 to AD 1200), Extended (*c.* AD 1200 to AD 1550) and Terminal (*c.* AD 1550 to AD 1675) Variants of the Middle Missouri Tradition and the Initial (*c.* AD 1300 to AD 1550) and Extended (*c.* AD 1550 to AD 1700) Variants of the Coalescent Tradition. The differences between and among these taxonomic units can be given organizational coherence by using the concepts of community and mode of production.

Theoretical constructs and units of analysis

By a community I mean any human aggregate composed of two sexes and a minimum of three generations whose day-to-day interaction with their natural and social environments has a knowable and discernible grammaticality – a consistency of structure that provides a modicum of predictability but is only in part determined by the content of the behaviour in and through which it is phrased. The archaeological evidence for a community should therefore consist of a set of time and space coincident artefact classes whose production and use implies, if it does not specifically require, the presence of young, adult and aged males and females. By insisting on artefact classes produced and/or used by two sexes and three generations we may assure ourselves of the basic data needed for inferring essential kin-type/kin-class and gender-mappings. Then too we may make a broad distinction between communities whose concepts of kin and gender are domestic-hearth focused and those that are not. In the case at hand, both Middle Missouri and Coalescent traditions are domestic-hearth focused. However, they are different with respect to the customary and I suppose preferred physical distance between separate domestic hearths. A juxtaposed domestic-hearth focus typifies the Middle Missouri tradition, a dispersed domestic-hearth focus typifies the Coalescent tradition. The former I argue promotes an emphasis on parent–child ties and the latter a stronger commitment to sibling ties, both of them actualized through a kin-based mode of production. By a mode of production I mean the customary way community labour and technology are organized and deployed (Wolf 1982: 73–7). A mode of production is therefore a mental blueprint that organizes the productive efforts of a community's inhabitants (see Kus 1984: 102–5). It is the blueprint for framing and answering such questions as who will decide what is to be done and when it is to be done. It is also the master plan that structures the flow of goods and services within and among communities. Buildings of varying external appearance can be drawn from the same basic blueprint by modifying room dimensions or relationships and/or by using different combinations of wood, brick, glass and paint. So, too, social architectures of differing appearance may be built from the same mode of production by modifying the kinds of goods and services produced and varying the routes and magnitudes of their distribution (McGuire 1992: 250). The mode of production, then, is an abstract analytical matrix that models social transactions and one whose elements may be systematically manipulated in the light of the available evidence. In so far as such a matrix is a springboard for making claims about human behaviour, it is useful (Krause 1989: 18).

However, it must be considered a bridge to interpretation, nothing more (McGuire 1992: 153).

In my universe of discourse, I may model the mode of production common to all communities from earliest (*c.* AD 1000) to latest (*c.* AD 1700) as kinship-based (Wolf 1982: 88–100). However, to do so will require a brief discussion of what I mean by kinship. I assume, for instance, that kinship is based on human biological and social needs. The most fundamental feature of all kinship systems, the recognition of parent–child links, depends on three biological facts: (1) human females bear few young at a time, hence an extremely high rate of infant mortality cannot be tolerated; (2) human infants are helpless for a relatively long time and therefore must be fed, sheltered and protected for an extended period; and (3) humans reach sexual maturity relatively late in their lives and thus they experience a prolonged period of biological and social dependency. In other words, children are born helpless and for a relatively long time must be nurtured and enculturated before they can assume a productive or reproductive role in the community. Differently put, humans are not biologically disposed to culturally appropriate behaviour, they must be socially programmed to do so.

However, social programming takes programmers. Some adults must be identified and committed to the task of childcare and enculturation. A universal and distinctly human means of achieving this end takes the form of presumed biological continuity (see Goodenough 1970: 3–38). Those adults presumed to share the essential relationship of biological continuity (however this may be conceptualized, symbolized and understood) with non-adults are identified as their parents by descent (see Fortes 1953). Thus relatives by descent are those persons, adult and child or adult and adult, joined by parent–child links, whether interpreted as taking matrilateral, patrilateral or bilateral form. Since the historic descendants of both Middle Missouri and Coalescent tradition peoples were matrilateral, most archaeologists have assumed a matrilateral descent idiom for the prehistoric bearers of both traditions and, I think, rightly so. I shall reserve the expression relatives by affiliation for those adults linked to children by an affinal tie to a parent by descent. Thus, we may distinguish between parents by descent and parents by affiliation. Finally, I construe full siblings as children with at least one common parent by descent. It should be obvious that a parent by descent link is primary; affiliation and sibling links are secondary. This is so because the recognition of affiliation requires the existence of a prior marriage tie, and siblingship the prior existence of a descent link.

A differential command of resources and benefits inheres in parent–child links, whether these be determined by descent or affiliation (see Radcliffe-Brown 1950: 1–85). The long period of infant care and enculturation requires that food, shelter and protection be provided through descent- or affiliation-based claims on the time and labour of adults. Such claims are reciprocal and typically result in long-term indebtedness. Adults must encumber their time and children must limit the independence of their action and borrow against their potential as unencumbered producers. In this sense all human children incur a social debt as a consequence of their biological needs (Radcliffe-Brown 1950: 27). It is through and by this form of social indebtedness that superordination/subordination relations are created and maintained and authority distributed within and sometimes among communities (see Leach 1961). Parent–child ties, for example, may be extended to form descent lines within a community (see Fewster, Chapter 11, this volume). When they are, they may be used to create and maintain an intra-community pattern of superordination/subordination that is reinforced by residential proximity and descent line interdependence in collective community enterprises. Then, too, parent–child links may be extended to tie separate communities one to another. In such cases, the extension of parent–child links, even if in large part metaphorical, carries with it the potential for an inter-community pattern of superordination/subordination, but this potential lacks the reinforcement provided by residential proximity and is subject to being further weakened by the emergence of separate and potentially conflicting community interests. Sibling ties may also be extended to reach kinsmen in collateral lines of descent both within and among communities. However, sibling ties are not as frequently marked by or as thoroughly saturated with the superordination/subordination element that permeates parent–child ties and as a consequence are potentially more egalitarian. When extended, they may be used to create a pattern of intra- and inter-community co-operation, albeit it often *ad hoc* in the sense of being historically or environmentally contingent. However, in any kinship-based mode of production, claims to the loyalty and labour of others may not exceed the extension of recognized parent–child, sibling and affiliative links. They are otherwise free to vary in response to a host of economic, social and political forces.

Since parent–child and sibling ties are universal, and since their historical descendants were so organized, there can be little doubt that ancient communities in the Middle Missouri were aggregates of consanguineal, affiliative and affinal kinsmen. That is, each community contained clusters of persons organized by virtue of interlocked parent–child and sibling ties, each related to others of similar kind by virtue of affinal links and affiliative parenthood. In sum, each community contained a network of affinal, descent and sibling ties that served as a charter for the distribution of rights and duties, privileges and obligations. Thus, through kinship, rights and duties were distributed to form an implicit labour-management system that was embedded in particular relations among people. Nevertheless, the ways such rights and duties were spread within and among clusters of relatives seems to have varied. Let me sketch the broader developmental patterning.

The Middle Missouri Tradition

A farming–hunting and harvesting economy, with concomitant ceramic, bone and stone tools, was brought to South Dakota in the twelfth century AD by bearers of the Middle Missouri Tradition (Lehmer 1954, 1971; Caldwell 1966; Caldwell & Jensen 1969). Middle Missouri Tradition peoples built side-by-side, semi-subterranean, long rectangular houses with ridge-pole supported A-framed roofs that rested on vertical timber-framed walls, both roof and walls covered with

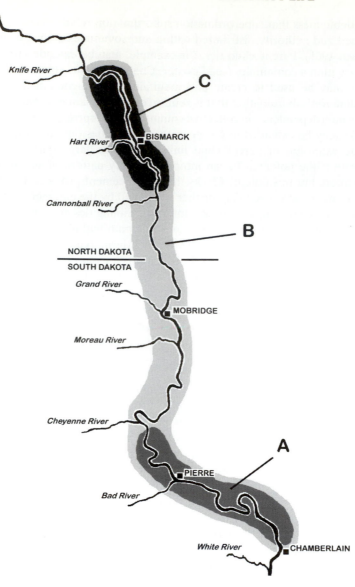

Figure 8.2   Geographic distribution of the Middle Missouri Tradition.

bundles of grass and a mantle of earth. These houses, from a dozen to 50 or more of them, were set in rows, each row facing the same direction (usually southeast) with entryways that opened on to linear lanes or pathways. The houses sat atop high L-shaped terrace spurs that overlooked the Missouri River's bottomlands and were bounded on three sides by steep ravines. The entire community was either surrounded by a palisade and/or palisade and ditch or was detached from the hinterland by a linear ditch backed with a wall of closely set upright posts (Lehmer 1971: 65–97).

The earliest Middle Missouri Tradition groups reached the Missouri River in the vicinity of Chamberlain, South Dakota. From here, the tradition was spread northward to the confluence of the Missouri and Cheyenne Rivers by agents of its Initial Variant. At least 33 Initial Variant sites have been recorded from the bluffs overlooking the Missouri River bottoms between Chamberlain and the Cheyenne River junction (Lehmer 1971: 65–97) (fig. 8.2 area A).

The social dynamics of this spread are still unclear but I suspect that population growth and dispersal linearized by both the prevailing pattern of kin relations and the distribution of defensible landscapes and farmable soils played an important role. Without bending the evidence, I may visualize the relationships among successive communities as those of parent to offspring with a weakly developed and periodically disputed pattern of superordination–subordination in inter-community relations that stimulated conflict. I say this because bearers of the Initial Variant of the Middle Missouri Tradition were the region's sole occupants (Lehmer 1971: 98). Yet the defensible locations chosen for community residences, the fortifications that accompanied them and the evidence for episodic violence among them (Lehmer 1971: 100–1) indicate a propensity for internecine warfare or at least the expectation thereof.

The Extended Variant of the Middle Missouri Tradition emerged about AD 1200 between the Moreau River and the North Dakota border and over the next 350 years spread both ideas and people to the north and south, pushing the Middle Missouri Tradition to its greatest extension (Johnson 1985: 11–14). 57 Extended Variant sites lie on the Missouri River bluffs between Chamberlain, South Dakota and the junction of the Knife with the Missouri in North Dakota (Lehmer 1971: 67) (fig. 8.2 area B). These sites were characterized by long rectangular, semi-subterranean, timber grass and dirt-covered houses in clusters of 12 to 50 or more, built side-by-side in rows with entrances opening on to lanes or pathways. Some of the smaller, northern frontier communities were unfortified but the ditches and palisades that surrounded those to the south were elaborate. They included raised bastions at each corner and along intervening sections of palisade wall, deep ditches and guarded entryways (Caldwell 1964: 2). The expansion of territory occupied by bearers of the Extended Variant was substantial but we may model its spread as follows. First, an in-migrant or frontier population was introduced that was characterized by a small unfortified or minimally fortified community. Second, population growth on the part of the parent led to the budding off of daughter communities. Third, the spatial separation of parent from offspring and the emergence of separate community interests undermined parent–offspring harmony and engendered competition. Fourth, fortifications were elaborated as a hedge against hostile forms of competition. Fifth, one or more of the competing communities were physically relocated to a different locality. Finally, this process was replicated in the new locality. Both initial and extended Middle Missouri Tradition communities may be viewed as kin-based corporations whose transgenerational corporate strength was enhanced by co-residence on the part of matrilaterally related males.

The Terminal Variant of the Middle Missouri Tradition, which spanned the years between AD 1550 and AD 1675, is marked by a dramatic contraction of area occupied, a major increase in community size, a reduction in the number of separate communities and the construction of the most extensive and elaborate of fortifications (Wood 1967; Sperry 1968). All nine Terminal Middle Missouri sites lie well north of the Grand River, in the Cannonball and Knife-Heart regions of North Dakota (fig. 8.2 area C). All are large, consisting of as many as 100 semi-subterranean, long rectangular houses built side-by-side in rows and interspersed with reasonably regular lanes or paths. Each was enclosed by deep, wide linear ditches backed with bastion-studded palisades. Lehmer (1971: 121–2) argues that these towns were composed of formerly separate communities whose inhabitants were expelled from South Dakota by an aggressive Coalescent Tradition expansion and moved northward to swell the populations of their North Dakota compatriots. In our kinship and tradition-driven model, these towns were social composites. That is to say, they were composed of formerly separate communities drawn together by the needs of defence and they now exhibited a multicorporate community structure. In Terminal Middle Missouri communities, the rows of houses were arranged about a central open space or plaza indicating, I suspect, an attempt to mediate the divisive pull of separate corporate interests through focusing the scheduling of social and ritual events on a public plaza. This much is implied by Wood's (1967) description of terminal variant or proto-Mandan cultural dynamics in which he attributes such historic Mandan integrative devices as the multiclan scheduling of ceremonialism, age-graded societies and the Okipa ceremony, to plaza-focused attempts to mediate competition between town segments. Let us now turn to a consideration of the Coalescent Tradition whose bearers are seen as responsible for these events.

The Coalescent Tradition

Middle Missouri specialists have identified the peoples of the Coalescent Tradition's Initial variant as immigrants from the Central Plains (Zimmerman 1985: 94–111). Initial Coalescent village sites were decidedly restricted in space and, with one possible exception, in time. They lay on flat, lofty terrace tops between the mouth of the White River and the Missouri/Bad River junction (fig. 8.3 area A). Most were occupied in the relatively brief interval between the fourteenth and sixteenth centuries (Lehman 1971: 111; Weakly 1971: 31). All these sites were accompanied by carefully engineered defensive perimeters composed of bastions, palisades and fortification ditches that enclosed dispersed dwellings that resembled box-like or dome-shaped mounds of earth with projecting rectangular entrance passages. The less than cohesive placement of lodges and their low average

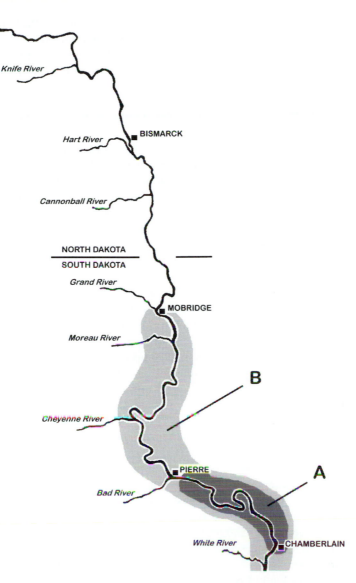

Figure 8.3 Geographic distribution of the Initial and Extended Variants of the Coalescent Tradition.

density per palisade-enclosed space (about one lodge per half hectare) may reflect the fact that each household seems to have been a separate unit of production and consumption tied to others in the community by a periodic, rather than daily, integration of separate domestic group interests. For this reason, some have argued that the fortifications were an *ad hoc* response to warfare that followed the construction of scattered households in areas of high military risk (Lehmer 1971: 125). Yet others have viewed this situation as a conscious attempt to retain the basic elements of a Central Plains community plan in a hostile social environment (Spaulding 1956: 68). Stark evidence for hostility comes from the Wolf Creek component of the Crow Creek village (Zimmerman & Whitten 1980: 100–9) where the remains of 500 slaughtered and mutilated villagers had been thrown into one end of the fortification ditch (Zimmerman 1985: 108).

Some Initial Coalescent populations in the Big Bend country occupied fortified settlements into the third, fourth and perhaps the fifth decades of the sixteenth century AD. However, others, identified as members of the Extended Variant of the Coalescent Tradition, began to disperse, in the process building unfortified settlements composed of small clusters or strings of earthlodges scattered along the river terraces and floodplains. At a slightly later date (perhaps the later years of the sixteenth century AD), related groups were building villages along the Missouri River as far north as the Grand River junction (Hoffman 1967: 63) and as far south as Lake Andes near the Nebraska/South Dakota border (Hurt 1952: 12) (fig. 8.3 area B). Like their Big Bend counterparts, these Extended Coalescent villages were straggling affairs with clusters of earthlodges scattered along the river's terraces. Lehmer (1971: 116) and others identified the Extended Variant community pattern as a reversion to the dispersed design of Central Plains folk. Nevertheless, this community plan was acted upon and 'linearized' by the centrifugal tug of the region's strip of farmable bottomland soils. There are, for instance, over 1000 recorded sites with a nearly continuous distribution within the 792 km of river bottom between the North Dakota/South Dakota border and the Niobrara River at the Nebraska line (Lehmer 1971: 115). Many of these sites are small and consist of a dozen or fewer lodge ruins. Those excavated carry a very thin mantle of debris (Wedel 1961: 185). Lehmer (1971: 116) observed that 'this implies that they were occupied for only short periods of time and that the Extended Coalescent population was generally a rather mobile one'. The Extended Variant people spread beyond the confines of the Missouri River trough. Extended Coalescent pottery has been reported from the Black Hills (Wedel 1947), the Angostura Reservoir (Wheeler 1957) and the White River Badlands (Hannus et al. 1984). In Montana, Extended Coalescent pottery has been collected from the Nollmeyer site (Krause 1995: 19–44) and from the Horse Butte Site (Ann Johnson, pers. comm. 1988). This kind of population spread and mobility fits the Central Plains Tradition model and, from the perspective being developed here, implies a weak transgenerational sense of corporateness on the part of non-co-resident matrilaterally related males.

Earlier generations of plains prehistorians tended to idealize the Extended Coalescent earthlodge by describing it as circular with a centrally located hearth, a superstructure composed of four beam-supporting central roof-support posts, a circular series of beam-supporting roof/wall posts, and a rectangular entryway frame. Yet, the floor plans of excavated lodge ruins indicate peripheral post arrangements approximating circles, rectanguloid shapes, rough ovals and lop-sided ovals (Lehmer 1971: 115). Some lodges may have had funnel-like entryways extending inward from the peripheral post line (Hoffman 1968: 6). The firepit is often not centered *vis-à-vis* the peripheral posts and the primary central supports are frequently difficult to define, leading some to speculate on a two-post alterna-tive for roof support (Hoffman 1968: 15). Lehmer (1971: 115) has suggested that 'some Extended Coalescent houses may have had teepee-like pole superstruc-tures'. In sum, Extended Coalescent houses seem to be a gesture to the ideal, far less regular in floor plan than both their Middle Missouri tradition counterparts and their Initial Coalescent predecessors, leading some to view them as *ad hoc* accommodations to a mobile lifestyle. In terms of our kin-driven model, they may be seen as reflecting the weakened transgenerational transfer of information that accompanied the residential spread of subsequent generations.

Extended Coalescent communities in the Big Bend country were not fortified, but along the frontiers to the north and south, fortifications appeared early in the span of settlement. With several exceptions, the fortified strong-points along the northern and southern frontier did not match the sophistication and complex-ity of their Initial Coalescent and Middle Missouri Tradition prototypes. The fortified areas were smaller and bastions, when constructed, were not set to pro-vide an enfilade. In the southernmost Extended Coalescent site, Scalp Creek, no bastions were found but the site contained an enclosing ditch and oval palisade. The Extended Coalescent fortifications along the northern frontier (with the ex-ception of those at the Payne and Davis sites) may have been no more than rallying points or redoubts for the peoples from surrounding farming hamlets (Caldwell 1964: 3).

In short, an explosive expansion of area occupied and the spreading out of local populations typified the Extended Variant of the Coalescent Tradition. The overall developmental patterning may be summarized as follows: (1) a Big Bend heartland characterized by dispersed unfortified settlements that, through popula-tion growth, provided the impetus for a northward, southward and westward expansion of area used and/or occupied; (2) fortified communities along both the northern and southern frontiers of occupation, with fortified villages emerging early in the south and a mixed pattern of redoubts and fortified villages character-izing the pattern of settlement in the north; and (3) a later lapse of fortifications along the southern but not the northern frontier. At this point, I think we must presume that the differences I have noted are kin and tradition-governed and are related to prior experience in different heartlands.

Coalescent Tradition antecedents

The Central Plains groups that migrated to South Dakota's Big Bend country were a product of earlier population shifts related to the advent of agriculture and the environmental and social pressures that accompanied a modification of the region's climate. The earliest Central Plains farmers, identified taxonomically as bearers of the Central Plains tradition, developed communities that reflect a reasonably sedentary lifestyle adjusted to the seasonal rhythm defined by integrating the needs of hunting and harvesting with those of maize, bean and squash agriculture. These communities consisted of isolated farmsteads and/or two to four house hamlets spread over the hills, terraces and bluffs that bordered the region's watercourses (Wedel 1986: 96–105). The dwellings in each were rectanguloid timber, grass, mud-plaster and dirt-covered structures. Most contain the detritus expected of formative stage, household-focused domestic life (Krause 1995: 312). Wood (1969: 105) has described Central Plains Tradition communities as 'neighborhoods composed of semi-independent homesteads or homestead aggregates'.

Elsewhere I have argued that as Central Plains Tradition communities grew and spread, parent households fissioned along generational lines as newly formed family units removed themselves from the parent hamlet or homestead to new and in most cases neighbourhood-peripheral locations (Krause 1982: 81). As they did so, the social, political and economic import of inter-generational kin links was undermined by the physical distance between parents and offspring but intra-generational kin links were strengthened through a socially and ritually intensified focus on the neighbourhood-wide exchange of ideas, food and other items. In other words, I suspect that the superordination–subordination relations inhering in parent–child links was substantially weakened by physical separation, while the more egalitarian relations inhering in affinal and sibling links may have been strengthened by periodic exchanges of goods and services. According to Baerreis & Bryson (1965), at about AD 1250 a favourable Neo-Atlantic period of abundant summer rainfall was interrupted by an abrupt change in atmospheric circulation, the introduction of greater amounts of cool, dry air, lowered temperatures and decreased precipitation. This climatic change seems to have intensified the budding-off process and stimulated the physical spread of Central Plains Tradition farming populations. Exchanges of food and other items that once promoted social solidarity within a hamlet and homestead neighbourhood now seem to have lapsed into a generalized inter-neighbourhood trade that protected its participants from the effects of local drought. The benefits of this strategy might assure its persistence. Blakeslee (1978: 139–43) sees this 'generalized' trade in foodstuffs, ideas, raw material and manufactured goods as instrumental in the 'mixing and sorting' of ideas and practices that created the Coalescent Tradition. I have argued that several centuries of modified climatic conditions stimulated several changes as follows: (1) an abandonment of farming communities in the western reaches of Kansas and Nebraska; (2) a southwest to northeast shift in the centre of population density in the middle reaches of Kansas and Nebraska; (3) a northward shift in the centre of population density along the eastern margin of the Great Plains; and (4) the Initial Coalescent intrusion into South Dakota's Big Bend country (Krause 1985: 27). Hence, it may be that those communities that represent the Coalescent Tradition's Initial Variant may have brought with them a social architecture that facilitated the geographic spread of households and household clusters.

Middle Missouri Tradition antecedents

The Middle Missouri Tradition heartland lay in southern Minnesota and north-western Iowa, a transition zone between the eastern Woodlands and the Plains proper. This area contained prairie grassland with wooded stream valleys near the eastern limit and it also lay within the range of plains bison herds (Lehmer 1971: 98–100). The most commonly accepted ancestors for the Initial Variant of the Middle Missouri Tradition are the Mill Creek villages along Iowa's Big and Little Sioux Rivers (Toom 1992: 125). Although the dynamics of Mill Creek community growth are not well understood, it is clear that concentrated populations built side-by-side timber-framed rectangular houses covered with grass and dirt. Anderson (1987: 529–31) has argued for an early pattern of large base settlements that lasted 100 years or more and that spawned and were surrounded by smaller and less permanent (30 years) 'budded-off' villages. He maintains that this early pattern was followed by an environmental stress-induced reconsolidation of budded with base villages and the emergence of elaborate fortifications that included dry moats, ramparts and palisades. Anderson attributes the complex defensive works to Oneota military pressure from the east and posits a concomitant emergence of Mill Creek war chiefs and military societies. Bozell and Ludwickson (1994: 147–8) argue for a coincident pattern of Mill Creek hostility to the west, asserting that:

> There appears to have been a profound cultural boundary at the Missouri River. There is very little evidence of 'friendly' contacts [between the Mill Creek inhabitants of western Iowa and Nebraska Phase representatives of the Central Plains Tradition in eastern Nebraska] in the form of cross-finds of pottery, etc. The Nebraska phase contraction along a 'front' opposing contemporary Mill Creek people in northwest Iowa, was synchronous with the retraction and aggregation of Mill Creek peoples into fortified villages.

They further maintain that interaction between Mill Creek and late Nebraska phase would have been hostile. It therefore seems reasonably clear that a commitment to warfare and a community pattern emphasizing parent–child links and the superordination–subordination relations that inhere therein has an ample precedent in the Mill Creek villages most likely to have been ancestral to South Dakota's Initial Middle Missouri Tradition communities.

Discussion

If the patterning I have outlined here is tenable, Middle Missouri archaeology presents a good dataset for assessing the conditions under which different social architectures accompanied the same mode of production. Both Middle Missouri and Coalescent Tradition peoples were immigrants and we may presume that both brought with them a body of knowledge and set of social practices shaped by prior experience. This prior experience is evident as follows. Both traditions were exposed to the 'linearizing' environmental effects of occupying the Missouri River trough and both responded by episodes of rapid population spread (the Extended Variants). They both utilized the region's natural resources as objects of labour and instruments of labour. Both responded to conflict or the threat thereof by constructing fortifications. Yet one, the bearers of the Middle Missouri Tradition, maintained a tenacious hold on the community design they first brought to the region. These settlements are typified by the geographic concentration of related households and a developmental patterning in which parent communities produced offspring that replicated their progenitors. This may be seen in a metaphorical sense as a sort of parent–child link-based vertical linearization or a transgenerational replication of uniformity. For the other population, the bearers of the Coalescent Tradition, a geographic concentration of related households was an *ad hoc* solution to special problems as a temporary solution. As soon as possible, Coalescent Tradition folk adopted a community plan typified by the geographic dispersal of households. In a metaphorical sense, these communities followed a sort of sibling link-based horizontal linearization or an intragenerational space-expansive organization of diversity.

Conclusion

In sum, I see the web of kinship as an infrastructure in which human ambition, individual initiative and a host of other forces, both external and internal, may shape into a mode of production. What is more, in Middle Missouri prehistory, different social architectures accompanied the same mode of production in the same natural environment and among peoples whose technologies were virtually identical. To achieve a more adequate understanding of this pattern, we must focus on the Middle Missouri and Coalescent Traditions as meaning-directed and socially negotiated sets of kin-based beliefs and practices rather than tool and efficiency determined bodies of information. Many of my colleagues will disagree. Nevertheless, if my efforts stimulate them to seek alternative and credible means to the same end, I shall have achieved worthwhile results.

References

Anderson, D. 1987. Toward a processual understanding of the Initial Variant of the Middle Missouri Tradition: the case of the Mill Creek Culture of Iowa. *American Antiquity* **52**(3), 522–37.

Baerreis, D. & R. Bryson 1965. Climatic episodes and the dating of the Mississippian Culture. *Wisconsin Archaeologist* **46**(4), 203–20.

Blakeslee, D. 1978. Assessing the Central Plains Tradition in eastern Nebraska: content and outcome. In *The Central Plains Tradition: internal development and external relationships*, D. Blakeslee (ed.), 134–43. Iowa City: University of Iowa Press.

Bozell, J. & J. Ludwickson 1994. *Nebraska Phase archeology in the South Bend locality*. Lincoln: Nebraska State Historical Society.

Caldwell, W. 1964. Fortified villages in the northern Plains. *Plains Anthropologist* **9**(23), 1–7.

Caldwell, W. 1966. The Middle Missouri Tradition reappraised. *Plains Anthropologist* **11**(32), 152–7.

Caldwell, W. & R. Jensen 1969. *The Grand Detour Phase*. Smithsonian Institution River Basin Surveys, Publications in Salvage Archeology 13.

Cooper, P. 1949. Recent investigations in Fort Randall and Oahe reservoirs, South Dakota. *American Antiquity* **4**(1), 300–10.

Cooper, P. 1953. *Appraisal of the archeological resources of Oahe reservoir, North and South Dakota*. Smithsonian Institution, Missouri Basin Project.

Fortes, M. 1953. The structure of unilineal descent groups. *American Anthropologist* **55**, 17–41.

Gibbon, G. 1984. *Anthropological archaeology*. New York: Columbia University Press.

Goodenough, W. 1970. *Description and comparison in cultural anthropology*. Chicago: Aldine.

Hannus, L., T. Nowak, J. Butterbroat, E. Leuck, R. Winham 1984. *1981 and 1982 survey and testing at the White Horse Creek Quarry, 39SH37, White River Badlands Regional Research Project*, vol. 2. Archaeological Laboratory, Center for Western Studies, Augustana College.

Hoffman, J. J. 1967. *Molstad village*. Smithsonian Institution River Basin Surveys, Publications in Salvage Archeology 4.

Hoffman, J. 1968. *The La Roche site*. Smithsonian Institution River Basin Surveys, Publications in Salvage Archeology 11.

Hurt, W. 1952. *Report of the investigation of the Scalp Creek site, 39GR1, and Ellis Creek site, 39GR2, Gregory County, South Dakota, 1941, 1951*. Pierre: South Dakota Archaeological Commission, Archaeological Studies, Circular 5.

Johnson A. 1985 Extended Middle Missouri sites in the Grand-Moreau region, South Dakota. *South Dakota Archaeology* **8/9**, 11–39.

Krause, R. 1972. *The Leavenworth site: archaeology of an historic Arikara community*. Publications in Anthropology 3, University of Kansas.

Krause, R. 1982. The Central Plains Tradition revisited. *Plains Anthropologist* **27**(95), 75–82.

Krause, R. 1985. Trend and trajectory in American archaeology: some questions about the Mississippian Period in southeastern prehistory. In *Alabama and the Borderlands: from prehistory to statehood*, R. R. Badger & L. A. Clayton (eds), 17–39. Tuscaloosa: University of Alabama Press.

Krause, R. 1989. The Archaic Stage and the emergence of Hopewellian ceremonialism in the southeastern United States. *Mississippi Archaeology* **24**(1), 17–34.

Krause, R. 1995. Attributes, modes, and tenth-century potting in north central Kansas. *Plains Anthropologist* **40**(154), 307–52.

Kus, S. 1984. The spirit and its burden: archaeology and symbolic activity. In *Marxist perspectives in archaeology*, M. Spriggs (ed.), 101–7. Cambridge: Cambridge University Press.

Leach, E. 1961. *Rethinking anthropology*. Monographs on Social Anthropology 22, London School of Economics.

Lehmer, D. 1954. *Archeological investigations in the Oahe Dam area, South Dakota, 1950–51*. Smithsonian Institution, Bureau of American Ethnology Bulletin 158/River Basin Surveys Papers 7.

Lehmer, D. 1971. *Introduction to Middle Missouri archeology*. Anthropological Papers 1, National Park Service.

Marx, K. 1977 [1867] *Capital: a critique of political economy*, vol. 1. Marx Library, New York: Vintage–Random House.

McGuire, R. 1992. *A Marxist archaeology*. San Diego: Academic Press.

Radcliffe-Brown, A. 1950. Introduction. In *African systems of kinship and marriage*, A. Radcliffe-Brown & D. Forde (eds), 1–85. London: Oxford University Press.

Spaulding A. 1956. *The Arzberger site, Hughes County, South Dakota*. Ann Arbor: Occasional Contributions from the Museum of Anthropology, University of Michigan.

Sperry, J. 1968. *The Shermer site (32EM10)*. Plains Anthropologist Memoir 5.

Toom, D. 1992. Radiocarbon dating of the western Initial Middle Missouri Variant: some new dates and a critical review of old dates. *Plains Anthropologist* **37**(139), 115–28.

Vogt, E. 1956. An appraisal of prehistoric settlement patterns in the New World. *Viking Fund Publications in Anthropology* **23**, 173–82.

Weakly, W. 1971. *Tree ring dating and archaeology in South Dakota*. Plains Anthropologist Memoir 8.

Wedel, W. 1947. Prehistory and environment in the Central Great Plains. *Transactions of the Kansas Academy of Sciences* **50**(1), 1–18.

Wedel, W. 1961. *Prehistoric man on the Great Plains*. Norman: University of Oklahoma Press.

Wedel, W. 1986. *Central Plains prehistory: holocene environments and culture change in the Republican River Basin*. Lincoln: University of Nebraska Press.

Wheeler, R. 1957. *Archeological remains in three reservoir areas in South Dakota and Wyoming*. Lincoln: report on file, National Park Service, Midwest Archeological Center.

Wolf, E. 1982. *Europe and the people without history*. Berkeley: University of California Press.

Wood, W. 1967. *An interpretation of Mandan Culture history*. Smithsonian Institution, Bureau of American Ethnology Bulletin 198/River Basin Surveys Papers 39.

Wood, W. 1969. *Two house sites in the Central Plains: an experiment in archaeology*. Plains Anthropologist Memoir 6.

Zimmerman, L. 1985. *Peoples of prehistoric South Dakota*. Lincoln: University of Nebraska Press.

Zimmerman, L. & R. Whitten 1980. Prehistoric bones tell a grim tale of Indian v. Indian. *Smithsonian* **11**(6), 100–9.

CHAPTER NINE

Temporalities of prehistoric life: household development and community continuity

Melissa Goodman

Introduction

In prehistoric contexts, structural remains often appear less ambiguous than the social relations that formed them. However, architectural forms are dictated by the social conventions and practical needs of their occupants and cannot be effectively treated as spatial, rather than social, relations. Many attempts to investigate household space have presented domestic behaviour in universal terms (e.g. Kent 1990b,c; Rappaport 1990). This approach is vulnerable to much of the critique that has been aimed at processual archaeology on the basis that generalization effectively denies cultural variability (e.g. Bawden 1990; Lawrence 1990). Certainly in contemporary and historical studies the household has been shown to be highly variable (e.g. Netting at al. 1984; Blanton 1993; see also Brück & Goodman, Chapter 1 and Price, Chapter 3, this volume). Tringham (1991) offers an alternative approach to the study of prehistoric households which allows for this variability to be considered. Her concern is that generalized approaches to households propagate genderless, faceless interpretations of prehistory. To address this she proposes that the social relations of households should be reflected in how houses were used because they form an important context where those relations were played out. In this way, houses can be seen to have a use-life related to the developmental cycle of the domestic group inhabiting it. This view of the households allows structural remains to be seen as participating in and reflecting the lives of prehistoric people.

Taking up Tringham's approach, this paper focuses on the household over the short-term at the scale of a human lifetime and asks how households change as their members change. An additional consideration is the manner in which these changes are co-ordinated within communities over the long-term, through the maintenance of common ways of creating and using domestic space over many lifetimes. In other words, viewing households over the short-term can help create a humanized view of prehistoric societies only if we are able to integrate this scale

145

of understanding into the longer-terms patterns we recover. This involves proposing mechanisms of transmission which link households and transcend the lives of individual community members. Examples from Andean ethnography and archaeology are used heuristically to indicate how this approach might be applied.

Before entering into this discussion, a few terminological considerations should be made. In this paper, the convenient if awkward term 'dwelling' will be used for the structural remains of residences both to escape the connotations of the more laden 'house' (see Brück & Goodman, Chapter 1, this volume; also Hodder 1990; Johnson 1990) and because it allows for variations in residential units by size, complexity and number of buildings. However, the more familiar term 'household' will be used in this chapter to emphasize that structurally defined units appear to signify indigenous social units regardless of their particular form (for the Andes see Stanish 1992: 18–23). It also reinforces the view that patterns in architecture exist through the co-ordination of human efforts through time. Households will be taken to encompass the combination of dwellings and their residents. This definition attempts to include human relations and spatial attributes without creating a focus on the details of either membership or domestic practices, which are contentious issues (for discussion see Brück & Goodman, Chapter 1, Price, Chapter 3, Brück, Chapter 4, this volume).

Prehistorian, prehistoric life, the ancestors

Individuals are usually absent from the archaeological record, and with them the details of how they changed and developed over the course of their lives. For this reason, archaeologists generally assume that limitations to the resolution of the data prevent us from accessing many aspects of prehistoric social relations. I should like to start by suggesting that this lack of resolution is also partially conceptual, arising from the relationship between prehistorian and the prehistoric people we study.

Without biographical information, prehistoric people are situated into a category which does not require individual identity and become *beings*, Tringham's 'faceless blobs'. It may not be too far-fetched to suggest that this ambiguous category resembles our own idea of 'the ancestors'. Here a distinction should be made between *our* ancestors, known from the genealogical tracking of named people with real biographies, and *the* ancestors who are viewed as a faceless collective. This may help explain the observation that archaeologists tend to view the past as genderless (e.g. Gero & Conkey 1991) and mainly adult (Safaer 1994).

One quality of 'the ancestors' is that they live on as symbols long after they have died, but in our perception of them they are also removed from their biological existences. Although as archaeologists we may encounter the remains of individuals, we mythologize their identities into a collective (the ancestors, the dead) and do not require reference to their actual births, experiences and deaths in order to talk about them. An advantage of subsuming prehistoric people into a static category is that we are removed from their mortality. However, it also releases archaeologists from a responsibility to relate the lives of prehistoric people to the realities of living. This is not to say that we forget that they had subsistence needs, but that these activities take on an automatic quality removed from an active context where perceptions change as individuals mature and decisions must be made.

It may not be surprising that we tend to mythologize people from the deep past when we consider that many non-literate societies act in a similar manner. In the familiar example of the Nuer, Evans-Pritchard (1940) explicitly addresses this process, 'Beyond the limits of historical time we enter a plane of tradition in which a certain element of historical fact may be . . . incorporated in a complex of myth' (ibid.: 107). This process is articulated in genealogical constructions by truncating actual genealogies to fit a fairly constant number of remembered ancestors be-tween historical individuals and mythical ancestors. This parallels the differences between *the* ancestors (mythical) and *our* ancestors (historical). As literate re-searchers we can access longer lists of named individuals. Nevertheless, this only defers the same process of mythologization to people beyond written records, the prehistoric folk.

A second problem with the separation in time between prehistorian and prehis-toric people is that we enjoy the perspective of seeing their lives encapsulated in a past that is somehow finished. This disengages people in prehistory from par-ticipation in changing presents, their own pasts and also futures. This argument is familiar from postprocessual critiques of the tendency to portray the past in static systemic models, which results in undervaluing the dynamic processes of change. It is also an implicit critique of depersonalizing the past because, if we follow cognitive psychologists, human beings *always* situate themselves in a pro-gressive present where events pass through a cycle from future potentiality to present experience to past reality (the temporal–perceptual cycle; see Gell 1992: 229–41).

At a certain point when things are too deep into the past, we fail to differentiate them, as with the divide between myth and history described above. If this lack of resolution is at work in prehistoric archaeology, no manner of improvement in recovery techniques will produce enough data to effectively 'fill the gap'. Data resolution is not the issue. The problem lies in the perception of the deep past as removed from us and no longer participating in the temporal–perceptual cycle. In effectively, if not explicitly, denying that past events were embedded in a living context, we encourage a static view not only because we mythologize past people but also because we fix their actions in a sequence of events which ignores that they came about amidst any number of other possible outcomes. This leads to the concern that since we are looking 'behind' us into the past we know the results of actions that may have been unknown to their agents which reinforces a tendency to see past action as necessarily giving rise to the consequences we identify (see Kovacik, Chapter 10, this volume). In effect, this removes prehistoric people from a role in decision-making.

These observations may help to clarify why discussions of time in archaeology have tended to favour the long-term which is seen as more suitable to the data (e.g.

Bailey 1982, 1987; Hodder 1987; Barrett et al. 1991; Barrett 1994). I suggest that for the study of households, explanation of long-term patterns must be understood within the context of processes at the level of human experience, otherwise we fail to address the mechanisms by which these patterns were created. This requires a closer look at both the diachronic processes of individual households and how individual households are linked within a community. The former will be discussed first in terms of household development.

The household developmental cycle

Although household development cycle models have been applied to archaeological contexts (e.g. Tourtellot 1988; Tringham 1984, cf.1991) there remain aspects of these models which have yet to be explored. A review of Fortes' (1958) seminal paper on the development of households over time provides an introduction to this theme. Limitations to this idealized model are then explored through anthropological critiques and ethnographic examples.

Fortes (1958) suggests that household development can be compared to the organic model of a lifetime in that change occurs in phases related to changes in the composition of the domestic group. The major changes he envisages include marriage, the birth of children, fission as mature offspring establish their own residences and the subsequent shrinking of the parental household as members leave and die. This reflects the fact that managing human ageing is one of the few universals in social life. As the household is a major locus of human activity, the impact of these changes are particularly relevant to households.

Fortes' model would lead us to expect synchronic variation between households across a cultural horizon reflected in dwellings at different stages of household development. Thus material differences between households can be expected regardless of household form (e.g. nuclear, stem, multiple family). Fortes distinguishes between a 'type' which is a static category and a 'phase' which refers to a distinctive period within the 'life-cycle' of a household. In archaeology, a type may be related to household forms and describe behavioural patterning in terms of architecture and features. In contrast, a household phase is primarily used where rebuilding can be demonstrated. However, although rebuilding phases are chronologically ordered, in archaeology they are not generally addressed in terms of change internal to the household as this model would imply.

Yanagisako (1979) has cautioned that households can mediate the impacts of household development through various strategies of household organization and thus obscure phases. She suggests that it may be better to assess the diversity between domestic units and their articulation rather than look for typologies. Variability between houses may represent important structuring principles related to household development but this can vary from site to site within a cultural horizon or within a single site between subgroups (i.e. as an expression of class). In archaeology this would encourage a careful assessment of synchronic variation across a site or cultural horizon before addressing diachronic change. This helps to ascertain the degree to which variation between households is a cultural norm and allows for the closer resolution of actual change through time.

Andean household development strategies

The developmental model represents a highly simplified vision of how households change. Additional considerations arise through closer examination of these processes in an actual community. This is shown through ethnographic examples from the Andes.[1] As real communities reflect various degrees of conformity to cultural ideals, the domestic cycle is far from homogeneous across the Andes and it must be stressed that the following summary is itself an idealized presentation of these processes (for greater discussion see Bolton & Mayer 1977). Andean dwellings vary in form but generally take the shape of compounds of structures which face into a patio. Many domestic activities such as grinding grain may take place either inside the structures or in the patio space. An economic strategy of direct access to land resources in different ecological zones, 'verticality', leads many Andean households to maintain dwellings of various types across a landscape such as small temporary huts in distant fields or permanent structures with seasonal use. Thus the contents of a single dwelling need not represent the whole of the household's resources nor are the activities of a household group necessarily coterminous with a single dwelling.

The formation of a new couple starts the Andean household cycle. Marriage may be seen as more a process than an event and can encompass several stages. A new couple usually takes up temporary residence with one member's parents before establishing an independent household and claiming inheritance (Lambert 1977: 8–12). This temporary stage is of variable length and may terminate before marriage. In some regions married couples may reside in the parental residence even after children are born (Weismantel 1989). These couples may start their own storage and hearth areas within the parental compound while still sharing meals with the parental group. This has obvious implications for the presence of such features as dual hearths in archaeological dwellings. When new couples establish their own households, residence is generally neolocal except for the child who inherits the parental compound. Even after establishing their own residence, the younger couple may exchange food with the parent household for an extended period. This suggests that the phases Fortes describes may appear rather ambiguous in the archaeological record. For example, different rooms within a dwelling take on different roles throughout their use-lives. This may be the case of a store room becoming a dormitory as children mature or the abandonment of a second hearth as the parental household divides. A shift of ownership of a dwelling from members of one generation to the next may result in the conservation or change of previous use patterns and can be quite difficult to ascertain in the archaeological record.

This idealized developmental cycle has focused on modern accounts from the Andes where marriage is exclusive. However, at the time of the Spanish conquest, it appears that polygamy was not uncommon among regional elites (Murra 1980: 93). Less affluent farmers may also have been polygamous as the earliest Spanish census documents include references to households in which two or more women have children by the same man (Mayer 1981). This practice was actively forbidden by Catholic missionaries and indigenous practices were quickly adapted to satisfy Spanish authorities (ibid.). Clearly the modern household development cycle outlined above would have been complicated by the inclusion of additional marriage partners. The paucity of references to this strategy in the archaeological literature may indicate the continuation of a bias against this household form. But the presence of such features as dual hearths in archaeological contexts may also have arisen from such polygamous households.

The variable time length of food-sharing between households of different generations demonstrates one way that households are linked within a community. There are a number of other Andean practices which effectively blur the boundaries between households. For example, the multiple marriage of siblings to the same family group allows for a subsequent sharing of household labour between siblings and the co-ordination of agricultural activities on family-held lands (Skar 1984). Distant kin and fictive kin also impact Andean household development patterns as illustrated through the example of the exchange of children and godparenting. Children born to a young couple while still residing in the parental dwelling may remain with the grandparents when the biological parents move house. These children are raised as their grandparents' children but still have a link with their biological parents. Andean godparenting also binds households both privately and in civic ritual obligations (e.g. Skar 1982: 198–205; Allen 1988: 87–91). Godparents enter into the households of their godchildren through financial contributions and by extending both households' social networks. The bond between the households of parents and their children's godparents is maintained through dense networks of labour exchange (see below). The intensity of these bonds takes on the role of fictive kin. Some elements of fictive kin may be precolumbian (Murra 1980).

These observations on Andean household patterns suggest that the boundaries between households are far from distinct and that the relationships between them change over time. Although the details of these processes may not be readily available in the archaeological record, the implications of this variability must be considered if we are attempting to 'read' the material patterns resulting from them. These observations complicate the use of household contents as indicators of wealth (e.g. Smith 1987) because we do not know to what degree variation between households is due to different stages of household development or, conversely, if observed differences are partially offset by the sharing of resources between households.

Households in communities

The links between households may also be seen in terms of the tension between the inward focus of domestic groups and the outward focus of the society as a whole (Fortes 1958). Within communities, the desires of individual households are constrained by the politico–jural power of the greater social group. The degree of household independence varies between societies and may be reflected in the degree of conformity in dwelling form and use. Although Hodder (1990) has discussed this tension in relation to prehistoric Europe, the subtlety of the relationship between independent household and community is not generally acknowledged. Archaeological models of households rarely suggest how they articulate together within the political organization of societies. This is curious because house form has been tied to cultural identity in archaeology for many years (e.g. Childe 1929).

For house form to be an essential expression of cultural identity, households within a community must share a common ideology which informs the construction of specific dwelling forms and the use of space within them. Although the degree to which a community adheres to a specific 'blueprint' may vary between societies or over time (Krause, Chapter 8, this volume), the fact that such patterns can be identified indicates that a supra-household form of transmission must exist. In other words, for such patterns to be maintained over time the common knowledge of a community must be expressed in ways that serve to link household groups through consensual cultural behaviour. By approaching transmission in this way, the long-term is broken down into acts that are repeated not only within individual households but also in the 'social space' between them. Again, an example from the Andes can provide more details to suggest how this can influence archaeological interpretation.

Supra-household alliances: the ayllu

The foregoing discussion suggests mechanisms by which households are enmeshed in larger social networks that connect them socially and economically. This focus will now be developed in relation to the institution of the *ayllu* in the Andes. The *ayllu* may be seen as the next level of social organization above the household and has no direct parallel in Western society.[2] I focus on this institution here because *ayllu* social organization illustrates a mechanism by which the activities of individual households are joined and co-ordinated over time. Although other societies may link households in less structured and formal ways, the *ayllu* is suggestive of the kind of supra-household social structures available to communities.

Much of what is known about the *ayllu* is composite, being drawn from modern community practices and ethno-historical documents. This general discussion of the *ayllu* highlights aspects of social organization related to household studies and is far from a complete description (for further discussion see Castro Pozo 1946; Alberti & Mayer 1974; Isbell 1978; Murra 1980; Mayer 1981; Skar 1982; Allen 1988). *Ayllu* members include immediate family, distant relatives, godparents, neighbours, friends and strategic allies. Within this network there are inevitably closer partnerships, such as between siblings, and relationships of obligation or duty. *Ayllu* membership is formal and situates individuals and households within a network of reciprocal obligations to group members.

It can be argued that *ayllu*s mediate two contrasting tendencies: reciprocity and social hierarchy. Andean reciprocity is an ideal that is expressed directly through labour organization (Alberti & Mayer 1974). Household and *ayllu* interact in complex systems of labour exchange. Without attempting an exhaustive discussion, indigenous Andean forms of labour exchange fall into several distinct categories. A division seems to be maintained between craft activities, which are carried out primarily by the household, and food production and construction activities (Sillar 1994). The latter activities are carried out in labour parties of *ayllu* members and careful note is made of who participates as this creates reciprocal obligations between households (Isbell 1978: 167–77). Labour exchange may be classified according to the degree of trust between the participants and their relative social positions. Labour exchange may be reciprocal, asymmetrical for food or goods, as communal dues or as tribute to elites and the state (Isbell 1978: 167–77; Skar 1982: 212–19; Stanish 1992: 24–5; Hastorf 1993: 52; Gose 1994: Ch. 1). Manipulation of reciprocal labour allows for differential access to resources by individual households. Thus although this system may be seen as equalizing, it is not egalitarian.

The communal aspects of the *ayllu* may be contrasted to the hierarchy and inequality that mark *ayllu* social organization (Isbell 1978). This tension is one of the aspects of the *ayllu* that serve to maintain its existence through time as the Inka, Colonial and Republican states have used *ayllu* networks as intermediaries of state power (Mayer 1981, D'Altroy 1987). The *ayllu* leadership allocates access to lands and water and also plays a central roles in local rituals. Political organization of *ayllu*s is complex and variable, but for the present discussion it is pertinent that obtaining formal positions within the community involves the resources of an entire household and their labour-exchange network, usually in the form of hosting feasts (Isbell 1978; Skar 1982; Allen 1988; Gose 1994). Participation in the *ayllu* heirarchy therefore relies on the ability of a household to draw on the resources and labour of other households. Thus the *ayllu* structure links households together economically and mediates their participation in higher levels of social organization such as the state.

For the purposes of this discussion, it is important that the sharing of labour between households is such that individuals may carry out activities related to the production and preparation of food in more than one household. Thus the independent status of households becomes problematic. Although the *ayllu* may be fairly unique to the Andes, it does illustrate how the activities of households may be co-ordinated within a community over time. This linking of households allows for the sharing of information on community ideals, such as the use of dwelling space, which may result in conformities of behaviour such as dwelling form.

The foregoing indicates that in order to address social practice at the household level, we must be able to theoretically tackle how these practices are co-ordinated within communities. This effectively limits the range of approaches available and may appear to renew a Durkheimian (e.g. 1915:7) emphasis on the collective nature of cognition as critiqued by Bloch (1977). However, I do not want to propose that this level of analysis reflects the human condition. It simply appears to strike a good balance in the interpretation of the archaeological record in terms of household practices. I now turn to examples of how these concerns might be applied to archaeology and propose an approach that allows household processes to unfold 'in their own time'.

Households in temporal perspective

As the presence of domestic traditions must involve transmission from generation to generation, these transgenerational processes reflect the temporal scale of the human experience (Fortes 1958; Bender 1967; Yanagisako 1979; Wilk & Rathje 1982). By focusing on the human life-cycle a link is created between universal conditions (e.g. the need for social reproduction) and the sociohistorical strategies of specific groups addressing these conditions. Thus I am not only concerned with what has been called 'living space' but also with 'living time'.

We call on social processes spanning generations when addressing such events as the periodicity of house-building and the ideology that governs their use. The living experience we recover is not that of the individual but of collectivities and the temporal structure of change relates to the human ageing process. This may be called 'generational time' where the focus is on the social network extant for households. This reflects the recognition that households are embedded in a web of cultural norms that specify such things as the use of domestic space and how they cope with changes as their members age. These patterns exist where we can see a particular construction and maintenance of dwellings reiterated across a cultural horizon. This implies a commitment to the reproduction of social ideals that function beyond any single individual's lifetime.

A focus on the social processes operating in the short-term helps to break up the chronologies we generate from artefacts used as markers for absolute or relative dating schemes which usually span centuries. Although we still cannot make assumptions about how time was perceived, this human's eye view provides a platform for developing an approach to both daily life and to the processes popularized by Giddens (1984) which structure social life through their transgenerational continuities and discontinuities. One way to approach this is to divide cultural chronologies into generations, which may be estimated at about 20 years. Although this heuristic notion of a generation may not reflect how generations were perceived in the past, this does permit phases and cultural horizons to be interpreted in terms of social practices and transmission.

In the field, attention to variations between households at different generational stages may be somewhat at odds with other aims of excavation. If we choose to see household variation as normal, it becomes difficult to resolve rank/ status differences between households from developmental phases. Assessing this concern may require a larger sample than the statistical minimum required for artefact analysis. Occupation which endures several generations may blur stages of development and decline if the same structures are in continual use. The continued use of dwellings is also a statement about the cultural management of human development and is one way that the variation between cultures to which Yanagisako (1979) has alerted us may be seen in the archaeological record.

Archaeological studies of the Andean household

Thus far this discussion has remained abstract and I now explore how this consideration may be applied to archaeological households using two examples from Peruvian archaeology. These examples illustrate what effect the integration of inter-generational models might have on interpretation in household-based research projects.

North coast, Peru

Bawden's (1982) study of the urban Moche settlement at Galindo (AD 600–750) found domestic remains reflecting a highly stratified community. The planned settlement appears to have been constructed rapidly after the fall of a massive temple complex at the culture's central site. A repetitive multiroom form is seen in all dwellings and Bawden suggests that this represents the use of an idealized template in the ordering of Galindo domestic space. Analysis of variability in dwellings by size, contents and location relative to town walls, subsistence resources and non-residential structures supports a convincing argument in favour of a society divided into four spatially defined social classes. The single-occupation site was exceptionally well preserved and virtually the entire expanse of the site was studied. In this case it would have been possible to assess synchronic variation between households within each social class. This variation could be used to determine if evidence of different household cycles characterized each class.

In a further study, Bawden (1990) compared dwelling form and settlement structure between cultural horizons by tracing a long sequence from the Salinar/Galinazo (200BC–AD 200) through the Moche (AD 200–750), including Galindo, and into the subsequent Chimu (AD 750–1450). The variable resolution of primary data prevented direct comparison of activity areas between these sites and limited the applicability of the detailed analysis performed on the Galindo data. However, Bawden identifies a tripartite sequence of domestic patterning from undifferentiated single rooms to segmented dwellings and a final return to the older patterning of undifferentiated single rooms. He ties this domestic patterning to concurrent political transitions as Moche political authority rose, went into decline and was later replaced by a new settlement organization.

Bawden sees the return to an older undifferentiated domestic form as evidence that 'social integration was deeply embedded in an already long tradition of integrative values derived from communally oriented principles grounded in specific cultural and mythical concepts in the Salinar – in simplistic terms "kinship organisation"' (ibid. 1990: 168). Price (Chapter 3, this volume) critiques assumptions about the centrality of the nuclear family that underlie this model. For my purposes, the maintenance of these ties over generations needs to be addressed in terms of the transmission of these ideas through time. The loosely defined 'traditional kinship principles' that Bawden proposes recall Bourdieu's (1990 [1980]) *habitus*, which may provide a mechanism for the preservation of these social forms.

However, this will not account for innovation between phases and mechanisms for ideological continuity throughout this long sequence (approximately 80 generations) which needs to be explained. Thus the relationship between the preservation of kinship structures and a normative household form is tenuous in Bawden's argument. It would be helpful to assess the mechanisms of transmission and explore continuities in other forms of material culture to explain how a consistent household ideology might have been maintained.

Political stratification is very clearly demonstrated throughout much of this sequence (e.g. in monumental burials) and there is a marked tendency towards settlement planning in the later periods (e.g. Galindo, Chan Chan). I suggest that if kinship alliances were preserved through the duration of this long sequence, then community organization must have taken on a more formal quality. If the primary social unit was a supra-household network, as in the *ayllu* model, this may have been preserved through the ability to interdigitate households with the burgeoning social hierarchy. For Galindo, the division of the site into neighbourhoods may also represent social units such as *ayllus* or even castes but this would have to be assessed against a more detailed study including, as Bawden notes, interpretation of the rich iconography. From these studies we can appreciate the macro-organization of dwellings within the settlement structure but have little information on shorter-term processes operating in the households themselves or the social mechanisms by which they are maintained.

Otora Valley, Peru

A second example is Stanish's (1989, 1992) study of household data in the Otora Valley, Peru (AD 1100–1475) to test models of 'zonal complementarity'. In order to assess inter-zonal interactions, he distinguishes between cultural phases marked by direct colonization, autochthonous cultural development and long-distance trade. Stanish chooses to distinguish between the household as the primary economic unit and the *ayllu* as the primary sociopolitical unit. This allows him to define the archaeological household in purely economic terms (Stanish 1992: 34–8). He proposes that structural variations in dwelling form indicate differences in ethnicity.

Ethnic identity is addressed in terms of ceramics recovered from funerary and domestic contexts. Stanish (1989: 12–13) suggests that ceramic finewares are poor ethnic markers as they are gathered from primarily funerary and non-domestic contexts where prestige goods display may favour an exaggerated emphasis on exotic goods. As the bulk of household remains are plainwares, he believes that they are more likely to reflect the ethnic affiliation of the group. However, in the absence of absolute dates for these sites, Stanish has relied heavily on exotic finewares to develop a relative chronology based on established ceramic sequences from other Andean regions. The Otora Valley plainware sequence was not analysed in sufficient detail to provide a record of shorter-term changes related to local ethnic development (for an excellent example see Bermann 1994).

Stanish relates the development of settlements in this region to colonial expansion in pursuit of agricultural resources. He concludes that the initial settlements in the Otora Valley were colonies of distant polities. The elaboration of local funerary rituals and prestige goods exchange over broad chronological periods are used to suggest a weakening of ties to the mother community. The later phase is seen as a local ethnic development and as this develops into a polity, long-distance trade links are established with groups outside the initial parent communities and a local social hierarchy becomes evident.

Again, well-preserved, single-occupation sites suggest several questions relating to generational cycles that could have been addressed. For example, in the earlier frontier phases, do we expect the resident group to represent the full demographic range found in established settlements? If these colonists were part of an *ayllu* in the mother settlement, would we expect them to be permanent, full-time residents of these settlements? To discuss this fully would require an assessment of the characteristics of pioneer communities. However, let me suggest that the first colonists were likely to have been young adults capable of making the long journey from the home territory and building settlements and agricultural systems from scratch. After these colonies were established, a more full demographic range could develop if exchange of personnel from the mother community was minimal. This development would promote the creation of a local social structure between settlement members such as between first and second generation colonists. Using this logic, the observation that nascent elites formed locally is not surprising, but follows from the fact that from the earliest periods, communities were planned allowing for the creation of potential leadership roles. As these settlements developed and expanded over time, local lineages or perhaps *ayllus* would become established as ties to the mother communities weakened. This reconstruction is intended to demonstrate how attention to short-term processes allows for a closer reading of the data and is far from conclusive. Closer examination of the processes of colonization of new lands will add to these discussions.

Implications for Andean archaeology

Several questions arise from these examples. In particular, the relationships between the household and developed social hierarchies have not been explored to their full potential. It is clear that the generational time approach is best suited to archaeological contexts with a horizon of well-preserved dwellings. Clearly refined chronologies will add to this application. In these examples, the local vocabulary of architecture and artefact assemblages that express household ideology can be related to small-scale social institutions. Where a social hierarchy or state structure exists, explorations of social networks that unite residential units may explain how individual households are able to integrate into these structures. Attention to these smaller social aggregates would help to identify the role of local communities in expansive social systems. Where a local sequence can be established, this can be used as a basis for understanding the expansion of states into provincial settlements (see Bermann 1994). This would help to demystify the enduring maintenance of cultural traditions. More research is needed into how these traditions are conserved from generation to generation in non-literate societies.

Conclusion

In archaeology, we have become comfortable with a long-term perspective that views culture change at the societal level. Much of the debate on time and temporality in archaeology is situated on longer-term processes (Bailey 1982, ibid.1987, Hodder 1987, Barrett et al. 1991, Barrett 1994). In contrast, the study of short-term processes requires attention to the nature of the individual in time with an emphasis on human experience (Thomas 1996). As prehistoric data is not resolvable to individuals, we must address the temporal spreading of individuals through time as they age and their social relationships change. In this discussion, I have suggested that to bridge the gap between a long-term perspective and the real life experiences of people in the past, the intricacies of household development should be explored. This allows archaeologists to open up discussion of inter-household social strategies below the state or societal level. It has been proposed that the incorporation of a generational time model into the study of prehistoric households can suggest mechanisms for the transmission of conserved ideology and mediate differences of scale in interpretation. Colonial situations may provide good data sets for this approach. Inter-household alliances are another strategy that can effectively be pursued, particularly in an Andean setting. I have looked to supra-household social institutions based on the Andean *ayllu* for clues into the strategies these societies have employed to manage the tension between the desires of the household and the greater society. Examples from Andean archaeology indicate that these aims are compatible with current research aims and provide impetus for a more detailed assessment of micro-scale processes.

Notes

1. Accounts of Quechua and Aymara social structure inform this discussion. The Inka spread Quechua as their imperial language and it has several modern variants. The Aymara form a different linguistic group from the Lake Titicaca area and have similar supra-household institutions. Although research indicates that the Quechua and Aymara may employ different systems of hierarchy and political economy (Browman 1996; Hastorf pers. comm.), this discussion will include material from both groups.
2. The term *ayllu* is not unambiguous in Andean society particularly because it can be used to describe variable portions of the population with reference to the speaker. For example, outside one's region the *ayllu* may represent the entire population of a valley wherein one lives but within that valley it may be used to refer to a smaller subgroup to which one identifies more closely. This nested quality is similar to the way English speakers use the term 'home'. For example, when abroad one may refer to one's city of residence as home but within that city one would refine this to a street or actual dwelling. Here I am using the term *ayllu* loosely to refer to a supra-household alliance and will not seek to evaluate this variation in actual usage of the term.

References

Alberti, G. & E. Mayer (eds) 1974. *Reciprocidad e intercambio en los Andes peruanos.* Lima: Instituto de Estudios Peruanos, Perú Problema 12.

Allen, C. 1988. *The hold that life has.* Washington, DC: Smithsonian Institution Press.

Bailey, G. 1982. Concepts of time in quaternary prehistory. *Annual Review of Anthropology* **12**, 165–92.

Bailey, G. 1987. Breaking the time barrier. *Archaeological Review from Cambridge* **6**, 1–10.

Barrett, J. 1994. *Fragments from antiquity.* London: Basil Blackwell.

Barrett, J., Bradley, R., Green, M. 1991. *Landscape, monuments and society.* Cambridge: Cambridge University Press.

Bawden, G. 1982. Community organization reflected by the household: a study of pre-Columbian social dynamics. *Journal of Field Archaeology* **9**, 165–81.

Bawden, G. 1990. Domestic space and social structure in pre-Columbian northern Peru. See Kent (1990a), 153–71.

Bender, D. 1967. A refinement of the concept of household: families, coresidence, and domestic functions. *American Anthropologist* **69**, 493–504.

Bermann, M. 1994. *Lukurmata.* Chichester: Princeton University Press.

Blanton, R. 1993. *Houses and households: a comparative study.* New York: Plenum.

Bloch, A. 1977. The past and the present in the present. *Man* [new series] **12**, 278–92.

Bolton, R. & E. Mayer (eds) 1977. *Andean kinship and marriage.* Washington, DC: American Anthropological Association, Special Publication 7.

Bourdieu, P. 1990 [1980]. *The logic of practice.* Oxford: Polity.

Browman, D. 1996. Evolving archaeological interpretations of Inka institutions: perspectives, dynamics, reassessments. *Latin American Research Review* **31**(1), 227–43.

Castro Pozo, H. 1946. Social and economico-political evolution of the communities of Central Peru. In *Handbook of South American Indians, vol. 2: The Andean civilizations,* J. Steward (ed.), 483–500. Washington, DC: Smithsonian Institution Bureau of American Ethnology Bulletin 143.

Childe, V. G. 1929. *The Danube in prehistory.* Oxford: Oxford University Press.

D'Altroy, T. 1987. Transitions in power centralization of Wanka political organization under Inka rule. *Ethnohistory* **34**(1), 78–102.

Durkheim, E. 1915. *The elementary forms of the religious life* (J. W. Swain, transl.). London: Allen & Unwin.

Evans-Pritchard, E. 1940. *The Nuer: a description of modes of livelihood and political institutions of the Nilotic people.* Oxford: Clarendon Press.

Fortes, M. 1958. Introduction. In *The developmental cycle in domestic groups,* J. Goody (ed.), 1–14. Cambridge: Cambridge University Press.

Gell, A. 1992. *The anthropology of time: cultural constructions of temporal maps and images.* Oxford: Berg.

Giddens, A. 1984. *The constitution of society.* Oxford: Polity.

Gero, J. & M. Conkey (eds) 1991. *Engendering archaeology.* Oxford: Blackwell.

Gose, P. 1994. *Deathly waters and hungry mountains: agrarian ritual and class formation in an Andean town.* London: University of Toronto Press.

Hastorf, C. A. 1993. *Agriculture and the onset of political inequality before the Inka.* Cambridge University Press: Cambridge.

Hodder, I. (ed.) 1987. *Archaeology as long-term history.* Cambridge: Cambridge University Press.

Hodder, I. 1990. *The domestication of Europe.* Cambridge: Cambridge University Press.

Isbell, B. J. 1978. *To defend ourselves: ecology and ritual in an Andean village.* Austin, TX: Institute of Latin American Studies, Univeristy of Texas at Austin.

Johnson, M. 1990. The Englishman's home and its study. In *The social archaeology of houses,* R. Samson (ed.), 245–57. Edinburgh: Edinburgh University Press.

Kent, S. (ed.) 1990a. *Domestic architecture and the use of space: an interdisciplinary cross-cultural study.* Cambridge: Cambridge University Press.

Kent, S. 1990b. Activity areas and architecture: an interdisciplinary view of the relationship between use of space and domestic built environments. See Kent (1990a), 1–8.

Kent, S. 1990c. A cross-cultural study of segmentation, architecture, and the use of space. See Kent (1990a), 127–53.

Lambert, B. 1977. Bilaterality in Andes. See R. Bolton & E. Mayer (1997) (eds), 1–27.

Lawrence, R. 1990. Public collective and private space: a study of urban housing in Switzerland. See Kent (1990a), 73–91.

Mayer, E. 1981. *A tribute to the household: domestic economy and the Encomienda in Colonial Peru.* Special Publication of the Institute of Latin American Studies, University of Texas at Austin.

Murra, J. 1980. *The economic organisation of the Inka state.* Greenwich, Connecticut: Jai Press Inc.

Netting, R., R. R. Wilk, E. J. Arnould 1984. *Households: comparative and historical studies of the domestic group.* Berkeley: University of California Press.

Rappaport, A. 1990. Systems of activities and systems of settings. See Kent (1990a), 9–20.

Safaer, J. Derevenski 1994. Where are the children? Accessing children in the past. *Archaeological Review from Cambridge* **13**(2), 7–20.

Sillar, W. 1994. *Pottery's role in the reproduction of Andean society.* PhD thesis, Archaeology Department, University of Cambridge.

Skar, H. 1982. *The Warm Valley People: duality and land reform among the Quechua Indians of Highland Peru.* Oslo: Universitetsforlaget.

Skar, S. 1984. Intrahousheold co-operation in Peru's Southern Andes: a case of multiple sibling-group marriage. In *Family and work in rural societies*, N. Long (ed.), 83–98. London: Tavistock Publications.

Smith, M. 1987. Household possessions and wealth in agrarian states: implications for archaeology. *Journal of Anthropological Archaeology* **6**, 297–335.

Stanish, C. 1989. Household archaeology: testing models of zonal complementarity in the South Central Andes. *American Anthropologist* **91**(1), 7–24.

Stanish, C. 1992. *Ancient Andean political economy.* Austin: University of Texas Press.

Thomas, J. 1996. *Time, culture and identity: an interpretative archaeology.* London: Routledge.

Tourtellot, G. 1988. Developmental cycles of households and houses at Seibal. In *Household and community in the Mesoamerican past*, R. R. Wilk & W. Ashmore. (eds), 97–120. Albuquerque: University of New Mexico Press.

Tringham, R. 1984. Architectural investigation into household organization in Neolithic Yugoslavia. Paper presented at the 83rd Annual Meeting of the American Anthropological Association, Denver, Colorado.

Tringham, R. 1991. Households with faces: the challenge of gender in prehistoric architectural remains. In *Engendering archaeology*, J. Gero & M. Conkey (eds), 93–131. Oxford: Basil Blackwell.

Weismantel, M. 1989. *Food, gender and poverty in the Ecuadorian Andean.* Philadelphia: University of Pennsylvania Press.

Wilk, R. R. & W. L. Rathje 1982. Household archaeology. *American Behavioral Scientist* **25**(6), 617–39.

Yanagisako, S. 1979. Family and household: the analysis of domestic groups. *Annual Review of Anthropology* **8**, 161–205.

CHAPTER TEN

Memory and pueblo space

Joseph J. Kovacik

Introduction

Settlement is one of those terms that archaeologists intuitively understand. We all think we know what a settlement is, what it looks like, and usually how to analyze it. However, I have to confess that I personally am not sure what exactly a settlement is. In this paper, I outline what I think about the social development of settlements, and how we can use a small segment of the material record to get at the changing dynamics of the history of the inhabitants of a settlement. For my purposes, then, I define settlement abstractly as a dynamic construction of space and time that preserves, or perhaps encapsulates, the collective memory of a group. In essence, this definition allows almost any trace of material to be both a settlement and the preserve of memory but, as I hope to show in later sections, it is the archaeological situations that display more complex conglomerations of material culture that interest me most, and have, I believe, the most potential for understanding the dynamic nature of society.

For my particular purposes here, I utilize almost exclusively animal bones, episodes of architectural construction and sediment deposits as my conglomerations of material culture. More specifically, I have tried to understand the relationships between carnivores and birds of prey and their placement within built structures. In recalling discussion with colleagues both in Cambridge and in the American Southwest, I have come to appreciate the concept of 'structured deposition' (Richards & Thomas 1984). In essence, the idea behind the concept of structured deposition is that some fragments of the archaeological record (deposits) were built up (constructed, structured) knowingly and with some level of intentionality in order to influence an outcome. In trying to build on the concept of structured deposition and make it my own, I have endeavoured to integrate it, make it more dynamic, by showing that in some cases deposition[1] is related to processes of memory. In particular, I argue that memory is directly linked to many of the actions embodied within the procurement and deposition of carnivores and birds of prey within a changing built environment, and that the structure of the patterns that are recognizable are linked to the transmission not only of knowledge about the animal, but to the cognitive position the animal holds and the dynamic it produces within the wider society.

160

Games

When thinking about the notion of settlements in the American Southwest, trying to see 'settlement' as a dynamic construction of space and time, settlements as the preservations of memory, I am often struck by the apparently static nature of the data. Of course, formation process studies tell us that the archaeological record is dynamic, always in a state of transformation and flux, but this does not help the analyst who simply sees a 'record'. How, then, to change our way of seeing the record (perhaps not physically, say with a special set of dynamic-inducing glasses), but in our minds? A game based on a simple definition of settlement and a quick example provide a clue.

Let me define settlement as a circumscribed segment of the landscape containing a humanly modified environment. For my purposes here let me take as 'a settlement' the prehistoric building of 29SJ627 in Chaco Canyon, New Mexico (fig. 10.1). Could this settlement also be defined as a technological project? I believe it can.

'A technological project is a fiction, since at the outset it does not exist, and there is no way it can exist yet because it is in the project phase' (Latour 1996: 23). Latour also writes that the above tautological statement:

frees the analysis of technologies [settlements] from the burden that weighs on analysis of the sciences [the archaeological project]. As accustomed as we

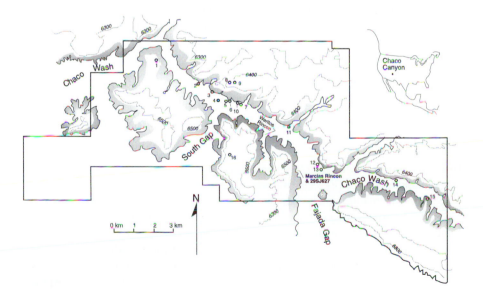

Figure 10.1 Schematic plan of Chaco Canyon, New Mexico, showing major sites and study areas: 1 Peñasco Blanco; 2 Casa Chiquita; 3 Kin Kletso; 4 Pueblo del Arroyo; 5 Pueblo Bonito; 6 Hillside Ruin; 7 Talus Unit; 8 New Alto; 9 Pueblo Alto; 10 Chetro Ketl; 11 Hungo Pavi; 12 Una Vida; 13 H. Q. Ruin; 14 Wijiji; 15 Shabik'eshchee Village; 16 Tsin Kletzin.

have become to the idea of a science that 'constructs,' 'fashions,' or 'produces,' its objects, the fact still remains that, after all the controversies, the sciences [archaeology] seem to have discovered a world that came into being without men and without sciences. Galileo may have constructed the phases of Venus, but once that construction was complete her phases appeared to have been 'always already present.' The fabricated fact has become the accomplished fact, the *fait accompli*. Diesel did not construct his engine any more than Galileo built his planet . . . no one would dare assert that the Diesel engine 'was always already there, even before it was discovered.' No one is a Platonist where technology is concerned. (ibid.) [my brackets]

If we throw out our preconceived ideas of settlement for the moment and think of 29SJ627 as a form of 'technology' made up from the combination of numerous technological acts and technologies, or acts of deposition, what we see is something that did not always exist, 'even before it was discovered'. The static picture of 29SJ627, as seen in composite in figure 10.2e, can be distilled into the more dynamic series shown in figure 10.2. What we see in phase 0 and prior are archaeological phases as yet undiscovered (unseen) by archaeologists, yet perhaps consisting of buildings, and prior to that, perhaps a patch of land that was as yet unbuilt upon by the prehistoric peoples of Chaco Canyon, yet still indeed existing for them.

The analysis of the settlement of 29SJ627, then, is the analysis of a technology that is dynamic now (remember those formation processes are still tearing 29SJ627 down, with the National Park Service stabilization crews trying to stop or slow those same processes), but was also dynamic in the past because the project had no beginning or end. The physical, geographic location of 29SJ627 has always existed, and as long as people were going through the canyon, that location was known to people. How and why that location became important enough to become a settlement is the focus of the following section.

Collective memory: definitions and how it can work in archaeology

In developing a theory for collective memory we can gain insight into the long-term maintenance of projects that are termed sites or settlements. Memory of a place and the maintenance of a memory is that which transforms a previously unknown location into a space with the potential for becoming a settlement. After a location is 'settled', memory acts as the agent to maintain the location's importance. How, then, can we identify material traces of prehistoric peoples' memories? The initial premise is that memories exist not solely within an individual but within the acting whole of a larger group, an idea formalized by Maurice Halbwachs before the Second World War.[2] The individual and the group are, in this scheme, inseparably bound together, and while the individual operates or acts the group supports; conversely while the group defines, the individual modifies. The concept of the group is also particularly well suited to prehistoric archaeology

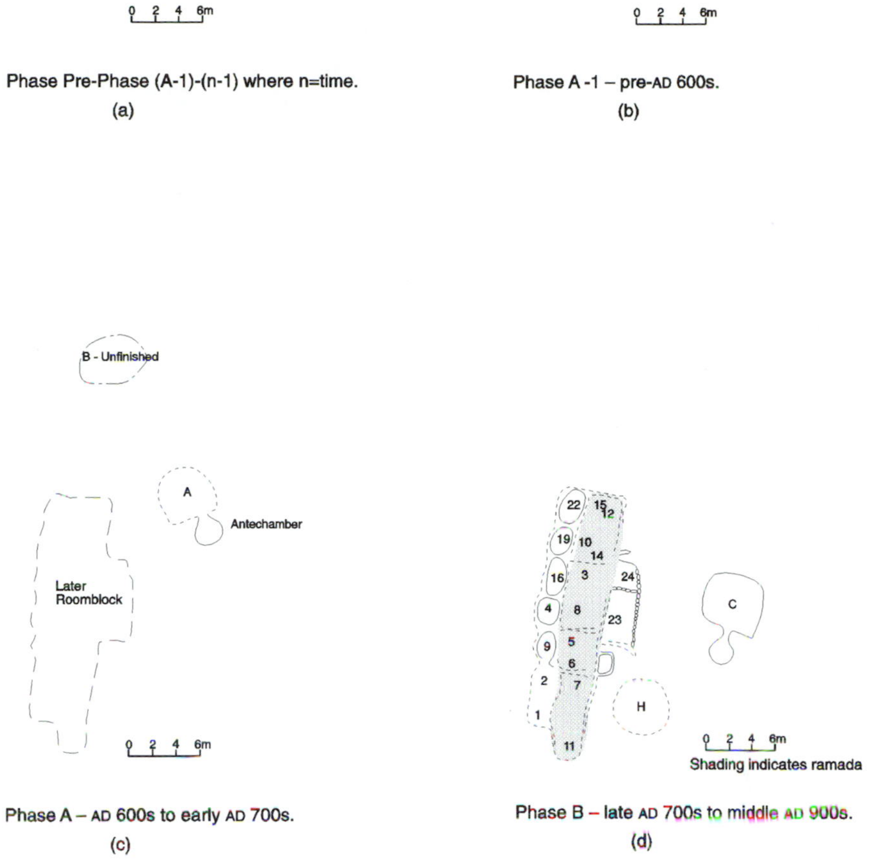

0 2 4 6m

0 2 4 6m

Phase Pre-Phase (A-1)-(n-1) where n=time.

(a)

Phase A -1 – pre-AD 600s.

(b)

B - Unfinished

A

Antechamber

Later
Roomblock

22 15
12

19 10
14

16 3 24

4 8
23

9 5
6

2 7

1

H

C

11

0 2 4 6m

0 2 4 6m

Shading indicates ramada

Phase A – AD 600s to early AD 700s.

(c)

Phase B – late AD 700s to middle AD 900s.

(d)

Figure 10.2 Construction episodes (phases) and final floor plan at 29SJ627, Chaco Canyon, New Mexico (adapted and modified from Truell 1992). *Continued overleaf.*

in which we are mostly unable to deal with the actions of single individuals (except perhaps in some cases of *chaînes opératoires*).

Memory is complex in that it is a combination of mental acts such as recognition, recall and articulation (Fentress & Wickham 1992: 26). To recognize something is to be able to identify it using previous knowledge, while recall is internal remembrance 'involving some form of mental presentation' (ibid.). Articulation is the communication of recollections (ibid.). Proust articulates it well as he recalls how he remembers:

But then, even in the most insignificant details of our daily life, none of us can be said to constitute a material whole, which is identical for everyone, and need only be turned up like a page in an account book or the record of a will; our social personality is a creation of the thoughts of other people.

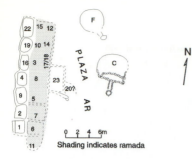

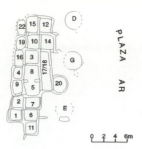

Phase C – middle AD 900s to early AD 1000s.

(e)

Phase D – middle 1000s.

(f)

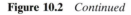

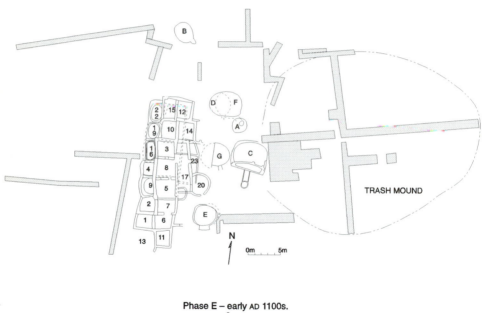

Phase E – early AD 1100s.
&
Phase E +(n+1) – time after Phase E (early 1100s) to the Present.

(g)

Figure 10.2   *Continued*

Even the simple act which we describe as 'seeing someone we know' is to
some extent a physical process. We pack the physical outline of the person
we see with all the notions we have already formed about him, and in the
total picture of him which we compose in our minds those notions have
certainly the principal place. In the end they come to fill out so completely

the curve of his cheeks, to follow so exactly the lines of his nose, they blend so harmoniously in the sound of his voice as if it were no more than a transparent envelope, that each time we see the face or hear the voice it is these notions which we recognize and to which we listen. (1989: 20)

The unarticulated effect of time on one's memories is illustrated in Proust's later discussions, but the process of filling in the details through interaction and discussion with others is obvious and maintained, touching on each of Fentress and Wickham's mental acts.

'We appeal to witnesses to corroborate or invalidate as well as supplement what we somehow know already about an event that in many other details remains obscure' (Halbwachs 1980: 22). The individual possesses memories of their past that are called on in the individual's present for a variety of purposes. However, these memories of our past do not exist in isolation. Rather, they are formed by our involvement, our membership, within a wider community of individuals. It is this interdependence, our inability to act outside of society, that makes *all* our memories collectively bound. Even if we experience an event 'alone', we are not *alone* for, as Halbwachs notes, our personal history is bound with others with whom we have 'lived', have had personal contact with, or even read about.

The situating of individual memories against one another does not necessarily make them memories of the collective. For a memory to become a significant part of the group's memory, for it to move into the 'foreground', remembrance of an event must concern the largest number of members of a group. These group memories 'arise out of group life itself or from relationships with the nearest and most frequently contacted groups' (Halbwachs 1980: 43). Examples of this are infinite and seem trivial when stated. It suffices that we all have memories shared with a wider group: our graduation from university, the Apollo landing, the opening of a new shopping mall, the closure of a local pub. Of course, each of these examples takes on different characteristics for each individual. Some are more widely shared while others exist within a limited sphere. It should be emphasized that it is not the group that actually remembers an event. Individuals remember in their own way and place varying degrees of importance on a specific memory. The collective memory is the abstracted essence of an event or plan or story that a group holds because of their common experience of witnessing the event. Again, it is by communicating, by remembering a shared memory within a group that a memory is corroborated and maintained.

'Every collective memory requires the support of a group delimited in space and time' (Halbwachs 1980: 84). The demarcation in space–time is what forms the basis of our archaeological assemblages. Grayson defines an assemblage as 'the entire set of . . . specimens [artefacts] from a given cultural or geological context, in which the defining context is provided by the analyst' (1984: 17; my addition in brackets). This definition allows for an assemblage's boundaries to be changed according to the analyst's needs. Thus, the material remains of a community's existence (a settlement) are presupposed by the presence of an archaeological assemblage existing in a specific space–time[3] (the present or the time of excavation), and this assemblage also represents the actions of those who operated in other specific space–times (the periods of the sites' occupations). It is because these space–times are recognizable by archaeologists and others that there is a thinly stretched line of continuity allowing for the investigation of memory.

A collective notion of time is essential for a theory of memory to operate effectively. Building on Durkheim, Halbwachs writes that:

> an isolated individual might, strictly speaking, be unaware of the flow of time and incapable of measuring duration, whereas social life implies that all men agree on times and duration and know well the conventions governing them. This is why there is a collective representation of time. (1980: 88)

While these general principals may reference astrological events and physics, 'society superimposes upon these general frameworks others especially suited to the conditions and habits of concrete human groups' (ibid.: 89). It is because of a group's shared perceptions of time that the patterning of memory, as present in the archaeological record, is recognizable. We must assume that at least some archaeological deposits are patterned because of the cyclic repetition of an event. These patterns arise because of a common temporal framework. Every person would know that this is the 'right time' for a specific event. While the accuracy with which we measure the passage of time today makes us hyper-dependent on our temporal framework, for the Chaco Anasazi their less fragmented yet accurate measurements would have created dependence nonetheless.

While memory is dependent on temporality, the ability to order things chronologically (past, present) is dependent on patterning (similarity in overall structure). 'Attributed differences arise from participation in common categories. By contrast the current within which thought flows in inner consciousness is not a homogenous milieu, since form is not distinguished from matter and container and content are one' (Halbwachs 1980: 94). Thus, the archaeological record is dependent on the interaction of time (obviously) and memory, for without the two there would be no patterning. And without patterning there would be no recognition either in the past or present of human action, reducing society to independent individuals each acting according to their own system, or to their own means (apologies to White 1959: 8).

Archaeology and the identification of memory

What would an archaeologically recoverable memory look like, and if we could identify it how would we know it even was memory-related? First, I should make clear that I do not think the actual memory of an event is preserved within the ground. Rather, traces or fragments of a series of actions associated with specific rituals and more mundane activities leave behind material remains. Some of the materials we recover were part of actions spurred on and framed by and within processes of memory, be it the need to maintain a specific link with the past, or to set forth in a new direction. Thus, the act of deposition, unless completely careless and unintentional (e.g. the loss of an object, although 'loss' is difficult to assess), is always in reference to a previous act. Another example is when soil is placed or moved but people do not realize there are artefacts within the soil – that is the soil is deposited intentionally but the artefacts within it are deposited unintentionally (secondarily). 'Each object appropriately placed in the whole recalls a way of life common to many men. To analyse its various facets is like dissecting a thought compounded of the contributions of many groups' (Halbwachs 1980: 129). The phrase 'each object appropriately placed' implies that fragments of material culture gain and provide meaning through their placement. Thus, an entire deposit, such as a trash mound, or a deposit based strictly on cyclic recognition need not be the only deposits worthy of carrying memory. Individual objects, individual fragments of meaningful wholes, become objects of remembrance when intentionally placed. Individuals or groups who place these single objects (or perhaps sets of objects of which only a few are recoverable archaeologically) reference the memory of how to place and what the placement will mean in the future. Because there is a limited set of both material and physical constraints the placements over time form recognizable patterns.

Because one act references other earlier acts we have patterning. In some cases, the aid of various analytic techniques reveals additional patterns (see Kovacik 1996: 80–98). In one sense, all patterns, no matter how complex and distant from the actual data, are traces of memory. While this may be true, I believe it is more accurate archaeologically to rely on a contextual analysis based on the observation of simple patterns that become apparent by close familiarity with the data, and not necessarily through complex statistical analysis.

If importance can be attached to specific deposits then specific objects should also carry importance. For example, from the ethnographic literature we know that the pueblo peoples placed importance on birds, and by extension on their feathers. Single feathers of specific birds were attached to 'prayer sticks' with the significance and power of the birds transferred to the made object and to the accompanying actions performed with the object (White 1932; Ladd 1963). A fragment from the whole represents the whole. While this is admittedly simplistic, in archaeological terms it means that in particular contexts, fragments or portions of complete, specific objects can be considered representative of the whole.

Mindeleff (1891) observed the founding of a Tusyan or Hopi house. After gathering the appropriate construction materials:

> The builder goes to the village chief, who prepares for him four small eagle feathers . . . These feathers are placed at the four corners of the house and a large stone is laid over each of them. The builder then decides where the door is to be located, and marks the place by setting some food on each side of it. (ibid.: 101)

After the house is completed, the builder then 'prepares four feathers similar to those prepared by the chief, and ties them to a short piece of willow, the end of which is inserted over one of the central roof beams. These feathers are renewed each year' (ibid.: 102).

These single objects prepared by both the chief and the builder are composites made up of fragments from a whole and *are representative of a larger whole*, that of the community. The initial foundation deposits link the house into the community. The initial foundation deposits are mirrored by the family, renewed on a yearly basis, referencing not only the coming of the sun (a practical expression of collective representations of time) but also the earlier foundation deposits.

When a house is 'ritually closed', what constitutes the ritual? Is the plastering of a new floor a ritual? Is the taking out of the trash, or the making of a new vessel, or the cooking of a meal a ritual? All five events take place within the mundane world. If we move house regularly, even seasonally, the movement in one sense becomes mundane activity. It becomes something that is done without necessarily thinking; the time of year when we move arrives, and we move. If people occupy several 'houses' within a year, and the house's use-life is short, should we not also assume that the houses would always be being closed and opened? The relative commonality of these occurrences implies that the actions are within the mundane sphere. The same is true of plastering a floor or cooking; the activities are common. Although the time scales of plastering and cooking are vastly different, both can be considered mundane. However, that the acts are performed regularly, mundanely, does not preclude them from incorporating acts of remembrance. The act of plastering references the past and would force the individuals or groups involved in the act to take note of what had come before; their reasons for replastering need to be integrated into a recalled framework of action. *Deposition is an act of remembrance, even when done in a mundane manner.*

Moving from situations of remembrance to acts of archaeological deposition done in remembrance is a subtle transformation. *Through the act of deposition we reference earlier objects and actions even though specific knowledge of what was has been forgotten.* How do we know this? We know this because we recognize patterns. Even though there is separation between events archaeologically, we observe patterns in the data. These patterns are not just distributed over space but within time. We know this to be true because seriation works. While seriation requires high frequencies of a particular class of objects to operate meaningfully, contextual methods (Hodder 1986: 118–45) allow analysis to function at the level of single objects. These single objects must have something else that ties them together besides physical similarity. For example a *mano* (grinding stone) in association with a *metate* is indicative of something different to a *mano* in the trash mound. However if we find *manos/metates* in rooms, and within specific places within each room, the *mano/metate* and room come to have more meaning: their association provides the other with meaning. The repetition of sets of objects within specific places over time–space is a pattern, with the pattern being recognizable and meaningful.

Patterns are the centre of the argument in archaeology; without them we would be lost. While I recognize that some patterns are the result of natural processes, I believe that most are tied to mundane practices that stem from the conscious or unconscious recollection, recall and articulation of memories. Coming back to these three acts, recollection, recall and articulation, and their conjunction with the archaeological record, carnivore and bird of prey bones again come to the fore-front of my mind because of their observable power. That these animals and their fragmented bodies play(ed) a part in contemporary pueblo life is indisputable; exactly how they were used, and what their meaning was in the prehistoric past is less tangible. As I show in the following sections, the use and deposition of carnivores and birds of prey at the site of 29SJ627, and indeed in Chaco Canyon, was circumscribed and specific. The power of the living animals appeared to be known and understood, and translated into their handling and deposition at crucial moments in the history of the site. That the patterns were recreated over genera-tions suggests that the memories too remained.

29SJ627 and the identification of memories

In this section I show that architectural construction, faunal remains and depositional practices come together in the production and reproduction of society through the processes of memory and transmission outlined above. The basic structure of the faunal collection from 29SJ627 is outlined contextually and statistically with several particular examples of specific depositional practice outlined.

Of all the sites excavated by the Chaco Center, only 29SJ627 provides informa-tion covering the whole of its occupational and spatial history. While there were problems during the excavations with complex stratigraphy, and with terminology in the report writing stage (see Editor's Preface in Truell 1992; T. Windes pers. comm.), these irregularities do not detract from the usefulness of the site.

29SJ627 is located in Marcia's Rincón on the south side of Chaco Canyon (fig. 10.1). It is in close proximity to various sites on the colluvial/alluvial plain just north of the confluence of Chaco and Fajada (Vicenti) Washes. These sites together form a cluster whose closest great pueblo neighbour is Una Vida, some 1.1 km east-northeast.

29SJ627 consists of 25 above-ground rooms, at least six pitstructures, several ramadas or covered areas, plazas or forecourt areas, a trash midden and many open-air pits and cysts (Truell 1992). The final site plan can be broken into five distinct construction phases (fig. 10.2). Each phase was defined according to vari-ations in architectural stratigraphy that correlated to building episodes. The build-ing episodes (phases) at 29SJ627 are similar to those derived for sites such as Chetro Ketl (Lekson 1978, 1984) and Pueblo Bonito (Lekson 1986), although for these sites the dating is much more specific and refined because of the abundance of dendrochronological information. Within each phase at 29SJ627 there is a series of re-flooring episodes, although re-flooring is limited to the above-ground room block only. The faunal remains collected from 29SJ627 total 4749 bones and bone fragments. The primary, or objective level of classification (at least in the western academic sense), and the point at which I begin my discussion, has already been performed by the Chaco Project (Akins 1981a,b,c,d,e,f, 1982, 1987, 1992; Gillespie 1981). The archaeological faunal remains from 29SJ627 were identified to genus, species or subspecies level and these data computerised by N. Akins, S. Emslie and J. Applegarth in 1978. Thirty-three taxa are represented within the collection. Rather than treating each individual species as unique, the species can be formally grouped into fewer categories according to objectively and subjectively defined criteria. I have argued elsewhere (Kovacik 1996) that there are five gross categories or 'groups' into which the majority of animals at 29SJ627, and indeed many southwestern sites, can be placed: these are rabbits, rodents, large mammals, carnivores and unidentified birds and identified birds. Each of these groups is exclusive of the other and is characterized by a minimum of traits defined and presented (with the exception of unidentified birds and birds to species) in considerable detail by Findley (Findley et al. 1975; Findley 1987).

If dealing solely with a written record that detailed Native American perspectives on a given animal, a direct comparison between the criteria naturalists use to identify species and the criteria Native Americans use to identify species could be performed. However, as archaeologists we realize that the past and the present are substantially separated in terms of what would have been important then, and that which is important now. For this reason, it was necessary to demonstrate that the 'groups' of animals and individual species themselves were treated differently from one another. Using a range of analytic techniques and a minimum of assumptions, I have shown conclusively that the groups of animals identified above are observable within archaeological materials (see Kovacik 1996).

In essence, the initial premise that animals and their remains played an active role in the consciousness and daily lives of the people of Chaco Canyon can be restated as: all species are treated in an identical fashion; therefore there will be no, or minimal (non-statistically significant), differences in the placement or handling of individual bones (handling includes variables such as where in the site the animal bones were located, in what position in the depositional sequence the animal bones were located, the presence of attributes indicating butchering or burning associated with cooking or other processing activities, or the selection of specific body parts). Alternatively and more abstractly: (1) all animals are drawn from a single population; and (2) because all animals are drawn from a single population they occupy the same 'place' in group/individual consciousness. Therefore the treatment (butchering and other processes) and placement of animals bones is independent of species. Instinctively we suspect these premises to be false. Thus, the question becomes can we show that specific animal species come from different populations and are exploited in different ways? Following from this, what meaning can be attributed to these different exploitations?

Intentional selection in archaeological situations hinges on the identification of certain elements as having a higher probability of being meaningful – or, more accurately, being used and deposited in meaningful ways. Aside from extrapolation from the ethnographic data and the associated lapse into ethnographic analogy and the transference of meaning generated in this present on to a distant past, what measures can provide us with evidence of how animals were conceptu-

Table 10.1 Percentage of all large mammal and rabbit elements and carnivore and raptor elements, Chaco Canyon, New Mexico; DF = 4, χ^2 = 428.28, p = 0.0001.

	Large mammals and rabbits		Carnivores and raptors	
	Count	%	Count	%
Head	2688	17.104	241	14.311
Rear legs	4915	31.274	430	25.534
Front legs/wings	2834	18.033	653	38.777
Articulated skeleton	20	0.127	6	0.356
Everything else	5259	33.463	354	21.021

alized and why they were deposited in the past? A simple percentage comparison of large mammal and rabbit elements plotted against carnivore and raptor elements proves a helpful first step in distinguishing intentional and unintentional acts of deposition. By taking into account all the recovered elements from sites excavated by the Chaco Center (Akins 1981a,b,c,d,e,f, 1987, 1992; Gillespie 1981), I have set up a baseline for further interpretations. Table 10.1 clearly illustrates that large mammals' and rabbits' body parts and carnivores' and raptors' body parts are present in different percentages in Chaco Canyon. Large mammals and rabbits have higher overall percentages of head elements, rear-leg elements and those elements that come from the shoulder, back and pelvis (the latter are represented in table 10.1 by the category 'everything else', which includes unidentified bones). Carnivores and raptors are more strongly represented by elements from the front legs and wings and, to a lesser extent, articulated skeletons (table 10.1). This distribution suggests that the bodies of carnivores and raptors and large mammals and rabbits were utilized (butchered or fragmented, and *by implication* deposited) in different ways. The inhabitants of Chaco Canyon seem to focus particular attention on the front legs and wings of carnivores and raptors, while directing less attention to these same portions in the case of large mammals and rabbits. The chi-square test on the data (DF = 4, χ^2 = 428.28, p = 0.0001) supports this argument.

The same approach, a percentage comparison, in this case comparing recovered materials with expected frequency, sheds light on the question of intentional deposition. Intentional deposits are often thought of as only encompassing those deposits deliberately (consciously) placed into excavated contexts. Thus, the fill within some pit features, such as a human burial and its associated grave goods, is easily considered intentional. Recent archaeological work, mostly stemming from individuals trained in Britain (Richards & Thomas 1984), has attempted to expand the concept of intentional deposition to a wider range of contexts by introducing the concept of 'structured deposition'. This concept allows a wider range of deposits to be thought of as intentional, with the correlation that at least a portion of the materials within structured deposits were intentionally included.

If we compare the recovered materials (table 10.1) to an expected distribution (table 10.2) in which all the bones from an individual animal are present – or the

Table 10.2 Expected percentage of large mammal, carnivore and raptor elements if a single, complete skeleton of a particular animal were recovered; data taken from Lyman 1994: 98, Table 4.1.

	Cervids with teeth		Cervids without teeth		Canids with teeth		Canids without teeth		Raptors	
	Count	%	Count	%	Count	%	Count	%	Count	%
Head	27	14.595	5	3.067	47	21.171	5	2.778	2	1.709
Rear legs	50	27.027	50	30.675	60	27.027	60	33.333	42	35.897
Front Legs/wings	52	28.108	52	31.902	58	26.126	58	32.222	24	20.513
Everything else	56	30.270	56	34.356	57	25.676	57	31.667	49	41.880

Table 10.3 Comparison of recovered versus expected percentage of skeletal elements.

	DF	χ^2	p
Recovered carnivores and raptors versus expected carnivores without teeth	3	30.25	0.0001
Recovered carnivores and raptors versus expected carnivores with teeth	3	16.62	0.0008
Recovered large mammals without teeth versus cervids without teeth	3	35.83	0.0001
Recovered large mammals with teeth versus cervids with teeth	3	12.50	0.0059

expected frequency based on the ideal situation of the number of bones found in different parts of the complete animal skeleton – we see that our recovered distribution remains statistically different from the expected (table 10.3). These results suggest that *in archaeological situations* (1) a specific animal was brought to the site incomplete; or (2) the observed distributions are biased because of sampling error as a result of inadequate excavation procedures and sample coverage.

Having already highlighted the potential for carnivores and raptors to signify meaningful behaviour, the presence of carnivores and raptors in specific contexts, in particular roof fall and fill, in contact with floors and to a lesser degree within sub-floor fill, suggests that materials within these deposits warrant our special consideration.

However, that a deposit is intentional does not exclude the potential for it to contain secondary materials or refuse. Schiffer defines secondary refuse as materials discarded other than at their place of original use (Schiffer 1972; 1987: 18, 60). He also states that 'habitation settlements produce mainly secondary refuse' (Schiffer 1987: 60) and notes in his re-examination of the Broken K Pueblo data (*contra* Hill 1970) that much of the material considered as primary or *de facto* refuse (the fills associated with floors in Hill's analysis) is more likely to be secondary refuse (Schiffer 1987: 323–38). Taking Schiffer's points on board, even if materials are redeposited, redeposition can be intentional, with this social act having both intended and unintended social consequences.

Table 10.4 Percentage of all large mammal and rabbit elements, and carnivore and raptor elements, by general context, Chaco Canyon, New Mexico; DF = 7, χ^2 = 2660.93, p = 0.0001.

	Large mammals and rabbits		Carnivores and raptors	
	Count	%	Count	%
Surface	1632	9.951	15	0.949
Fill	9554	58.256	874	55.281
Roof fall and fill	207	1.262	183	11.575
Floor fill	2196	13.390	14	0.886
Floor contact	983	5.994	212	13.409
Sub-floor fill	1687	10.287	88	5.566
Other	48	0.293	189	11.954
Unknown	93	0.567	6	0.380

Table 10.5 Percentage of large mammal and rabbit elements, and carnivore and raptor elements, by structure type at 29SJ627, Chaco Canyon, New Mexico; DF = 7, χ^2 = 525.70, p = 0.0001.

	Large mammals and rabbits		Carnivores and raptors	
	Count	%	Count	%
Back	728	13.653	92	10.222
Middle	477	8.946	137	15.222
Front	1083	20.311	225	25.000
Pitstructure	731	13.710	154	17.111
Kiva	1160	21.755	29	3.222
Plaza	517	9.696	17	1.889
Midden	356	6.677	49	5.444
Other	280	5.251	197	21.889

Approaching the deposition of faunal remains within Chaco Canyon with an appreciation for the potential of intentional and meaningful materials being incorporated into larger secondary deposits opens up new possibilities for analysis. The ethnographic literature (Mindeleff 1891; White 1932; Beaglehole & Beaglehole 1935; Benedict 1935; Ortiz 1969) and the symbolic importance of animals suggest that in archaeological contexts carnivores and raptors may be treated and deposited differently from large mammals and rabbits. Table 10.1 indicates that we should be aware of the importance of carnivore and raptor front legs and wings, while table 10.4 suggests we should pay special attention to roof fall and fill, the deposits on floors and sub-floor fill contexts.

A final table (table 10.5) shows the distribution of large mammal and rabbit elements and carnivore elements as percentages within the different types of spaces at 29SJ627. What we see at 29SJ627 is a more general distribution of large mammals and rabbits (i.e. the distribution is more even than the carnivores and raptors), with carnivores and raptors concentrated in middle and front rooms in addition to pitstructures and the contexts designated 'other' (almost wholly the areas 'behind' the site). Again, these data indicate that large mammals and rabbits and carnivores and raptors have not only different spatial distributions, but that these distributions are representative of overall room significance. The distribution of animal groups within rooms may also be linked to the degree to which a particular space is predominately for private or public use.

Conclusions

The animal bones from 29SJ627 could be occurring in fill between floors, or any other contexts for that matter, because they were unintentionally included in the matrix. The elements could have been lying around on the surface or in trashy areas when the materials were eventually procured for use within rooms. Thus, the carnivore and raptor materials might have been unintentionally included in secondary deposits. Consequently, all deposition is intentional regardless of the materials used; only the consequences are intended or unintended. However, the limited range of contexts and the limited range of included elements suggests that the materials were first intentionally selected prior to deposition. This means that they were removed from the animal and kept separate prior to deposition, with the intention of producing a desired outcome. The step of selection is therefore separate from the act of deposition. The data indicate intentionality in species selection, while the limited range of contexts in which intentionally selected deposits are located suggests that carnivores and raptors are 'rare', although this rarity does not automatically imply symbolic deposition. It is possible that different animals are located by species/body part because of different ways of processing carnivores, raptors, large mammals and rabbits, and because of the possibility that these groups were processed in different places. However, the limited range of carnivore and raptor elements leads me to suggest that while different ways of processing different species, in different places, may have affected the distribution of a given species within a site, these processes were not the direct cause of the observed distributions.

Looking to the ethnographic data on hunting and butchering practice at Hopi (Beaglehole 1936), we remember that the bodies of eagles (ribs, sternum and vertebra) were not brought back to the site. Instead, the bird was butchered in the field with the body buried immediately; only the skin, feathers, wings, head and legs were brought back to the site. If the same general process of butchering was active in the case of the Chaco Anasazi, a wing and leg-dominated raptor distribution could indicate that the animals were butchered elsewhere with only a limited portion of the animal returned to the site.

If the birds and carnivores were processed off-site, the fact remains that they were deposited at 29SJ627 within a limited range of contexts. The small range of contexts implies yet again that the carnivores and raptors were powerful and that the elements we recovered were also powerful. The distribution also implies that some portions of these animals may have been too powerful for any individual to control and that these elements were best disposed of elsewhere.

While we cannot conclusively state that because bird or carnivore elements are used ethnographically in activities related to the founding of place, to make an identity or to bring rain, they must also have been used prehistorically for the same reasons, there is compelling evidence from 29SJ627 to suggest intentional action behind the handling and patterning of many species. Reviewing the above data on the birds, we can make several generalizations: from the 31 or so species of bird that could be present, only seven are represented at 29SJ627, six not including *M. gallopavo* or turkey. The 'other' six species of bird show no evidence of cooking or eating (see also Akins 1992), and any disarticulation of body parts (i.e. removing the wings or legs from the body) was performed with skill and care, as indicated by the placement and range of butchering marks on some elements (Akins 1981a,b,d,e,f, 1987, 1992). For example Akins notes for Pueblo Alto that 'Tiny cuts on the proximal ulnas of several species of hawks from Plaza 1, Grid 30 . . . suggest systematic disassociation and use of the wings' (Akins 1987: 503). From the ethnographic data, I noted that only the heads, wings feet and skin of hawks and eagles were returned to the site with the remainder of the animal buried at the place of its killing (Beaglehole 1936). These two examples of skilled butchering, one archaeological and the other ethnographic, illustrate the intentionality behind the social and symbolic treatment of animals.

In terms of settlement as a technological act, we see that the spatial development of any site is complex. However, what we often forget is that development took place over generations and that the first individuals to build at a site, in this case 29SJ627, would not have foreseen the consequences of their building. Little would they have known that over 300 years later, people would still be living at the site: people not necessarily related to them but people who maintained their own identity through the actions of those first inhabitants.

What I have established in this chapter is that specific animals and groups of animals were treated with care and prepared for an active role in the lives of the people of 29SJ627. The role specific animals played at 29SJ627 is a simple one: the hunting, killing, preparation and deposition of carnivores and raptors focused human action on the maintenance of links with the history of the site, and the formulation of relationships between contemporary people. That I have focused mainly on animals in no way implies that other classes of material remains cannot be used to understand memory. Rather for me animals appeared to be the easiest way into questions of memory and depositional practice because of their obvious symbolic potential. Thus I would suggest that animals be utilized as a first step in building the puzzle of a settlement's social structure. Other material remains that have a high potential for carrying and transmitting symbolic meaning, even in fragmented form, can then be added to the animals and architecture. Obvious examples would be those materials directly related to animals and their procurement and processing (projectile points, cooking vessels and tools especially suited to butchering are just three examples). The important point is that no class of material culture exists in a vacuum. As archaeologists we study how material culture interrelates, and how these relationships inform us about both the conscious and subconscious nature of the past and present. These pasts and presents, as socially motivated constructs, are becoming our collective memories.

Notes

1. In this paper, I use 'deposition' to mean the intentional placement of any material object. This includes sediments that may unintentionally contain objects of material culture (this is often termed secondary refuse: Schiffer 1987).
2. *La Mémoire Collective* was published posthumously in 1950 by Presses Universitaires de France.
3. The hyphenated phrase 'space–time', as I use it, embodies the coexistence of all material in both space and time simultaneously. This extends to my usage of the term 'phase', 'settlement', 'artefact', etc. In other words, as analysts we usually situate material culture into particular and separate temporal and spatial spheres. By situating materials into space–time I mean to argue that all materials are dynamic always, including after deposition or construction, when materials often take on a static appearance.

References

Akins, N. J. 1981a. *Analysis of the faunal remains from 29SJ724.* Santa Fe: Branch of Cultural Research, National Park Service.
Akins, N. J. 1981b. *The faunal remains from 29SJ299.* Santa Fe: Branch of Cultural Research, National Park Service.
Akins, N. J. 1981c. *The faunal remains from Shabik'eshchee village (29SJ1659).* Santa Fe: Branch of Cultural Research, National Park Service.
Akins, N. J. 1981d. *An analysis of the faunal remains at 29SJ423.* Santa Fe: Branch of Cultural Research, National Park Service.
Akins, N. J. 1981e. *The faunal remains from 29SJ1360.* Santa Fe: Branch of Cultural Research, National Park Service.
Akins, N. J. 1981f. *The faunal remains from 29SJ628.* Santa Fe: Branch of Cultural Research, National Park Service.
Akins, N. J. 1982. Perspectives on faunal resource utilization, Chaco Canyon, New Mexico. *New Mexico Archeological Council Newsletter* **4**, 23–8.
Akins, N. J. 1987. Faunal remains from Pueblo Alto. In *Investigations at the Pueblo Alto complex*, F. J. Mathien & T. C. Windes (eds), 445–650. Publications in Archaeology 18F, Chaco Canyon Studies. Santa Fe: National Park Service.
Akins, N. J. 1992. An analysis of the faunal remains from 29SJ627. In *Excavations at 29SJ627, Chaco Canyon, New Mexico: vol. II. The artifact analysis*, F. J. Mathien (ed.), 319–70. Reports of the Chaco Center. Santa Fe: Branch of Cultural Research, National Park Service.
Beaglehole, E. 1936. *Hopi hunting and hunting ritual.* New Haven: Yale University Press.
Beaglehole, E. & P. Beaglehole 1935. *The Hopi of second Mesa.* Menasha, WI: Memoirs of the American Anthropological Association 44.
Benedict, R. 1935. *Zuñi mythology.* Columbia University Contributions to Anthropology 21. New York: Columbia University Press.
Fentress, J. & C. Wickham 1992. *Social memory.* Oxford: Blackwell.
Findley, J. S. 1987. *The natural history of New Mexican mammals.* Albuquerque: University of New Mexico Press.

Findley, J. S., A. H. Harris, D. E. Wilson, C. Jones 1975. *Mammals of New Mexico*. Albuquerque: University of New Mexico Press.

Gillespie, W. B. 1981. *Faunal remains from 29SJ629*. Santa Fe: Branch of Cultural Research, National Park Service.

Grayson, D. K. 1984. *Quantitative zooarchaeology: topics in the analysis of archaeological faunas*. New York: Academic Press.

Halbwachs, M. 1980. *The collective memory* (trans. Ditter, F. J. Jr. & V. Y. Ditter). London: Harper & Row.

Hill, J. N. 1970. *Broken K Pueblo: prehistoric social organisation in the American Southwest*. Tucson: University of Arizona.

Hodder, I. 1986. *Reading the past: current approaches to interpretation in archaeology*. Cambridge: Cambridge University Press.

Kovacik, J. 1996. *A social/contextual archaeology of Chaco Canyon, New Mexico: collective memory and material culture amongst the Chaco Anasazi*. PhD thesis, Department of Archaeology, University of Cambridge. Also on file at the Chaco Culture Archive, Albuquerque.

Ladd, E. J. 1963. *Zuñi ethno-ornithology*. MA thesis, Department of Anthropology, University of New Mexico.

Latour, B. 1996. *Aramis or the love of technology* (trans. Porter, C.). Cambridge, Mass.: Harvard University Press.

Lekson, S. H. 1978. *An evaluation of the dendrochronology of Chetro Ketl*. Manuscript on file at Chaco Culture Archive, Albuquerque.

Lekson, S. H. (ed.) 1984. *The architecture and dendrochronology of Chetro Ketl, Chaco Canyon, New Mexico*. Albuquerque: Division of Cultural Research, National Park Service.

Lekson, S. H. 1986. *Great pueblo architecture of Chaco Canyon, New Mexico*. Albuquerque: University of New Mexico Press.

Lyman, R. L. 1994. *Vertebrate taphonomy*. Cambridge: Cambridge University Press.

Mindeleff, V. 1891. *A study of pueblo architecture in Tusayan and Cibola*. Reports of the American Bureau of Ethnology, vol. 8. Washington DC: Government Printing Office.

Ortiz, A. 1969. *The Tewa world: space, time and becoming in a pueblo society*. Chicago: University of Chicago Press.

Proust, M. 1989. *Remembrance of things past: 1*. London: Penguin.

Richards, C. & J. Thomas 1984. Ritual activity and structured deposition in Later Neolithic Wessex. In *Neolithic studies: a review of some current research*, R. Bradley & J. Gardiner (eds), 189–218. Oxford, British Archaeological Reports, British Series 133.

Schiffer, M. B. 1972. Cultural laws and the reconstruction of past lifeways. *The Kiva* **37**, 148–57.

Schiffer, M. B. 1987. *Formation processes of the archaeological record*. Albuquerque: University of New Mexico Press.

Truell, M. L. 1992. *Excavations at 29SJ627, Chaco Canyon, New Mexico: vol. I. The architecture and stratigraphy*. Santa Fe: Branch of Cultural Research, National Park Service.

White, L. 1932. *The pueblo of San Felipe*. Menasha: American Anthropological Association.

White, L. 1959. *The evolution of culture*. New York: McGraw-Hill.

CHAPTER ELEVEN

The uses of ethnoarchaeology in settlement studies: the case of the Bamangwato and Basarwa of Serowe, Botswana

Kathryn Jane Fewster

Introduction

The aim of this chapter is to explore some of the means by which ethnoarchaeology can help to address archaeological problems about settlement. It is not disputed that ethnoarchaeology has been a useful subdiscipline of archaeology for the past few decades, and recent changes in the questions being asked of prehistoric settlement (many of which are outlined in papers in this volume) have made the potential contribution of ethnoarchaeological research ever more important. Here, I use the results of my own ethnoarchaeological fieldwork among the Bamangwato and Basarwa (San) of Botswana to discuss some of this potential. For the purposes of this paper I define settlement as the entire repertoire of domestic and political architecture because, as will be shown, these so-called 'categories' of structures work together as a symbolic whole for the Basarwa and the Bamangwato, and any one category would make less sense if studied as an isolated 'type'.

I argue in this chapter that ethnoarchaeological research such as my own can help us to view prehistoric settlement in a way that many studies have suggested it to be – as space that is created to have social meaning and that also serves to reinforce that meaning (Moore 1982, 1986; Barrett 1988, 1994; Richards 1988; Hodder 1990; Tilley 1994). In order to do this, I discuss the domestic and political architecture of the Bamangwato of Serowe in terms of the coherent patterning that is present in structures ranging from the hearth shelter to the main court, or *kgotla* building. I also analyze this patterning in terms of generational time and structure and agency (Giddens 1979, 1984) to show how an understanding of settlement is enriched when the short-term temporal element is considered. I then go on to discuss the domestic and political architecture of the Basarwa who live on the edge of Serowe and show that the different and inverting principles by which these

178

people pattern their structures confirms much of what is argued for the
Bamangwato. I also discuss the nature of interaction between these two groups
and its physical manifestation in material culture. This leads on to a discussion
about the means by which the traditional presentation of archaeological data can
serve to obscure the questions that are currently being asked of those data. I then
show that analogies from the present can be applied at different levels and in
different areas of settlement studies. Ethnoarchaeology can be used as a generator
of ideas (following Ucko 1969); alternatively it can be used to show that long-held
beliefs about settlement structures and their relationships to people may be wrong
(the *spoiler* approach of Yellen 1977) and in this chapter I make some empirical
criticism of certain settlement principles (after Flannery 1986) that have been
accepted for a long time. I also demonstrate how ethnoarchaeology can be used to
make specific comparisons between past and present settlement structures by
applying the results of my research to the Epipalaeolithic site at Moita do
Sebastião in Portugal. I discuss the limitations and possibilities of an analogy
such as this. It will be argued that research that has emphasized the importance of
a consideration of social and material context in an understanding of settlement
architecture (Moore 1982; Parker Pearson 1982; Richards 1988; Hodder 1990) is
upheld in that the application of specific analogies to isolated archaeological data
is less than satisfactory. In order to do this, some of the detail of the Bamangwato
and Basarwa and their domestic and political architecture is first outlined.

The Bamangwato of Serowe

Serowe is the capital of the largest of eight Setswana-speaking tribes in Botswana,
the Bamangwato. The capital was founded in 1902 as a result of the secession and
subsequent migration of part of the tribe from the former capital at Shoshong (Old
Palapye). The location of Serowe was dictated largely by the presence of two rivers
that now exist as dry river beds for most of the year but that flood when the rains
arrive in October. The Bamangwato are agro-pastoralists and operate an unusual
three-way pattern of settlement that consists of discrete areas for the cultivable
lands, the cattle posts and the village. The village itself, of which Serowe is an
example, is occupied fully only during the winter months of July, August and
September (Hitchcock 1985; Schapera 1943).

Bamangwato settlement architecture

The Bamangwato kgotla building

The Bamangwato of Serowe have a hierarchical political structure that remains
operative despite the adoption of the British system of local government at Independence in 1966 (Colclough & McCarthy 1980). The traditional political system
consists of a pyramid of headmen at the pinnacle of which is the hereditary

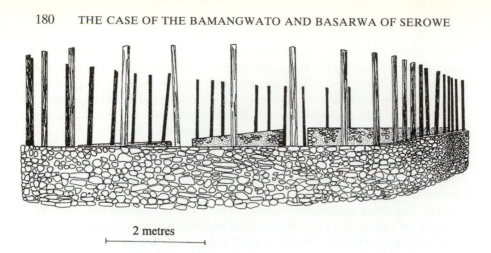

2 metres

Figure 11.1   The main Bamangwato *kgotla* building in Serowe.

position of tribal chief. The chief has repeated opportunity to maintain contact
with the tribe and demonstrate his skill as an orator, a judge and a leader at regular
kgotla meetings. All male members of the tribe are entitled to attend and participate in these meetings (Schapera 1938). The building in which the main
Bamangwato *kgotla* meetings are held in Serowe is an oval, or horseshoe-shaped,
structure of wood and stone located towards the edge of the community (figs 11.1
and 11.2). Each of the wards of Serowe (representing both political and physical
units of settlement – see below) has its own smaller *kgotla* building over which the
ward headman presides (Schapera 1938). These *kgotla* buildings are situated at the
centres of the wards.

Bamangwato wards

Bamangwato wards themselves are horseshoe-shaped arrangements made up of
individual compounds that butt on to one another (fig. 11.3). It can be seen that in
order to fit into the ward pattern, individual Bamangwato compounds must assume a particular shape: rectangular in plan and slightly squashed at the end that
forms the inner wall of the horseshoe. The compound itself has opposed entrances
with one at the squashed end of the trapezium which leads to the inner ring of the
ward horseshoe and the centrally placed ward *kgotla*, and the other on the longer
wall of the trapezium which leads to the outer ring of the ward horseshoe, other
wards, and the rest of the village (fig. 11.4). Each of the two walls of the compound
that do not carry entrances are attached to other compounds above and below it in
the horseshoe sequence. The two compounds situated at the 'neck' of the horseshoe, which each have only one compound butting on to them from above, form
exceptions. One extended family of 100–200 people typically inhabits a
Bamangwato ward and each of the compounds that make up the ward house
approximately ten people.

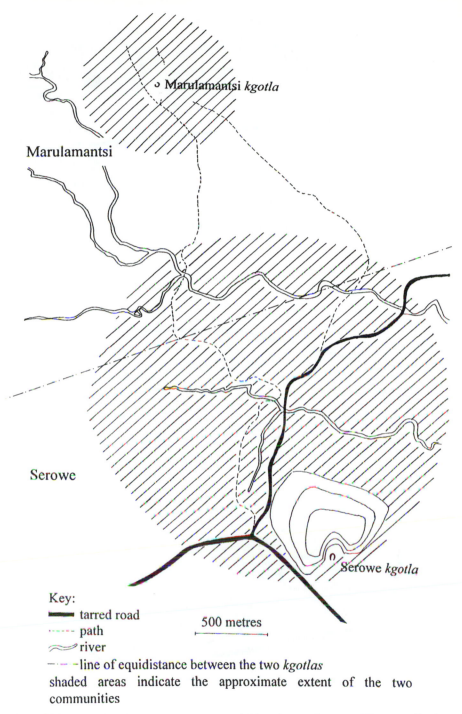

Figure 11.2 Map showing Serowe and the neighbouring settlement of Basarwa (San) at Marulamantsi.

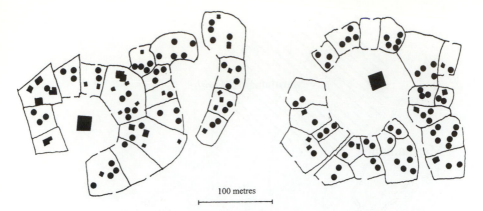

100 metres

Figure 11.3   Examples of Bamangwato wards in Serowe with central *kgotlas*.

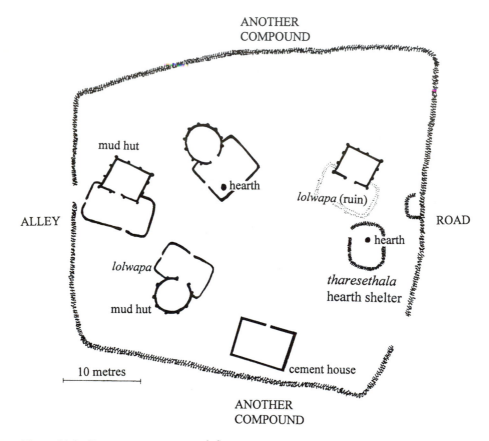

Figure 11.4   Bamangwato compound, Serowe.

Figure 11.5 Bamangwato hearth structure, Serowe.

Bamangwato hearth enclosures

The pattern of a horseshoe-shaped structure holding something at its centre is repeated at three distinct levels of Bamangwato settlement architecture. The first two levels have already been mentioned: the main *kgotla* building which holds the chief and the men of the tribe inside it at tribal political and judicial meetings, and the ward horseshoe which holds the ward *kgotla* inside it (itself containing the headman and the men of the ward inside it at ward political and judicial meetings). The third level at which this pattern can be observed is within Bamangwato compounds themselves: Bamangwato hearth enclosures are typically horseshoe-shaped structures of planted euphorbia with the hearth placed in the middle (fig. 11.5). The hearth enclosures themselves are usually located towards the edge of the compound (fig. 11.4).

The coherence and social implications of Bamangwato patterning

A schematic representation of these three levels of settlement architecture is shown in figure 11.6. The left-hand column of the figure refers to the Bamangwato whose settlement structures have been described above. The right-hand column refers to the settlement structures of the Basarwa, which will be discussed below. To take the Bamangwato first: it can be seen that there is coherence in both the shape of the three structures and their location with regard to other structures. These three levels of architecture have been chosen for analysis because they also denote social and political coherences. The hearth for the Bamangwato is the focus

Level of sturcture	Bamangwato	Basarwa
Hearth shelter: ❖ Located towards the edge of the compound for the Bamangwato ❖ Located towards the centre of the compound for the Basarwa	Nuclear family/non-family 	Nuclear family/non-family 
Kgotla building: ❖ Located towards the edge of the community for the Bamangwato ❖ Located towards the centre of the community for the Basarwa	Men/women Bamangwato/ Non-Bamangwato 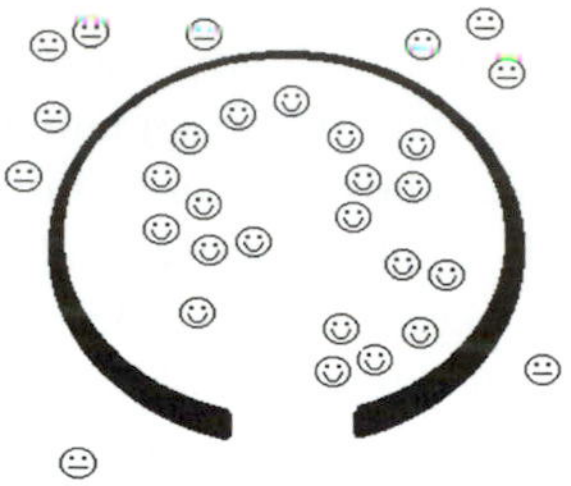	Men/women Basarwa/ Non-Basarwa 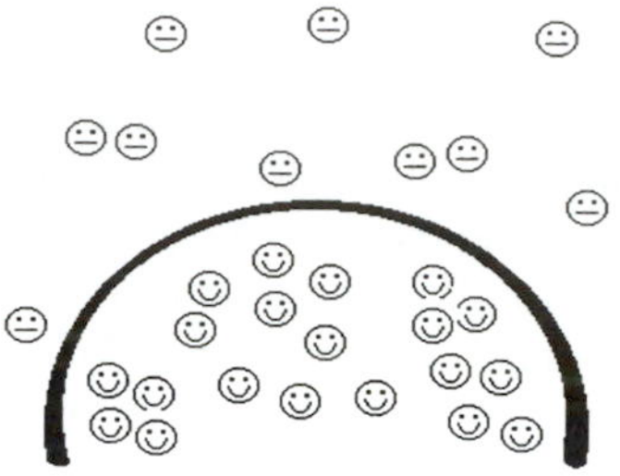
Ward horseshoe	Ward members (extended family)/non-ward members 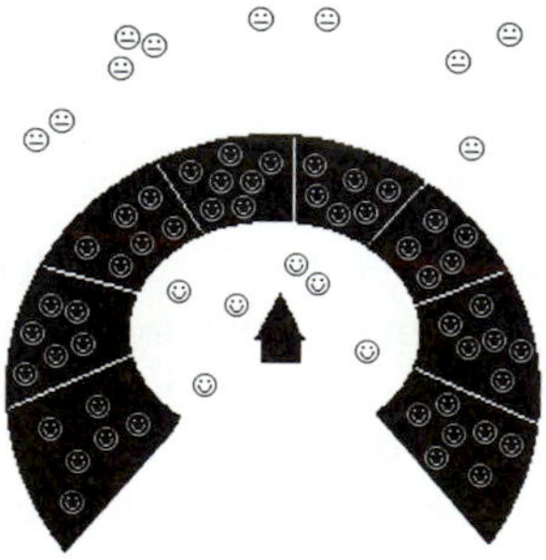	Not present

Figure 11.6 Settlement architecture and social relations – Bamangwato and Basarwa.

of family social life. Cooking and chatting takes place at outside hearths and not, according to Western expectation, inside houses or huts. It is at the hearth, therefore, that messages are conveyed about who is 'family' (the immediate family in this case) and who is 'non-family'. The second level of structure – the main *kgotla* building – represents the expression of social and political messages regarding gender and tribal identity. As the hearth is the heart of family life, so is the main *kgotla* the heart of community life. Whether one may enter the main *kgotla* horseshoe or whether one must stay outside depends on whether one is a man or a woman, an adult or a child, a member of the Bamangwato tribe or not. Finally, the ward *kgotla* represents the heart of ward life, or the heart of the extended family, and the same structural symbolism is used to determine that there is to be a choice of who is to be included and who is to be excluded.

In this way, my own research confirms much of what has been argued in recent studies of settlement archaeology: settlement space is constructed according to the social and political concerns of the architects (Moore 1986; Barrett 1988; Richards 1988; Tilley 1994). What is more, ethnoarchaeology can help to elucidate the principles by which this process takes place because of the potential offered in ethnoarchaeological studies to both observe settlement structure and to ask the architects why structures were built the way they were. This study also confirms much of what was suggested by other ethnoarchaeologists who showed through their work that material culture conveys a set of symbolic meanings when viewed *as a cohesive whole* (Moore 1982; Parker Pearson 1982; Richards 1988). The example above shows that subdivisions within the field of settlement archaeology into categories such as domestic architecture and monumental architecture would have obscured the cohesive symbolism of the *kgotla*, hearth and ward had Serowe been an archaeological site.

Bamangwato ward structure and generational time, structure and agency

Another point that was made very clear as a result of this research was the importance of a consideration of generational time and structure and agency in an analysis of settlement data. The Bamangwato ward has been described above in synchronic terms. However, for the Bamangwato of Serowe, settlement structure and social and political structures are related in a way that would make little sense if the concept of time – more specifically, generational time – were left out of the equation (Giddens 1979, 1984).

As has been shown, the Bamangwato ward horseshoe consists of a series of individual compounds that butt on to one another to make the whole (fig. 11.3). The ward itself is both a political and a structural unit. The political ward is made up of one large extended family (100–200 people) of which the headman is the senior male member (Schapera 1938). Which members of the family inhabit which particular compound of the ward horseshoe is a matter dictated by the rules of hierarchy. The headman and his family live in the bell of the horseshoe and his

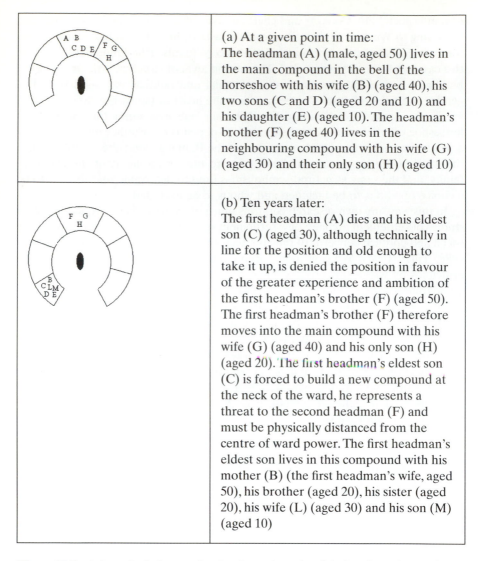

	(a) At a given point in time: The headman (A) (male, aged 50) lives in the main compound in the bell of the horseshoe with his wife (B) (aged 40), his two sons (C and D) (aged 20 and 10) and his daughter (E) (aged 10). The headman's brother (F) (aged 40) lives in the neighbouring compound with his wife (G) (aged 30) and their only son (H) (aged 10)
	(b) Ten years later: The first headman (A) dies and his eldest son (C) (aged 30), although technically in line for the position and old enough to take it up, is denied the position in favour of the greater experience and ambition of the first headman's brother (F) (aged 50). The first headman's brother (F) therefore moves into the main compound with his wife (G) (aged 40) and his only son (H) (aged 20). The first headman's eldest son (C) is forced to build a new compound at the neck of the ward, he represents a threat to the second headman (F) and must be physically distanced from the centre of ward power. The first headman's eldest son lives in this compound with his mother (B) (the first headman's wife, aged 50), his brother (aged 20), his sister (aged 20), his wife (L) (aged 30) and his son (M) (aged 10)

Figure 11.7 A hypothetical example: the domestic and political cycle – changes in the Bamangwato ward over generational time. *Continued overleaf.*

closest male kin live in the compounds on either side of him. The pattern continues, with the most distant kin of the headman occupying the compounds that form the neck of the horseshoe. When a temporal element is added to the understanding of the Bamangwato ward, the links between the domestic cycle (Goody 1971; Moore 1986) and social, political and physical structure can be seen most dramatically. A much simplified hypothetical example that demonstrates the possible implications of the temporal sequence has been set up in figure 11.7.

(C) Ten years later:

The second headman (F) dies and his only son (H) (aged 30), already in residence in the main compound and without an uncle to contest the position, becomes the next headman. He stays in the main compound with his mother (G) (the second headman's wife), his own wife (I) (aged 20), and their two sons (J and K) (aged 1 and 2). The first headman's eldest son (C) (aged 40) relinquishes hope of gaining the headmanship in his father's ward. He and his brother (D) (aged 30) construct a new ward with the help of any of the first headman's extended family who wish to join them. This new ward buds off their father's ward. The first headman's eldest son (C) is the headman of this ward and lives in the main compound with his wife (L) (aged 40) and his son and daughter (M and N) (aged 20 and 10 respectively). The first headman's eldest son has his own brother (D) (aged 30) and sister-in-law (O) (aged 20) living in the compound adjacent to him. One generation has passed. The ward cycle which is at once a family cycle, a social cycle, a political cycle and a structural cycle (in the physical sense of the word) can begin again.

Figure 11.7   *Continued*

As well as showing the relationships between political structures and space, the hypothetical example shown in figure 11.7 also helps to show something of the relationship between individual actors, structural positions and place. For example, the individual actions of the second headman (F) and the first headman's son (C) has an effect on their relationships to one another as people and may even threaten the stability of that particular ward, but their feuding never threatens the structural position represented by the headmanship itself. The physical structure or settlement pattern made by the Bamangwato ward horseshoe forms another example. Although various actors change their spatial positions in the ward horseshoe as the headmanship nears to or recedes from them, the symbolism of the residences themselves do not change. The main compound remains the main compound whoever resides in it, be his a weak or illegitimate claim to the position. The point at which this permanence of physical structure is threatened by the actors involved is when the first headman's son (C) gathers enough kin to set up a budding ward. But even then, the new ward follows the original structural pattern and the new headman (C) legitimizes his power by occupying its main compound.

Although this example suggests that the process described is a cyclical one, it should also be noted that while cyclical elements are at play, the cycle involved is not fixed or predetermined. The role of individual actors is important in influencing the manner in which these structures are actually played out. Agency can bring variation within the confines of political and social structures. An example of this is provided in the case of the ambitious brother (F) to the first headman (A). Had this man chosen not to contest the position, the first headman's son (C) would have inherited the position. Conversely, the process is not fixed or cyclical because the actions of individuals can bring about structural change. An example of this is provided in the case of the first headman's son (C) who built a new ward – a new political and structural unit – as a result of the actions of his ambitious uncle (F).

Bamangwato and Basarwa interaction

Support for much of what has been said up to this point regarding the symbolism running through Bamangwato domestic and political architecture is given by the domestic and political architecture of the neighbouring Basarwa (San). A group of around 300 Basarwa are settled on the edge of Serowe village at a location that is known as Marulamantsi. These Basarwa have stopped hunting within the past generation and are now engaged in a diverse strategy of subsistence that includes the gathering of wild products and relationships of trade and labour with their Bamangwato neighbours (see Vierich 1982; Hitchcock 1989; Kent 1992). Much of the trade and labour is concerned with agro-pastoralism. The Basarwa frequently herd Bamangwato cattle (*mafisa*) and work in fields owned by the Bamangwato (*majako*); they produce agricultural equipment to trade with the Bamangwato and they collect the wild grass and wood for poles used in Bamangwato house construction.

Although the lives of the Basarwa and the Bamangwato are intimately entwined and would appear in simple economic terms to be mutually dependent, the attitudes of the respective groups with regard to each other are paradoxical. Whereas the Basarwa express opinions about their Bamangwato neighbours that often describe them as 'family' to whom they are close yet distinct, the Bamangwato of Serowe frequently refer to the Basarwa as inferior, 'less-than-human' (largely as a result of their inability to farm) and '*tennyanateng*' (which may be translated as 'far, far away').

The Basarwa who have settled near the Bamangwato of Serowe have taken on the belief system of the Bamangwato, which involves witchcraft and sorcery, almost wholesale (see Guenther 1975) and they have adopted the political system of the Bamangwato partially but not wholly. It is surprising therefore, that although the Basarwa at Marulamantsi participate in many of the agro-pastoral activities of the Bamangwato of Serowe, few of them have adopted agro-pastoralism for themselves, despite at least three generations of intensive interaction between the two groups (see Fewster 1994 for further discussion). As was shown in other studies of interaction (Dennell 1985; Zvelebil & Rowley-Conwy 1986), it was possible in my own research to observe the differential adoption of aspects of social and economic attributes by the Basarwa living near Serowe as being reflected and reinforced in the material culture of the group. One of these indicators was settlement architecture. The coherence of Bamangwato settlement patterning (described above) is reinforced by the observation that the neighbouring Basarwa use different and inverting principles to organize the structures of their own settlement.

Basarwa settlement architecture

Basarwa hearth structures

The hearth structures of the Basarwa who live on the edge of Serowe often consist of crescents (as opposed to horseshoes) of planted euphorbia (fig. 11.8). These shelters are located in the centres of compounds (fig. 11.9) in contrast to Bamangwato hearth structures which are located towards the edges of the compounds (also see figure 11.6).

The Basarwa kgotla building

The pattern of the Basarwa hearth structure is monumentalized in the form of the *kgotla* building which is a semi-circular or crescent-shaped structure of wood and stone located at the centre of the community (figs 11.10 and 11.2). It should be noted that the *kgotla* is itself a representation of the Bamangwato concept of hierarchical politics that the Basarwa do not generally share, but that has been partially adopted by, or imposed on, the Basarwa living on the edge of Serowe within the past 20–30 years. That the Basarwa had transformed the Bamangwato concept of *kgotla* by constructing the building according to the principles dictated by the shapes of their own hearths and not those dictated by the shapes of the Bamangwato hearths is a material indication of the paradoxical or ambiguous political position of the Basarwa with regard to the Bamangwato of Serowe. Following Hodder (1990), it could also be argued that the symbolism of the Bamangwato architecture, which involves almost total enclosure in the form of the horseshoe, might allude to agro-pastoralist values such as enclosure, territoriality or an embrace of the *domus*. Concomitantly, the symbolism of the

Figure 11.8 Basarwa hearth structure, Marulamantsi.

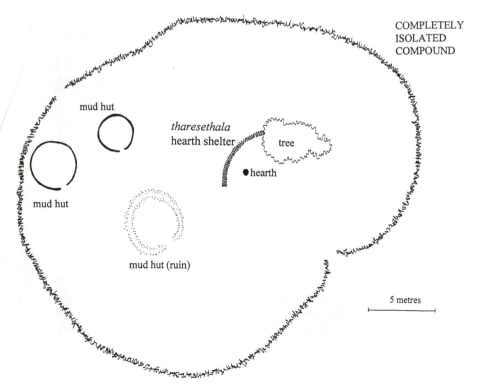

COMPLETELY
ISOLATED
COMPOUND

mud hut

tharesethala
hearth shelter

tree

● hearth

mud hut

mud hut (ruin)

5 metres

Figure 11.9 Basarwa compound, Marulamantsi.

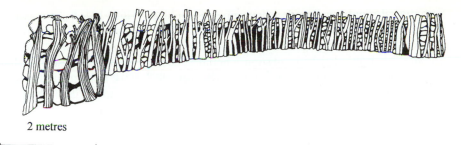

2 metres

Figure 11.10   The Basarwa *kgotla* building at Marulamantsi.

crescent-shaped structures of that Basarwa at Serowe may denote an adherence to hunter–gatherer values in the form of an openness to the *agrios*, the wild.

Basarwa wards

The Basarwa at Marulamantsi do not arrange their compounds into wards. This is confirmed by the shape of individual Basarwa compounds which are irregular and do not follow the pattern described above for Bamangwato compounds (Fig. 11.9). The fact that Basarwa compounds are not arranged into wards is another facet of the partial and ambiguous adoption of the Bamangwato political system. Although the *kgotla* building has been adopted (and adapted) by the Basarwa at Marulamantsi, the Bamangwato political system is not complete without the fundamental principle of the grouping of extended families into political and structural wards. Thus the physical structures can be taken as good indicators of the ambiguities of political and social interaction in this case.

Implications for archaeology – the presentation of data

Another question that is raised as a result of first-hand ethnoarchaeological research is whether it would be possible to reconstruct the social and political relations between the two communities described above from a study of the domestic and political architecture alone and without the aid of living informants, i.e. whether it would be possible to understand some of the meanings of the material culture described above if Serowe were an archaeological site. For example, the word *tennyanateng* – used by the Bamangwato of Serowe to describe the Basarwa as far, far away – refers not to a physical distance but to a social, or emotional distance. It could be suggested that if Serowe and its neighbouring settlement were archaeological sites, they would probably be mapped and presented in terms of a plan. Such a plan would demonstrate that the two communities were 5 km apart which might appear very close. Thus, this method of presenting would give the observer no clue about the emotional distance perceived by the

Bamangwato and the Basarwa themselves (Gould & White 1974). As it is this emotional distance that is the key to understanding Basarwa and Bamangwato relations, the data would need to be viewed in some way other than as sites on a plan. This reminds us to question whether the aims of current research that seeks to view settlement as social practice (Barrett 1988, 1994; Barrett and Fewster 1998) and to elucidate the social *intent* of settlement architecture (Tilley 1994) can be fulfilled if data continue to be presented for analysis according to etic principles only (see also Johnson 1993).

The word 'plan' in the English language is used in two ways. In the context in which it is most often used in archaeology, this means simply 'a view from above'. In more general terms, the word plan implies *intent*, an intention, an outline or a blueprint for future action. The word has both temporal and spatial connotations. In the presentation of much archaeological data, the spatial connotation of the word 'plan' has been emphasized over the *action* implied by the word and its temporal associations. As advances in settlement studies call increasingly for a view of social space as the dynamic outcome to human action and relations, it might be borne in mind that the method of presenting data can actually serve to obscure the questions that are being asked of the material.

Finally, the view from above may in fact hinder an important aspect of current research in settlement archaeology: territoriality. If the communities of Basarwa and Bamangwato at Serowe were archaeological sites excavated as they are today, it might be tempting to regard the main *kgotla* buildings of the two communities as territorial markers because they are the most visible and substantial structures of the entire settlement repertoires of the two communities. Having done that, we might argue the boundary line between the two groups might feasibly be drawn equidistant from each *kgotla* building. However, this is not where the actual boundary lies for the Basarwa and Bamangwato of Serowe (fig. 11.2). The potency of the *kgotla* symbolism is not to do with some kind of monumental muscle-flexing at the frontier between the two communities. Rather the *kgotla* building of each community has been situated in its right place *within* the community and the 'right place' is defined according to the settlement principles of each respective community. Thus, for the Basarwa, the 'right place' for the *kgotla* building is at the centre of the community and, for the Bamangwato, the 'right place' for the *kgotla* building is at the edge of the community. Only an appreciation of settlement architecture at all levels and in context, ranging from the hearth to the ward structure, would show that territory is being asserted in a manner more subtle and ultimately more potent than simply the distance between monuments.

Implications for archaeology: the spoiler approach

Yellen (1977) argued that there were many ways in which analogies from the present could be used to illuminate the past. One such method is the 'spoiler' approach, which demonstrates through ethnoarchaeological research that things might not have been the way archaeologists have suggested they might have been in the past. This form of analogy became pertinent when my own empirical observations showed that in the following example archaeological principles about settlement that had been held to be 'true' were not, in fact, universal. Flannery (1986) examined the connection between sedentism and the origins of agriculture by means of a comparison between house structures in Mesoamerica and the Near East in both the ethnographic literature and the archaeological context of the two areas. He summarized other peoples' work on the same to the following:

   (a) $10\,m^2$ of house space is available for each individual in societies of 'Neolithic type'.
   (b) Circular dwellings are usually associated with nomadic societies and rectangular dwellings are usually associated with sedentary societies.
   (c) Through time rectangular dwellings replace circular dwellings in many archaeological contexts around the world.
   (d) Circular structures are more quickly and easily constructed than rectangular dwellings and it is easier to add extra units to rectangular dwellings than to circular dwellings (this in part is Flannery's explanation as to why circular huts are associated with nomadic societies and rectangular huts with sedentary societies).

My own ethnoarchaeological fieldwork showed that none of these principles hold true for the two communities at Serowe: according to my sample, 'Neolithic-type' Serowans have on average $15\text{--}16\,m^2$ of hut space per person. They use both circular and rectangular huts and have done so for a long time. Circular huts take about as long to build as rectangular huts, and the rectangular huts of both the Bamangwato and the Basarwa rarely have units added on to them. When the family expands, new huts are built. This shows that if ethnoarchaeology is to be effectively applied to settlement studies, not only is there a need for constant re-evaluation of ideas about past settlement in the light of new data collected among contemporary societies, but information collected from present societies must also be subject to scrutiny.

An archaeological example: the application of a specific analogy

Another way in which ethnoarchaeological research can be used to help with problems concerning prehistoric settlement is by making specific comparisons between contemporary architecture and that of the past. For example, the crescent-shaped windbreak, which is marked out by postholes at the Epipalaeolithic site of Moita do Sebastião in Portugal, is uncannily reminiscent of some of the structures described above for the Basarwa living near Serowe (fig. 11.11). What is more, the windbreak is some 10 m long – too large to be an individual hearth shelter – and could represent a communal structure and perhaps something similar to the Basarwa *kgotla* described above. Although ethnoarchaeology can 'prove' nothing about the past, its value is in allowing the archaeologist (myself, in this case) to view the structure at Moita do Sebastião as a socially meaningful space and in generating a series of questions about that space that might otherwise not

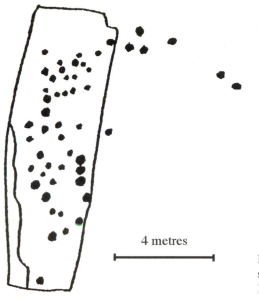

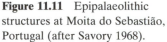

4 metres

Figure 11.11   Epipalaeolithic
structures at Moita do Sebastião,
Portugal (after Savory 1968).

have been asked. We might be inspired by the ethnoarchaeological case study
described above to ask who was allowed inside the space at Moita do Sebastião
and who was excluded, what this meant in terms of social and political relations
and how these relations might have altered within the space of a generation.

At a later stage, the semi-circular structure at Moita do Sebastião was replaced
by a similar-sized rectangular structure (fig. 11.11). It could be argued that the later
structure represents a different symbolic concern: an almost complete enclosure of
the internal space. According to the principles outlined in the ethnoarchaeological
example above, it could also be argued that the symbolism of this change from
openness to boundedness reflected a change from hunting and gathering to farming (see Hodder 1990).

However, one problem with the application of analogy to archaeological data
such as these is that the structures at Moita do Sebastião represent an isolated
example, removed, as a result of postdepositional process, from the whole context
of material culture of which it was a part. As was stated above, settlement structure
is better understood in context (Moore 1982; Parker Pearson 1982; Richards 1988;
Hodder 1990). It is also difficult to elucidate the time difference between the two
structures at Moita do Sebastião, thus reducing our understanding of the changes
in the structures that were brought about as a result of generational time.

Conclusion

This paper has explored some of the ways in which ethnoarchaeology can be used
to address archaeological problems about settlement. Ethnoarchaeology has

played an important part in archaeological reconstruction in general but new approaches to the archaeology of prehistoric settlement, many of which are outlined in chapters in this volume, have made the potential contribution of ethnoarchaeological research ever more pertinent. In this chapter, I have used the results of my own ethnoarchaeological fieldwork among the Bamangwato and Basarwa of Serowe, Botswana, to discuss some of the ways in which ethnoarchaeology can be used to enhance the study of prehistoric settlement. I have defined settlement as the entire repertoire of domestic and political architecture because these structures work together as a symbolic whole in Serowe and cannot be subdivided into the type of categories that might have meaning for the archaeologist, but would not have meaning for the Bamangwato and the Basarwa themselves. Although it has not been a subject of this paper, funerary architecture would also be included in the definition of settlement for the same reason. It was argued that research that has stressed the importance of a consideration of social and material context (Moore 1982; Parker Pearson 1982; Richards 1988; Hodder 1990) in an understanding of settlement architecture is upheld by the results of the ethnoarchaeological case study in Botswana. I have also analyzed the settlement patterning of the Bamangwato in terms of generational time and structure and agency (Giddens 1979, 1984) to show that our understanding of settlement, for the Bamangwato ward in particular, can be increased when the short-term temporal element is considered.

I have argued that ethnoarchaeological research such as this example can help us to view prehistoric settlement in a way that many studies have suggested it to be: space that is created to have social meaning and that also serves to reinforce that meaning (Moore 1982, 1986; Barrett 1988, 1994; Barrett and Fewster 1998; Richards 1988; Hodder 1990; Tilley 1994). In order to confirm this I have discussed the domestic and political architecture of the Bamangwato and the Basarwa in terms of the coherent patterning that is present in the hearth shelter, the *kgotla* building and the ward. This physical patterning corresponds to social and political relations both within the groups of Bamangwato and Basarwa and also serves to highlight ambiguities of interaction between the two groups. This led on to a short discussion about the way in which the traditional presentation of archaeological data as a two-dimensional plan can obscure the questions that are currently being asked of those data. It was suggested that if new questions are to be asked of settlement data, new ways of presenting data should be sought – ways in which more thought might be given as to what may have been meaningful for the prehistoric inhabitants as opposed to what has meaning only for the archaeologist–analyst.

I then showed that analogies from the present can be applied at different levels of analysis. Ethnoarchaeology can be used as a generator of ideas (following Ucko 1969), in the same way that it was used in this chapter in the application of the results of my ethnoarchaeological research to the Epipalaeolithic site of Moita do Sebastião in Portugal. Alternatively, ethnoarchaeological results can be used to show that ideas about the past may have been wrong (the *spoiler* approach of Yellen 1977) and in this chapter I made empirical criticisms of settlement principles (after Flannery 1986) that have long been accepted. I also showed how ethnoarchaeology can be used to make specific comparisons between particular settlement structures in the past and in the present, again using the archaeological case study of Moita do Sebastião. At all levels, the limitations and possibilities of analogy were discussed, and it was concluded that while ethnoarchaeological research is an invaluable tool for prehistoric settlement studies in general, those analogies that incorporate as much contextual information as possible – archaeological and ethnoarchaeological – are likely to be more informative than those that regard isolated aspects of material culture.

References

Barrett, J. C. 1988. Fields of discourse: reconstituting a social archaeology. *Critique of Anthropology* **7**(3), 5–16.

Barrett, J. 1994. *Fragments from antiquity: an archaeology of social life in Britain, 2900–1200 BC*. Oxford: Blackwell.

Barrett, J. & K. J. Fewster 1998. Stonehenge: *is* the medium the message? *Antiquity* 72, 847–52.

Colclough, C. & S. McCarthy 1980. *The political economy of Botswana*. London: Oxford University Press.

Dennell, R. W. 1985. The hunter/gatherer–agricultural frontier in prehistoric temperate Europe. In *The archaeology of frontiers and boundaries*, S. W. Green & S. M. Perlman (eds), 113–39. London: Academic Press.

Fewster, K. J. 1994. Basarwa and Bamangwato interaction in Botswana: implications for the transition to agriculture in European prehistory. *Archaeological Review from Cambridge* **13**(1), 83–103.

Flannery, K. V. (ed.) 1986. *Guila Naquitz: archaic foraging and early agriculture in Oaxaca, Mexico*. London: Academic Press.

Giddens, A. 1979. *Central problems in social theory: action, structure and contradiction in social analysis*. London: Macmillan.

Giddens, A. 1984. *The constitution of society: outline of a theory of structuration*. Cambridge: Polity Press.

Gould, P. & R. White 1974. *Mental maps*. New York: Penguin.

Goody, J. (ed.) 1971. *The developmental cycle in domestic groups*. Cambridge: Cambridge University Press.

Guenther, M. 1975. The trance dancer as an agent of social change among the farm Bushmen of the Ghanzi district. *Botswana Notes and Records* **7**, 161–7.

Hitchcock, R. K. 1985. Water, land and livestock: the evolution of tenure and administrative patterns in grazing. In *The evolution of modern Botswana*, L. A. Picard (ed.), 84–121. London: Rex Collings.

Hitchcock, R. K. 1989. Modelling Kalahari hunter–gatherer subsistence and settlement systems: implications for development policy and land use planning in Botswana. *Anthropos* **84**(1), 47–62.

Hodder, I. 1990. *The domestication of Europe*. Cambridge: Cambridge University Press.

Johnson, M. 1993. *Housing culture: traditional architecture in an English landscape*. London: UCL Press.

Kent, S. 1992. The current forager controversy: real vs. ideal views of hunter–gatherers. *Man* **27**, 45–70.

Moore, H. L. 1982. The interpretation of spatial patterning in spatial residues. In *Symbolic and structural archaeology*, I. Hodder (ed.), 74–9. Cambridge: Cambridge University Press.

Moore, H. L. 1986. *Space, text and gender: an anthropological study of the Marakwet of Kenya*. Cambridge: Cambridge University Press.

Parker Pearson, M. 1982. Mortuary practices, society and ideology: an ethnoarchaeological study. In *Symbolic and structural archaeology*, I. Hodder (ed.), 99–113. Cambridge: Cambridge University Press.

Richards, C. 1988. Altered images: a re-examination of Neolithic mortuary practices in Orkney. In *The archaeology of context in the Neolithic and Bronze Age: recent trends*, J. C. Barrett & I. A. Kinnes (eds), 42–56. Sheffield: University of Sheffield.

Savory, H. N. 1968. *Spain and Portugal: the prehistory of the Iberian peninsula*. London: Thames & Hudson.

Schapera, I. 1938. *A handbook of Tswana law and custom*. Oxford: Oxford University Press.

Schapera, I. 1943. *Native land tenure in the Bechuanaland Protectorate*. Lovedale: Alice.

Tilley, C. 1994. *A phenomenology of landscape: places, paths and monuments*. Oxford: Berg.

Ucko, P. J. 1969. Ethnography and archaeological interpretation of funerary remains. *World Archaeology* **1**(2): 262–77.

Vierich, H. 1982. Adaptive flexibility in a multi-ethnic setting: the Basarwa of the southern Kalahari. In *Politics and history in band societies*, E. Leacock & R. Lee (eds), 213–22. Cambridge: Cambridge University Press.

Yellen, J. E. 1977. *Archaeological approaches to the present: models for reconstructing the past*. New York: Academic Press.

Zvelebil, M. & P. Rowley-Conwy 1986. Foragers and farmers in Atlantic Europe. In *Hunters in transition: Mesolithic societies of temperate Eurasia and their transition to farming*, M. Zvelebil (ed.), 67–93. Cambridge: Cambridge University Press.

CHAPTER TWELVE

Debating marginality: archaeologists on the edge?

Robert Young & Trevor Simmonds

In 1987, Blaikie and Brookfield isolated three broad categories of marginality: sociopolitical, ecological and economic (Blaikie & Brookfield 1987a: 20). It has struck us quite forcibly that most archaeological discussions of 'marginality' and the 'margin' have followed these divisions, either consciously or subconsciously, often privileging one category above the others. However, we hope to show below that such categorizations of, and approaches to, marginality are not mutually exclusive. Conversely, we do not believe that where one form of marginality can be identified, the others must necessarily also be in place.

Most archaeologists have a clear ecologically/economically determined view of the 'margin'. Peripheral areas and strict economic marginality often tend to be defined in absolute terms on the basis of a simple binary (centre/periphery) opposition. However, we believe that attempts to discuss 'marginalities' using these categories also make the crucial and erroneous assumption that the societies being studied are bounded, isolated, monolithic units without social and economic contacts beyond their immediate spheres of activity and influence. We dispute the fact that such societies exist today and that they ever really existed in pre-history. We argue that any discussion of marginality (however defined) and of people's perception of it in the past must be broader and more context-orientated than a strict application of Blaikie and Brookfield's categories might allow. In this contribution, we set out first to examine Blaikie and Brookfield's three categories of marginality in detail, beginning with highly deterministic notions of ecological/environmental marginality. We then move on to economic approaches to the margin and finally we deal with what we believe to be the most difficult aspect of the 'margin' to discuss archaeologically: conceptions of sociopolitical marginality. Along the way, we try to highlight the overlaps in the three approaches.

In the second part we attempt to move the debate forward and examine, through one archaeological case study, how simplistic views of marginality have straightjacketed the nature of much discussion. We suggest that if archaeologists, historians and historical geographers wish to develop a more nuanced understanding of the nature of aspects of 'marginality' and of potential human responses to it, they need to consider the 'total' environment with its rich interplay of political, social, economic and ecological elements.

Ecological/environmental marginality

Very simply, ecological/environmental marginality can be defined in terms of the overall distribution of a species within a particular landscape or zone of a landscape. The onset of marginal conditions occurs when, for example, a plant or an animal approaches the limits of a habitat or environment in which its successful reproduction is possible. Beyond that limit, the ripening of particular plants is impossible and certain animals may not be able to obtain enough food for self-maintenance. The definition assumes that the inhabitants of such marginal zones do not possess the technological knowledge and/or ability to alter the material conditions of their existence to their advantage.

As will be obvious from the discussion that follows, we are very wary of an uncritical acceptance of this notion of marginality and its application to episodes of human activity. By defining 'marginal' zones of human occupancy solely on the basis of environmental criteria (see below for examples), we believe that some writers have sought to divorce these areas from their adjacent communities. This has the effect of excusing these writers from any consideration of the mediating effects that socioeconomic interdependence or co-operation can have on detrimental environmental change. It also provides an easy dataset (i.e. settlements and activity areas seen in isolation) on which to apply generalizing theories of climatic stress and environmental deterioration. A good example of this approach can be seen in a paper by Burgess (1985) that will be discussed below. This employs an extreme interpretation of the role of climatic stress on populations in 'marginal' areas (see also Young & Simmonds 1995).

A good example of the application of this concept can be found in the work of the historical geographer M. L. Parry on the Lammermuir Hills of Scotland. Parry (1975, 1985) adopted an ecological/environmental definition of marginality, employing the combined criteria of altitude and temperature to draw up limits beyond which the maintenance of an arable agricultural regime became a marginal activity. Long-term climatic trends were identified between AD 1000 and AD 1700, with a cooling phase between c. AD 1250 and AD 1530, and a cold phase extending from c. AD 1530 until AD 1700. Parry associated both of these phases with the gradual abandonment of the uplands. Despite the fact that the archaeological and historical dating of the settlements under study is not clear, Parry assumed that the economic threshold of the area was based solely on the growth requirements of particular crops. He largely ignored any economic strategy other than arable farming, and the only method of coping with changing local environmental conditions discussed is the retreat to the next limit of cereal cultivation.

However, it must be emphasized that societies, like crops, also have their own environmental/ecological thresholds. These thresholds are neither absolute nor universal because, unlike crops, human societies possess the ability to bring about more complex or specialized economies. Any threshold effect is thus dependent, as we show below, on the particular socioeconomic form dominant at any one point in time. This realization clearly demands a more complex approach to the study of socioeconomic and environmental context.

The archaeological implications of ecological marginality for settlement and subsistence are, at one level, dependent on the relationship between human communities and the biota affected by marginal conditions. However, to grasp these implications fully, archaeologists and historians must try to examine the total economic basis of a society and its relationship with its resources (Bailey 1989: 12–13). In this context, the overlap between economic, ecological and sociopolitical marginality should be obvious. For example, regions of poor or degrading soil that became incapable of cereal growth may have developed specialized economies to complement the requirements of the wider economic nexus (as Bailey 1989: 11) has argued for the English medieval upland economy; see also Young & Simmonds 1995).

The general points raised above should make us wary of the ready acceptance of the kind of 'sustainable threshold' approach to marginality and settlement development embodied in much archaeological writing. In ecological terms, both core and periphery are seen in isolation and the possible social and economic links between the two are largely unexplored (for broader scale approaches that emphasize the non-ecological aspects of 'peripheral' or marginal areas, see Champion 1989). We need to be clear about what constitutes the ecological core of an economy and how it articulates with other aspects of economic and social activity, before making hard and fast statements about its margins (Bailey 1989; Campbell 1990: 83).

Economic marginality

Archaeological discussions of economic marginality usually focus on the relative economic potential of a given piece of land and its capacity to provide sufficient yields (invariably of grain) to meet a group's food requirements. The basic principle of diminishing returns, with the emphasis on inputs of labour and social capital, has been seen by many as a useful criterion for assessing marginality. The point at which subsistence yields from a region barely match the labour input into that region is the 'economic margin'. This is an approach with which most practising archaeologists and economic historians would readily identify.

We suggest that this approach towards marginality, with its obvious overtones of economic formalism, embodies within it all the difficulties that we have outlined above in our discussion of the ecological/environmental margin. It rarely considers the flexibility of economic systems. The identification of marginality in economic terms is dependent, again, on both the dominant mode of production and existing levels of demand, yet there is often little discussion of the importance of social relations of production (labour, social capital, communal decision-making and exchange). Nor is there any acknowledgement of the possibility that societies may radically alter the means of production in relation to either changes in the material conditions of production or the social relations of such a system. The same soils and environments can hold very different economic potentials, depending on the social and technological capacity of a society. Blaikie & Brookfield (1987a: 17) have argued for the realization of an integrated approach to the study of people/ land relationships in marginal areas that values the flexibility of production and decision-making in developing economies.

Sociopolitical marginality

A sociological approach to marginality often identifies groups or activities that lie outside the culturally defined norms or rules of behaviour of a society. These people or activities constitute a sociological 'other', external to the main body of society (Mizruchi 1983; Shields 1991). The criteria for assessing this kind of 'otherness' or marginality are subject to constant change and modification. This suggests that monolithic or static models of marginality may be inappropriate in an archaeological or historical context, a point that we develop throughout this chapter.

The existence of socially marginal or 'liminal' groups is well documented in the literature of social anthropology. There are indications that some of these groups may perform vital functions on the margins of society (see Fewster, Chapter 11, this volume). Welbourn, for example, describes the role of one such group in a tribal society, the Marakwet blacksmiths of northwest Africa (Welbourn 1981). The Pokot, their neighbours, are pastoral, aggressive, and depend on the Marakwet as a market for their cattle and as a source for the procurement of metalwork. Metal objects produced by the Marakwet smiths are used by both groups to mark symbolic distinctions between different social categories and although the smiths are held neither in contempt nor esteem, they are set apart from Pokot society. Their 'otherness' is clearly shown by a whole range of social taboos associated with them (Welbourn 1981: 36; Yadeta 1985). Rowlands, using information gathered from a detailed survey of the social anthropology of metalworking and smithing, coupled with wide-ranging archaeological analysis, has postulated a similar marginal role for metalworkers in Bronze Age Europe (1971: 210–33). This connection between the marginal status assigned to groups and the socioeconomic value of their products suggests that the fortunes of such groups are intimately bound up with those of other, supposedly more complex, social formations.

Such an approach may be broadened through the recognition of a political element in the definition of marginal groups. Even within single social units, such as tribes, the social relations of production may be such that groups are marginalized from the products of their labour and enterprise. This point allows us to break away from the notion that 'marginal' groups are necessarily a minority. Such groups may just as easily comprise the majority, yet at the same time they may be situated outside the frameworks of political negotiation that govern the distribution or redistribution of goods and services. In the political economies of the New Guinea Highlands, for example, men clear the trees, fence the land and plant certain crops, whereas women weed the land and break down and rebuild compost mounds. Women till, plant and harvest as well as raising pigs that are the focus of the economy. However, the labour of men is deemed the more important here, since it seemingly creates improvements and capital, whereas the women's labour, which clearly maintains the smooth running of the economy, is marginalized. It is in fact seen as repetitious, appearing to create no capital or social gain from cycle to cycle (Allen & Crittenden 1987: 145–56). This is a clear case of a large section of the population being marginalized in terms of undermining the 'value' of its economic contribution because of accepted, socially constructed values and dominant male ideology. All this reinforces the politics of gender oppression.

Social marginality may bear no strict resemblance in spatial terms to the location of producers, so we must avoid a simple extrapolation of sociopolitical complexity from what are often seen archaeologically as regional concentrations of settlement or production sites on distribution maps. The evidence suggests that marginality, in the context of the present discussion, is politically defined within groups, classes and larger regional formations. Accordingly, social or political marginality will affect the position of these groups within the socioeconomic nexus through differential access to labour, resources, subsistence goods and markets. Social marginality, then, is more a product of social distance than spatial location (cf. Fewster, Chapter 11, this volume). This is an important point to establish if we are to examine in greater detail the functionings of socioeconomic systems in economically or ecologically marginal areas.

Aspects of the Marxist social formulation may help us to explore possible correlations between groups marginalized from the products of their labour, or socially marginal groups, and the location of these groups in marginal or economically restricted areas of land. The class conflict approach clearly allows us to integrate these various aspects of marginality. Here, it is argued that the spatial marginalization of individuals or groups occurs through sociopolitical mechanisms at the instigation of a dominant class or interest group. A more insidious process is the gradual securement of prime land by these groups, forcing others into less productive or economically/environmentally 'marginal' locations (Blaikie & Brookfield 1987a: 23). At a more practical level, isolated groups in geographically remote or inaccessible areas may find that participation in markets or inter-group contact is more difficult. In some ways, social and economic concepts of the margin therefore have important convergences.

The dialectical nature of the relations of production should encourage us to examine the effects of environmental stress on the position of producers in marginal areas within the socioeconomic nexus. By drawing on the relations of this wider nexus, groups can counter changes in the material base in order to maintain and reproduce existing socioeconomic structures within their localities (we return to this point below in our discussion of the work of Andrew Fleming and our application of his ideas to Bronze Age northern Britain). People can also reorganize the means of production at the local and regional level.

In the preceding discussion we pointed out some of the problems that previous approaches and understandings of the 'margin' have raised. We now make some suggestions that might broaden the discussion. The key to such progress, we believe, lies in a more integrated approach to the problem of 'marginalities'.

Integrative approaches to marginality: space, society and environment

Human perceptions of environment

Communities invariably identify those areas of land that will best serve the subsistence needs of the group in the light of existing cultural knowledge, in terms of varied maintenance strategies, and the available technology. These are all facets of a learned cultural repertoire, and progress is made through time by the gradual accretion of new experiences.

As suggested above, the simplistic reading off of sociopolitical complexity from the apparent concentrations of archaeological debris should be avoided. In this context, the landscape may be seen as a series of activity-related areas or places that are exploited to satisfy the social and subsistence needs of a community. Evans (1985) has discussed the role of 'places' in landscape archaeology, suggesting that the landscape should not be seen as a mere reflection of the subsistence organization of a society, but as a potential map of its cultural vision. He criticizes the assumption that 'places' must equate with activities (debris) and therefore 'sites', since this 'ignores the temporal, cultural and cognitive recognition of places through which they may exist as loci of meaning and not necessarily as foci of activity. In effect, places are locations where culture has humanized 'nature'' (ibid.: 81). Although we have some sympathy with this view, it is unhelpful to denigrate the usefulness of activity-related sites in this way, as all interventions in the landscape are, through their location and the nature of any possible material remains, potentially indicative of attitudes towards the natural environment.

Approaches to the logic of social space developed by behavioural geographers may help provide a fuller understanding of the way in which societies perceive marginality. Such approaches may also form a valuable accompaniment to any discussion of economic organization. Environmental stress or economic reorganization are often recognized in retrospect but they are not necessarily identified as such at the time. A subsistence economy does not always visualize the future in linear developmental terms, and the organization of production often operates on a yearly cycle, as a 'round of time' rather than an 'arrow of time' (Blaikie & Brookfield 1987b: 35). Similarly, an individual or a group's perception of environmental change may be restricted to the experience of a generation. Ignorance of environmental change is widespread (ibid.: 36). Indeed, some processes of environmental degradation show little significant effect until a resilience threshold is passed or the sensitivity of an area is increased. A good contemporary example of this phenomenon might be the West's belated grasping of the global implications of rainforest destruction or the cumulative impact of CFCs and other pollutants on 'global warming'.

The realization that environmental change may go unnoticed is important as it provides a different insight into why particular groups might continue to use, and even to intensify their use of, sensitive areas of the landscape in the face of ecological degradation. It also forms a useful adjunct to demographically driven models of marginal land-use, suggesting that population pressure on resources does not wholly explain the continued use of economically marginal areas. In this context, the continued use of an increasingly less-productive environment may be indicative of the 'maintenance of tradition', or may be a manifestation of a group's increasing sense of attachment to a particular locale.

Tuan (1974, 1984) has demonstrated how pre-industrial societies, such as the Aivilk Eskimos, are more finely tuned to their environment than groups living in the industrialized West. At the most basic level of perception, people develop greater acuity in relation to their surroundings, particularly in harsh environments. The Aivilk people have a minimum of 12 terms for winds and a similar number for snow; they can navigate for miles in a featureless landscape on the basis of wind direction, texture of snow and so on. Among the Aivilk, 'environmental stress' is clearly not necessarily experienced as such, and the impact of worsening climatic conditions may be partly negated by the increasing sense of place that a community feels towards the local surroundings and topography.

Social spatialization?

The important work of Shields (1991) on the perception of social and geographical boundaries lends itself to archaeological and historical geographical discussions of the 'marginalization' of places, areas and regions in terms of their perceived socioeconomic and environmental characteristics. Shields defines 'social spatialization' as 'the ongoing construction of the spatial at the level of the social imaginary (collective mythologies, presuppositions) as well as interventions in the landscape (for example the built environment)' (ibid.: 31).

The concept of social spatialization is also applicable to discussions of the natural environment, since such a framework integrates societal perceptions of environment and space with the idea of discernible interventions in geographical space over time. These interventions are the product of socially meaningful activities and are significant in that attitudes towards the environment and society reflected in spatial forms may be defined. Seen in this light, it becomes obvious that perceptions of marginality are culturally determined and that they are reproduced through the construction of 'space myths'. The cultural logic of space finds expression through language, which serves to reinforce attitudes to an area, and these attitudes in turn may be transformed into tangible actions and institutional arrangements. They may even alter strategies for the regional development of a particular institution.

We also suggest that *time* plays an essential role in the development of cultural perceptions of landscape, environment and marginality. Peripheral areas should not be defined in absolute terms on the basis of the simplistic binary opposition noted in our introduction, but by the continued formation or reinstatement of cultural perceptions through time by individuals and groups. If such a pattern of domains, places and potentials is culturally produced, then the necessity of temporal repetition and the role of cultural tradition negates the idea that such patterns are intuitive, naturalized productions. As Evans (1985) has observed, the process of formation and reinstatement of perceptions is in essence both historical and cumulative.

In this context, Gold (1982: 44–67) has discussed various definitions and applications of the concept of territoriality as a facet of human social behaviour. Ethnological approaches to the study of this manifestation of social organization are frequently rigidly functionalist. Territoriality is defined as a mechanism for ensuring security, a predictable supply of food and a reproductive network (e.g. Jochim 1976; Winterhalder 1981: 66–98). It is therefore seen as innate in the social make-up of animal and human groups.

An alternative approach suggests that the nature of territoriality is culturally learned and that the rules, symbolisms and mechanisms that govern and prescribe it are culturally embedded (Hodder 1987). Spatial organization is therefore also a reflection of attitudes towards, and perceptions of, environment and other people, rather than a simple index of population pressure, resource distribution or core/periphery relationships. As such, it may be bound up with types of production and social organization rather than scales of difference.

Settlement scale and group organization

Concepts such as quality of life and cultural development may play a large part in the way societies (and social elites in particular) organize themselves in areas of restricted economic potential. An awareness of this point allows us to suggest possible relationships between social organization, economic strategies and the environment of an area.

Fleming (1985) has discussed the types of social organization that we may envisage in later prehistory in various parts of Britain by relating settlement evidence to land tenure and patterns of collective organization. This work has implications for the study of marginal areas in that we may postulate the units of social organization that may occur outside archaeologically observable 'centres' of occupation, such as Wessex. Fleming's fieldwork (ibid.) on Dartmoor (an upland area in Devon that has been viewed by many as marginal on ecological/environmental and economic grounds) identified scattered houses, small hamlets and field systems dating to the second millennium BC. Fleming suggests a socioeconomic model for these communities in which the 'household' is the main unit of labour. A 'household' is defined as a nuclear or small extended family occupying one or two houses set within the fields farmed by the family. Kinship structures link these households into wider groups. Thus, what appears at first sight to be a dispersed settlement pattern of isolated units, possibly reflecting the physical marginalization of families within the landscape, may in fact be a closely linked society made up of localized groupings (ibid.: 131). Significantly, the settlement pattern will still appear as dispersed in terms of its distribution over the land, but social relationships within the system promote a much closer association of individuals in terms of action.

Fleming (ibid.) draws on the rural sociological models of Rees (1968) and of Arensberg & Kimball (1948). These researchers have argued that a farmstead is not simply an outlier of a nucleated community but forms a focus in its own right. The integration of farmsteads into interdependent social networks does not require the existence of a dominant centre with managerial functions; rather, this results from the nature of the relationships between the farmsteads themselves. Fleming examines the processes through which distinct, behaviourally linked social groupings are formed within this network of kinship and affinal ties (1985: 93–4). For a variety of reasons, individuals may command sufficient respect to form wider relationships because people related to them perceive that an 'advantage' may be gained through the reciprocal arrangements on which the system functions.

If the household is seen as a primary level of social organization, Fleming suggests that secondary levels of organization are represented by economic co-operation between households located in the neighbourhood, or groups of households from different neighbourhoods (ibid.: 132). At this level of secondary organization, activities such as harvesting could be carried out by groups from different farms. Rees (1968: 59), Emmett (1964), and Arensberg & Kimball (1948) all attest to this form of co-operation among rural communities this century in the British Isles, even with the advent of mechanization. Fleming is at pains to point out that this form of reciprocity may well have been even more pronounced in prehistory (1985: 133).

Furthermore, in addition to contact at the level of basic socioeconomic organization, anthropological literature indicates that even geographically or socially isolated groups may establish vital, if periodic, long-distance links with other groups and communities. Groups in marginal areas are likely to foster and maintain such contacts, particularly under conditions of either restricted economic potential or social and environmental stress, in effect increasing the socioeconomic capacity of the community.

In this context of socioeconomic interdependence and co-operation, Fleming (1985) notes that archaeological techniques that define socioeconomic thresholds through the examination of settlement location and function (most notably site-catchment analysis) must take into account social factors such as the pooling of labour. For example, the geographical proximity of kin may be contrived to allow sufficient labour for 'collective' work to be drawn up (ibid.: 133).

Fleming's work offers a refreshing insight into alternative approaches to the study, conceptualization and analysis of marginality. By linking social, spatial, economic and environmental aspects of settlement and land-use, he has raised issues that archaeologists and historical geographers of all periods should consider. For us, his work is a key indication of the integrated direction that archaeological studies of the 'margin' should take. Armed with Fleming's observations, and the lessons drawn from the discussion above, we can now offer a reinterpretation of the settlement and subsistence record of the Borders region of northern Britain in the later Bronze Age.

Reinterpreting the 'margin'

Three major settlement forms have been identified in the Borders region of northern Northumberland and southern Scotland: unenclosed settlements, palisaded settlements or 'stockaded farms', and hillforts. The work of Jobey (1985), Gates (1983), Halliday (1985), Topping (1981, 1989a, 1989b), Burgess (1984, 1985) and van der Veen (1992) is central to debates about settlement development and land-use in the region.

Traditionally, it was believed that unenclosed settlements preceded the development of enclosures. For example, Burgess (1984: 161) argued that the development of palisades was indicative 'of a period in which a dispersed population concentrated into progressively fewer but larger protected settlements'. Regarding the general distribution of these settlements in the Borders area, Gates has shown that the palisades and hillforts usually occupy positions better suited for defence than unenclosed settlements, and sometimes they occupy areas of higher absolute altitudes (Gates 1983: 119).

These settlement data have been interpreted in two ways. On the one hand, they are suggested to reflect settlement dislocation and discontinuity as a result of increasingly marginal economic and environmental conditions. On the other, they are regarded as clear evidence for the continued occupation of the area, reflecting local adaptive strategies in relation to the changing situation.

Colin Burgess has been one of the main proponents of the argument for settlement discontinuity and/or abandonment. In three contributions (1984, 1985, 1989), he has suggested that the uplands of the Borders region were deserted towards the end of the second millennium BC as a result of an economic/population/environmental catastrophe brought about by changing climatic conditions. He argued that in the early part of the second millennium BC, population increase, linked to ameliorating climate, resulted in the extension of settlement areas beyond the lowlands of Britain on to upland 'marginal' soils. This expansion is confirmed by the work of others such as Bradley (1978).

However, the mild climatic episode came to an end in the late second millennium BC (the Penard period, c. 1250–1000 BC). Burgess attempted to assess the implications of this cessation, arguing that climatic deterioration would have reduced the growing season for crops by more than five weeks. The altitudinal levels at which crops would have ripened may have fallen by as much as 50 metres, and Burgess suggested an overall decline of about 150 metres between the twelfth and seventh centuries BC (1985: 200).

Using the highly deterministic and formalistic reasoning embodied in Parry's research discussed above, Burgess argued that the result of this process was a 'dramatic retreat and dislocation of settlement and agriculture' (ibid.: 205) in both uplands and lowlands in the late second to early first millennium BC. If this really was the case, then we might expect to see some manifestation of this retreat in the pollen record. However, an analysis of the available data from Northumberland and the Borders does not substantiate this point (Young & Simmonds 1995).

Burgess (1989) has developed the desertion theme by attempting to link changes in population numbers and settlement patterns with known natural events, in this case volcanic eruption (see also ibid. 1985). Here, he was building on the work of Baillie on the adverse climatic impact of known volcanic eruption episodes (1989, 1991a,b). Burgess (1985) argued that as a result of the climatic changes brought about by this volcanic activity, there was a 300-year hiatus between the demise of upland open settlements and the emergence of palisaded sites in the first millennium BC. The case for desertion was, again, based on Parry's thinking, with a major plank in Burgess's argument being that the chronology of the excavated settlements in the region supported the notion of discontinuity. However, we have argued elsewhere that Burgess's use of radiocarbon dates is selective and that (as with the pollen data) the available dates do not substantiate his case (Young & Simmonds 1995).

We can find no real support for the idea of massive upland desertion in the Borders region in the late second and early first millennium BC. On the contrary, we would agree with Jobey (1985: 184) that 'the settlement lacuna which existed before the erection of protective palisades now no longer exists' in the Borders region. Gates (1983: 118) further asserts that 'there is no basis . . . for assuming that the uplands were deserted in the early first millennium as a consequence of climatic change'. This is not to deny that climatic change did take place towards the end of the second millennium BC, but upland abandonment was only one possible response to such change in what archaeologists have perceived (like Dartmoor) to be an economically/environmentally marginal area. In fact, Jobey (1985: 189) pointed to at least 25–30 recorded palisades and hillforts in the eastern Borders that lie at similar heights or at altitudes greatly in excess of those occupied by the highest of the known earlier unenclosed settlements.

Higham (1986: 122–3) has discussed the possible function of palisades and has suggested that they may be linked with a developing emphasis on pastoral farming. Far from being an indicator of a *decline* in living standards, as implied by Burgess, it may be that with the development of palisades in the locations described by Jobey, we are seeing a complex social and economic response to climatic change involving the wider integration of different landscape zones into the economic system. We have discussed this in detail elsewhere (Young & Simmonds 1995). Suffice it to say here that some of the points raised above relating to human perception of environmental change, especially those points relating to Fleming's work on Dartmoor, may be of direct relevance to the Borders situation. Rather than dispersed, highly unstable outliers of 'core' areas, what we may in fact be looking at in the upland settlement record of the Borders are dynamic systems of social and economic organization in economically and environmentally marginal areas.

The results of survey work by Topping (1989a,b) have an important bearing on this debate. He has shown that 'cord rig' – the narrow ridged remains of early cultivation that is being increasingly discovered in the Borders region – spans a broad timescale that probably covers the contentious period under discussion (Young & Simmonds 1995). Topping proposes a socioeconomic model for Later Bronze Age–Iron Age Northumberland according to which relative levels of cultivation directly reflect the socioeconomic preferences of the occupants of certain settlement types. He suggests that unenclosed sites, which are invariably linked with small-scale plots, exhibit less of a preference for cereals than those linked to formal fields (notably enclosed sites and forts). Topping argues that specialist economies may have developed: the subsistence economies of unenclosed settlements may have been very different to those of enclosed sites and forts, with the former laying more stress on 'wild' resources and the latter on more 'domesticated' food sources (1989a: 150).

However, far from lending itself to a clear interpretation of two economic regimes working side by side, we suggest that the results of Topping's survey work support the argument for continuity and organized adaptation in the light of changing circumstances in the area. It certainly seems to substantiate the argument that there was no hiatus in the settlement record in the Borders.

The evidence from the unenclosed settlements would seem to fall into a similar pattern to that suggested by Fleming's work on Dartmoor. There appears to be no rigid system of land division associated with these settlements (Gates 1983; Topping 1989a,b), but there is an emphasis on irregular plots. It might certainly be the case that the 'household' was the main centre of economic and social activities in the Borders at this time. The spacing of some of the unenclosed settlement sites within the landscape is also of interest, given Fleming's observations about co-operation and labour-pooling (see above). Even if only a third of those unenclosed sites known in areas such as the Till/Breamish Valleys and the Upper Tweed (Jobey 1985: 185, fig. 10.5, 188, fig. 10.7) were contemporary, their distribution would still allow for the kinds of reciprocal labour exchanges and collective decision-making processes hypothesized by Fleming. The complex series of developments leading to the construction of palisades might well be seen as the response of social groups with a developed sense of 'place' to changes in the material conditions of their existence.

As a result of Topping's recent work, we can also now assert that the development of the first clearly recorded formalized fields and field systems is contemporary and associated with the appearance of palisaded settlements. However, writing in 1986, Higham pointed out the apparent *lack* of fields associated with palisades. He also argued that the occupants of these sites were pastoralists (ibid.: 122). It may certainly be true that the function of the palisade was to control stock or to exclude animals from areas specifically designated for human habitation, but the more recent discovery of formalized boundaries around fields in the vicinity of palisaded settlements (e.g. High Knowes B: Topping 1989a) may also support the idea of diversity in the economic base of these sites. Such field boundaries are best seen as a means of keeping large numbers of animals (greater than those previously grazed around upland settlements) off still-prized crops.

The switch to a 'mixed ranching' style of economy over the long timespan suggested by the existing radiocarbon chronology (which shows an overlap in the use of palisades and unenclosed sites: Young & Simmonds 1995) is precisely the kind of complex adaptation we might expect in the light of our earlier discussion about the nature of marginality and people's gradually developing perceptions of their immediate environment. Linked to this, we might also suggest that flight in the face of increasingly adverse weather conditions would be the *last* recourse – not the first – for communities who had invested several generations of effort into making a living on the so-called 'margin'. In this situation, collective activity might still have been the norm, although by the end of the Iron Age in the region we can certainly see the emergence of a more hierarchical social structure (Higham 1986; Topping 1989a: 145–9).

We believe that the preceding discussion has achieved the aims set out in our introductory paragraphs. The margin is a contentious area in which to work, and we hope that the debate continues and that it involves more archaeologists.

References

Allen, B. & R. Crittenden 1987. Degradation in a pre-capitalist economy: the case of the New Guinea Highlands. In *Land degradation and society*, P. Blaikie & H. Brookfield (eds), 145–56. London: Methuen.

Arensberg, C. M. & S. T. Kimball 1948. *Family and community in Ireland*. Cambridge, Mass.: Harvard University Press.

Baillie, M. G. 1989. Do Irish bog oaks date the Shang Dynasty? *Current Archaeology* **10**, 310–13.

Baillie, M. G. 1991a. Marking in marker dates: towards an archaeology with historical precision. *World Archaeology* **23**, 233–43.

Baillie, M. G. 1991b. Suck in and smear: two related chronological problems for the 1990s. *Journal of Theoretical Archaeology* **2**, 12–16.

Bailey, M. 1989. The concept of the margin in the Medieval English economy. *Economic History Review* **42** (2nd series), 1–17.

Blaikie, P. & H. Brookfield (eds) 1987a. Defining and debating the problem. See Blaikie & Brookfield (1987c), 1–26.

Blaikie, P. & H. Brookfield (eds) 1987b. Approaches to the study of land degradation. See Blaikie & Brookfield (1987c), 27–48.

Blaikie, P. & H. Brookfield (eds) 1987c. *Land degradation and society*. London: Methuen.

Bradley, R. 1978. *The prehistoric settlement of Britain*, London: Routledge & Kegan Paul.

Burgess, C. B. 1984. The prehistoric settlement of Northumberland. In *Between and beyond the walls: essays on the prehistory of north Britain in honour of George Jobey*, C. B. Burgess and R. Miket (eds), 126–75. Edinburgh: John Donald.

Burgess, C. B. 1985. Population, climate and upland settlement. See Spratt & Burgess (1985), 195–230.

Burgess, C. B. 1989. Volcanoes, catastrophes and the global crisis of the late second millennium. *Current Archaeology* **10**, 325–9.

Campbell, B. M. S. 1990. People and land in the Middle Ages 1066–1500. In *An historical geography of England and Wales*, 2nd edn., R. A. Dodgshon & R. A. Butlin (eds), 69–121. London: Academic Press.

Champion, T. C. (ed.) 1989. *Centre and periphery: comparative studies in archaeology*. London: Unwin Hyman.

Emmett, I. 1964. *A north Wales village: a social anthropological study*. London: Routledge & Kegan Paul.

Evans, C. 1985. Tradition and the cultural landscape: an archaeology of place. *Archaeological Review from Cambridge* **4**, 81–93.

Fleming, A. 1985. Land tenure, productivity and field systems. In *Beyond domestication in prehistoric Europe*, G. Barker & C. Gamble (eds), 129–46. London: Academic Press.

Gates, T. 1983. Unenclosed settlements in Northumberland. In *Rural settlement in the Roman North*, P. Clack & S. Haselgrove (eds), 21–42. Council for British Archaeology Group 3.

Gold, J. R. 1982. Territoriality and human spatial behaviour. *Progress in Human Geography* **6**, 44–67.

Halliday, S. P. 1985. Unenclosed settlement in the east and south-east of Scotland. See Spratt & Burgess (1985), 231–51.

Higham, N. 1986. *The northern counties to AD 1000*. London: Longman.

Hodder, I. 1987. Converging traditions: the search for symbolic meanings in archaeology and geography. In *Landscape and culture*, J. M. Wagstaff (ed.), 134–45. London: Blackwell.

Jobey, G. 1985. Unenclosed settlements of Tyne-Forth – a summary. See Spratt & Burgess (1985), 177–94.

Jochim, M. 1976. *Hunter–gatherer subsistence and settlement: a predictive model*. London: Academic Press.

Mizruchi, E. H. 1983. *Regulating society: marginality and social control*. London: Collier Macmillan.

Parry, M. L. 1975. Secular climate change and marginal land. *Transactions of the Institute of British Geographers* **64**, 1–13.

Parry, M. L. 1985. Upland settlement and climatic change: the medieval evidence. See Spratt & Burgess (1985), 35–49.

Rees, A. D. 1968. *Life in the Welsh countryside*. Cardiff: University of Wales Press.

Rowlands, M. J. 1971. The archaeological interpretation of prehistoric metalworking. *World Archaeology* **3**, 210–33.

Shields, R. 1991. *Places on the margin: alternative geographies of modernity*. London: Routledge.

Spratt, D. & C. Burgess (eds) 1985. *Upland settlement in Britain: the second millennium BC and after*. Oxford: British Archaeological Reports, British series 143.

Topping, P. 1981. The prehistoric field systems of College Valley, north Northumberland. *Northern Archaeology* **2**, 14–33.

Topping, P. 1989a. The context of cord rig cultivation in later prehistoric Northumberland. In *From Caithness to Cornwall: some aspects of British field archaeology*, M. Bowden et al. (eds), 145–58. Oxford: British Archaeological Reports, British Series 209.

Topping, P. 1989b. Early cultivation in Northumberland and the Borders. *Proceedings of the Prehistoric Society* **55**, 161–79.

Tuan, Y. 1974. Space and place: humanistic perspectives. *Progress in Geography* **6**, 211–52.

Tuan, Y. 1984. *Topophilia: a study of environmental perception, attitudes and values*. New Jersey: Prentice-Hall.

van der Veen, M. 1992. *Crop husbandry regimes: an archaeobotanical study of farming in northern England 1000 BC–AD 500*. Sheffield: J. R. Collis Publications (Archaeology Monograph 3).

Welbourn, D. A. 1981. The role of blacksmiths in a tribal society. *Archaeological Review from Cambridge* **1**, 30–41.

Winterhalder, B. 1981. Foraging strategies in the boreal environment: an analysis of Cree hunting and gathering. In *Hunter–gatherer foraging strategies: ethnographic and archaeological analysis*, B. Winterhalder & E. A. Smith (eds), 66–98. Chicago: University of Chicago Press.

Yadeta, G. 1985. *Dynamic processes of development in marginal areas: a case study from the Pokot of north-west Africa*. Malmo: Liber Forlag.

Young, R & T. Simmonds 1995. Marginality and the nature of later prehistoric settlement in the North of England. *Landscape History* **17**, 5–17.

Index